Coming to Terms

Coming to Terms

THE RHETORIC OF NARRATIVE
IN FICTION AND FILM

Seymour Chatman

Cornell University Press

ITHACA AND LONDON

International Standard Book Number 0-8014-2485-2 (cloth)
International Standard Book Number 0-8014-9736-1 (paper)
Library of Congress Catalog Card Number 90-55119
Printed in the United States of America
Librarians: Library of Congress cataloging information
appears on the last page of the book.

To Barbara and Mariel
for being there

Contents

Acknowledgments   ix
Introduction   1
1. Narrative and Two Other Text-Types   6
2. Description Is No Textual Handmaiden   22
3. What Is Description in the Cinema?   38
4. Argumentation in Film: *Mon oncle d'Amérique*   56
5. In Defense of the Implied Author   74
6. The Implied Author at Work   90
7. The Literary Narrator   109
8. The Cinematic Narrator   124
9. A New Point of View on "Point of View"   139
10. A New Kind of Film Adaptation: *The French
    Lieutenant's Woman*   161
11. The "Rhetoric" "of" "Fiction"   184
    Notes   205
    Index   235

Acknowledgments

I AM GRATEFUL to the participants in the 1989 NEH Summer Seminar on Narrative in Fiction and Film (and especially to Marcia Thompson) for their comments on the manuscript. I also appreciate the input of my dear friends Robert Alter and Ernest Callenbach. Above all, I thank Wallace Martin for generous suggestions about both the general plan of the book and particular details of several chapters.

Chapter 1 appeared originally in abbreviated form as "The Representation of Text-Types," *Textual Practice* 2 (1988), 22–29. A portion of Chapter 3 appeared in "What Is Description in the Cinema?" *Cinema Journal* 23 (Summer 1984), 4–11. A portion of Chapter 6 appeared as "The Pajama Man," in *The State of the Language II*, edited by Leonard Michaels and Christopher Ricks (Berkeley and Los Angeles: University of California Press, 1989). Chapter 11 appeared in an earlier version under the same title in *Reading Narrative*, edited by James Phelan (Columbus: Ohio State University, 1989), pp. 40–52. I am grateful to all concerned for permission to include these portions in the present volume.

S.C.

Coming to Terms

Introduction

"Narratology" is a word that Henry James would have deplored, though he might have found merit in its objects of concern. After twenty years, I still feel something of an ironic twinge when I see it in print. A "science" of narrative seems an unlikely, even a slightly shady pursuit. But, of course, "—ology" can also mean "theory of," and who, these days, would dare fault theory? In any case, we can take heart from the fine work on narrative theory and its applications to literature and cinema published during these years.[1]

This book is concerned with the terms of narratology and of text theory in general. It assumes that every discipline needs periodically to examine its terms. For terms are not mere tags: they represent—in some sense, even constitute—a theory. By scrutinizing its terms, we test and clarify the concepts that a theory proposes. Through that clarification we can better decide whether they help or hinder our work.

Though the book treats a variety of subjects, it strives to incorporate them in a unified commentary on narrative terminology from two perspectives. The first perspective, informing the first four chapters, is external, considering the relations of Narrative—in particular, fictional Narrative—to other kinds of discourse or "text-types." This is less a general theory of the text than a set of distinctions that clarify Narrative's position among the text-types. Further, to explain how other text-types such as Argument and Description fit within the Narrative framework—and vice versa—I propose the concept of textual "service."

The next six chapters of the book approach narratology from an internal perspective. Following the order of my *Story and Discourse*[2] (and other recent narratological studies), they examine concepts and formulations that remain controversial: the implied author, the nature of the narrator (including the differences between literary and cinematic narrators), the concept of character "point of view" or "focalization" (which, I argue, deserves a better name—I propose "filter"), and the distinction between "unreliable narration" and what I call "fallible filtration." Throughout, I cite examples from both literature and film. I feel a special responsibility to discuss cinematic narrative in greater detail than I did in *Story and Discourse*; critics were right to question the subtitle "Narrative Structure in Fiction and Film," since that book gave film all too short shrift. Film seems particularly important to narratology at this juncture if we are to formulate the general principles of Narrative as well as its actualizations in various media. Only a general narratology can help to explain what literature and cinema have in common, narratively speaking, and only a good sense of that commonality will permit us to understand what is distinctively cinematic or literary.

Finally, both external and internal perspectives lead me to attempt a synthesis by reformulating Wayne Booth's conception of "rhetoric of fiction."

Chapter 1 attempts a distinction among three kinds of discourse or text-type—Narrative, Description, and Argument (with passing mention of the text-type traditionally called "Exposition") and illustrates how each of these may subserve the others. To correct the centuries-old prejudice that Narrative somehow dominates Description, I argue that no text-type is intrinsically privileged. Most texts utilize one overriding text-type, but it is generally subserved by other text-types. Narration can just as easily function at the service of Description as vice versa. Chapter 2 considers Description in greater detail, both as a text-type in its own right and in its interrelation with Narrative.

In Chapters 3 and 4 I take up the question of non-narrative text-types in the cinema. Most theoretical discussion of cinema, both as technique and as institution, has presupposed its total commitment to Narrative, and it is true that the vast majority of films—at least commercial films—are totally dedicated to story-telling. But if we want to extend our powers of textual analysis from literature to the cinema, we need to look at the cinematic ramifications of the other text-types as well. Chapter 3 considers Description in the cinema, a question apparently made difficult by the nature of the medium itself. Some believe that a film cannot describe at all. They argue that the act of describing as such—the evocation of the properties of objects for their own sakes—cannot occur in the cinema precisely because every last detail is *already* totally visible. I respond to that claim in several ways.

Chapter 4 illustrates the possible relations of Argument and Narrative in the cinema. It first examines the traditional moralistic use of Narrative in the movies. The films of Frank Capra come immediately to mind, their theses often announced in their very titles: *You Can't Take It with You*, *It's a Wonderful Life*. These films bear an archaeological relation to cinematic Modernism similar to that borne by fables or eighteenth century novels to the modern and postmodern novel. But in the quite different context of the European art cinema, films can accommodate textual mixes no less complex than those of modern novels. I illustrate with an analysis of a film whose textual structure is delightfully quirky: Alain Resnais's *Mon oncle d'Amérique* (1982).

In moving to an internal perspective, I turn to problems still brewing within the precincts of narratology proper. I skip over issues that seem reasonably settled (such as the relation of storytime to discourse time, and the greater facility of literary narrative for rendering the mental life of characters); interested readers will find sufficient citations in the notes, as well as in such works as Martin's and Prince's, to explore these topics as they wish.

Chapters 5 and 6 attempt a defense of the "implied author" against various kinds of attack; Chapter 5 defends in a theoretical way; Chapter 6 offers examples of the explanatory power of the concept. I intentionally assemble examples of the greatest possible diversity, foraging even into the intellectually murky world of magazine advertising.

Next, I deal with what I once called the "transmission" of the story. Chapters 7 and 8, on literary and cinematic narrators respectively, reexamine the distinction between mimesis and diegesis and argue for a definition of Narrative broad enough to stress that which plays, films, and novels have in common. They attempt to demonstrate that plot (the double chrono-logic), character, and setting are uniquely characteristic of Narrative among the text-types, that these occur in "shown" no less than in "told" texts, and hence that at a certain level in the textual hierarchy the similarities between performative and discursive narratives is more important than their differences. I contend that stories performed on stage or screen are no less "narratives" than those told by literary narrators. At the most abstract textual level, they are more like epics, novels, and short stories than they are like arguments or descriptions. A theatrical play is first a narrative and only second a mimetic rather than diegetic text. I argue this point at length, to help settle the problem of such concepts as the "cinematic narrator." I agree with theorists who assert that movies cannot generally be said to be "told," but, I contend, that does not mean that they are not narrated—and if they are narrated, they possess narrators. (It will be seen that this represents a retraction of my argument, in *Story and Discourse*, for the existence of "non-narrated" narratives.)

Chapter 9 continues the discussion begun by Henry James and brought up to date by Wayne Booth and Gérard Genette, about the name and nature of "point of view." Further ramifying Genette's crucial distinction between "Who narrates?" and "Who sees?" I propose that we devise separate terms for the "point of view" of the narrator (which I call "slant") and that of the character (which I call "filter"). Again, more than names is at stake. I argue that the term "focalization," for example, simply shifts the ground of the problem without solving it. Narrators do not "see" things in the story world in the same way that characters do; hence, any term that is applied indiscriminately to purveyors of discourse on the one hand and inhabitants of story on the other will blur our hard-earned distinction between "Who tells?" and "Who sees?" I further argue that the term "unreliable" is appropriate to narrators only, that the parallel phenomenon among characters needs another term. I propose "fallibility."

Chapter 10 leaves general narratology to take up a medium-specific issue: the question of the film adaptation of novels. I am particularly concerned with *imaginative* film adaptation, the kind that manages to translate literary features, such as narrator's commentary, which are not easily suited to the medium. I pick as my example the stunning film version of *The French Lieutenant's Woman*. The chapter is concerned not with the notorious and, to me, hollow issue of "fidelity" to the original but rather with the distinctive means by which the two media flesh out narrative features.

Having resolved certain pressing narratological questions, at least to my own satisfaction, I examine in Chapter 11 each of the terms in Booth's famous title and try to answer the question "In what sense can we genuinely speak of a 'rhetoric' of fiction: that is, why should we call what theorists of fiction do 'rhetoric,' rather than something else?" I argue that "rhetoric" is most meaningful in its traditional sense of "suasion," provided we understand that the term addresses not only the content but also the form of narratives.

Attempting to clarify and rationalize the terminology of a field as sophisticated and comprehensive as narratology is not easy, and I do not shoulder the responsibility lightly. Where I differ with colleagues, I do so out of respect for their efforts and conclusions. If in the heat of arguing my own views I seem to belittle theirs, I apologize in advance. Clearly the house of narratology, like the house of fiction itself, has many mansions. Different formulas have different strengths, some of which a partisan account always risks neglecting or even misrepresenting. I present mine for the sake of continuing a debate that has kept narratology one of the livelier topics on the academic scene.

A final note about the discussion of films: I have not used production stills or frame reproductions to illustrate my discussion. I feel that they too often render static an art that is, after all, still properly called the "movies." Instead, I have chosen examples readily available on videotape. My ideal reader not only owns a VCR with a good stop-action mechanism but has a charge account at a richly endowed video rental store.

CHAPTER 1

Narrative and Two
Other Text-Types

"W HAT IS NARRATIVE?" is not the same question as "What is *a* narrative?" For several years, my concern has been the type of discourse, or "text-type," that we call "Narrative." I have come to realize that Narrative, like most things, is best understood in contrast to what it is not. One place to locate Narrative is within the boundaries setting it off from other kinds of texts.[1] To advance our understanding of Narrative in fiction and film, we need to think about the properties of those other kinds.[2] In the process, we shall better understand the differing ways in which literature and film utilize the text-types in general.

It is customary to distinguish Narrative from three other text-types: Argument, Description, and Exposition. But the distinction between Exposition and the others is somewhat problematic. Exposition is usually defined as the "act of expounding, setting forth, or explaining" (*American College Dictionary*) or "discourse . . . designed to convey information or explain what is difficult to understand . . . apart from criticism, argument and development" (*Webster's Third New International Dictionary*). But, some rhetoricians believe, there can be no expounding or explaining that does not entail a degree of description and of argumentation. Expounding is descriptive to the extent that it inventories properties of the subject expounded; and it is argumentative to the extent that it implicitly urges that the situation or object expounded *is* as presented. Still, we tend to characterize as "expositions" arguments that are somewhat less than forensic and descriptions, especially of abstract issues, that entail logical organization.[3]

6

Fortunately, my own purposes are sufficiently served by the three terms Narrative, Description, and Argument. Since these terms also support different and sometimes conflicting senses, I capitalize the words when I refer to the class of text-types and use lower case to stand for individual examples of those types.

Let me define the sense of "text" I have in mind. I wish to distinguish it as one of two kinds of communicative objects. Already in Lessing we find a distinction between communications in spatial and in temporal media.[4] By "text" I shall mean any communication that *temporally* controls its reception by the audience. Thus, texts differ from communicative objects such as (non-narrative) paintings and sculptures, which do not regulate the temporal flow or spatial direction of the audience's perception. It is true that it "takes time" to view a painting or a statue, but such time is not governed by the artifact. A (non-narrative) painting presents itself all at once, so to speak, and we are free to scan or "read" it in any order we prefer (from left to right, top to bottom, center to periphery, detail to overall effect). Further, there is nothing in the painting or sculpture to inform us when the reading process should begin or end. A text in my sense, however, requires us to begin at a beginning *it* chooses (the first page, the opening shots of a film, the overture, the rising curtain) and to follow its temporal unfolding to the end it prescribes. Of course, I am not referring here to literal physiological processes but rather to the temporal "program" inscribed in the work. Recent experiments in psychology show that the actual eye movements involved in reading pictures do not differ radically from those involved in reading printed pages. As Marianna Torgovnick points out, psychologists "have shown that the eye does not really perceive paintings holistically, nor really perceive words sequentially."[5]

Clearly, it takes time to get one's bearings when looking at a painting. "The perceiving of a work of art," explains Rudolf Arnheim, "is not accomplished suddenly. More typically, the observer starts from somewhere, tries to orient himself as to the main skeleton of the work, looks for the accents, experiments with a tentative framework in order to see whether it fits the total content, and so on. When the exploration is successful, the work is seen to repose comfortably in a congenial structure, which illuminates the work's meaning to the observer."[6]

Text theory is concerned not with ocular physiology or psychology, however, but with the structure of discourse. Paintings *present* themselves as if they were holistic, verbal narratives as if they were linear. They do so regardless of how any given spectator or reader goes about perceiving any given work. The structure is one thing, the perception another. Temporality informs narrative texts in a way that it does not inform paintings (or non-narrative verbal texts, for that matter).[7] Temporality is involved only in the spectator's *work* in perceiving a painting; it is not part of the painting itself. But temporality is immanent to, a component of, narrative texts. The control exerted by a verbal (or other) narrative has no counterpart in the experiencing of a (non-narrative) painting or sculpture. The reader or spectator who skips pages or fast-forwards the videotape or goes out for a smoke during the second act must somehow learn, by inquiry or inference, what has transpired in the interim.

Music, too, is a time-regulating structure and hence a "text" in my sense. In classical Western music, for example, penultimate dominant chords generally call for resolving tonics, and to that extent they control listeners' expectations. But musical textuality is of a different sort than verbal textuality. Most aestheticians argue that music is not semiotic (or at least not "micro-semiotic"). It offers no constancy of reference between each of its elements—notes, phrases, movements—and something else in the real or an imagined world so that we think of the first as signifier and the second as signified. Most other texts, however, do make such reference; they entail a linked continuum of referential signs. "Cat" signifies one referent and "sat" another and "mat" a third, and "the cat sat on the mat" forms a semantic composite of the three.

The two different kinds of communications, textual and non-textual, may perform *at each other's service* (just as the various text-types can operate at each other's service, as I shall argue). Thus, a reproduction of a famous painting hung on a stage backdrop may subserve the dramatic text of words, gestures, and movements. Or the crescendo from a well-known piece of music may subserve the visual and auditory film images to intensify the feeling that the plot is coming to a head. Of course, in this "servile" function, the painting and the musical passage lose something of their autonomy. It is hard to focus on the purely musical structure of Mozart's overture to *The Marriage of Figaro* or the "Blue Danube Waltz" when they accompany cinematic narratives (the first, for example, "over" shots in *Trading Places* to establish the cushy life of a young commodities broker; the second in *2001* to suggest the grace with which a spaceship settles onto its moon-landing pad). Movie music is pretty much co-opted; indeed, if we started *listening* to the score, it would probably mean that we had lost interest in the narrative.

But my subject is the relation not of textual to nontextual communications but of Narrative to other text-types. As has been clearly established in recent narratology, what makes Narrative unique among the text-types is its "chrono-logic," its doubly temporal logic. Narrative entails movement through time not only "externally" (the duration of the presentation of the novel, film, play) but also "internally" (the duration of the sequence of events that constitute the plot). The first operates in that dimension of narrative called Discourse (or *récit* or *syuzhet*), the second in that called Story (*histoire* or *fabula*).[8] In traditional narratives, the internal or story logic entails the additional principle of causality (event *a* causes *b*, *b* causes *c*, and so on) or, more weakly, what might be called "contingency" (*a* does not directly cause *b*, nor does *b* cause *c*, but they all work together to evoke a certain situation or state of affairs *x*).

Non-narrative text-types do not have an internal time sequence, even though, obviously, they take time to read, view, or hear. Their underlying structures are static or atemporal—synchronic not diachronic. For instance, Arguments are texts that attempt to persuade an audience of the validity of some proposition, usually proceeding along deductive or inductive lines. Descriptions render the properties of things—typically, though not necessarily, objects visible to or imaginable by the senses. They "portray," "depict," or "represent." Though the term can apply to abstractions and other nonvisible entities, Description is often considered the verbal analogue to painting or drawing. As Michel Beaujour has noted, however, "describe" is often used in English in a very loose sense, blurring all possible distinctions of the kind I am trying to make. The dictionary, Beaujour observes, "offers some puzzling synonyms, which are italicized in the following list: represent, delineate, *relate*, *recount*, *narrate*, *express*, *explain*, depict, portray."[9]

If Description is treated as synonymous with Narrative (or Exposition), then obviously no more can be said. But we are not doomed to such a terminological impasse. It is precisely the function of theory building to coin new terms and to regulate old ones, not in a prescriptive or proscriptive spirit but simply in an effort to facilitate communication. We are not the slaves of language (as some contemporary theorists dolefully contend) but its masters, and we can decide what we are talking about and how best to talk about it.

Description is sometimes thought of as a sort of casual contiguity. In the expression "describing our thoughts," for example, the implication is of a more or less random array, fantasies lying cheek-by-jowl with cognition and conceptualization. But as we shall see, Description is not merely a "random" text-type; it generally has its own logic.[10]

Argument is the text-type that relies on "logic," at least in the informal sense; it may employ not the strict "demonstrative" logic of the syllogism but rather the softer one of the rhetorical enthymeme. Or the logic may be inductive, or perhaps analogous.[11] But unlike Narrative chrono-logic, Argumentative logic is not temporal. And unlike Description, Argument rests not on contiguity but on some intellectually stronger, usually more abstract ground such as that of consequentiality.[12]

These text-types crosscut the distinction between fiction and nonfiction. All three can inform both nonfictional and fictional texts. For example, "The Gettysburg Address" and Pare Lorentz's documentary film *The River* are nonfictional arguments; "To His Coy Mistress" and "A Modest Proposal" and most Hollywood World War II feature films are fictional ones.[13]

By "text-types," further, I mean something other than genres. Genres are—at least in one sense of the word—special subclasses or combinations of text-types. However one defines them, novels, novellas, short stories, mysteries, and Westerns are generic subclasses of the Narrative text-type. A Theophrastian character is a subclass of Description. A sermon is a subclass of Argument. And so on.

The text-types routinely operate *at each other's service*. "Ozymandias" is ostensibly a description, what the "traveller from an antique land" saw, but the overriding structure is an argument whose proposition is something like *sic transit gloria mundi*. The catechistic "Ithaca" episode of *Ulysses* is an argument at the service of the overall narrative. Narrators of novels routinely digress to describe or argue, describers to narrate or argue, and arguers to narrate or describe. (I shall exemplify each process below.)

The study of texts is at once simplified and enriched by the notion of service. Text-types are underlying (or overiding) structures that can be actualized by different surface forms. This concept accounts for textual complexity in a more satisfactory way than the assumption that everything is right there on the surface. To say, for example, that one of Aesop's fables is a narrative simply because it "tells a story" obviously misses its most important property. In its surface form a fable is a narrative, but clearly the narration is at the service of a "moral"—that is, an argument. As Susan Suleiman puts it, such texts are "founded on [the] illocutionary verb [of] demonstrating."[14] Obviously, all narratives—indeed all texts—are immersed in ideology, though some may try to conceal or deny it. But from the textual point of view, it is important to distinguish between the implication of an ideology and the urging of a thesis. Clearly *Ulysses* or *The Magic Mountain* or *8 1/2* do not "argue" an ideology.[15]

We need a clear understanding of the difference between the broad discourse function of each text-type (its overriding textual intention, be it Narrative, Descriptive, or Argumentative) and any textual actualization or manifestation, whether a sentence in a verbal text or a configuration of lines in a cartoon or a shot in a film. The following are examples of text-types at each other's service.

Argument

La Fontaine's fable "Phoebus and Boreas" recounts the battle between the North Wind and the Sun over which one can more quickly cause a traveler to remove his cloak:

> [Boreas] whistled, whirled, and splashed,
> And down the torrents dashed
> . . . all to doff a single cloak.
> But vain the furious stroke;
>   The traveller was stout,
>   And kept the tempest out . . .
> And as the fiercer roared the blast,
> His cloak the tighter held he fast.
> The sun broke out, to win the bet;
>   He caused the clouds to disappear,
>   Refreshed and warmed the cavalier,
> And through his mantle made him sweat,

> Till off it came, of course,
> In less than half an hour;
> And yet the sun saved half his power.—
> So much doth mildness more than force.[16]

La Fontaine's fable uses Narrative at the service of Argument. The argument is that of the carrot and the stick: seduction is more effective than aggression. To bend others to your will, accommodate your demand to the needs of their behavior. (The point is not the difference between the two natural forces: the wind could have blown very gently or not at all, leaving it to the heat of exertion to prompt the man to remove his cloak; the sun, on the other hand, could have lost by starting out *too* hot, in which case the man might have quickly sought shelter without even thinking about his cloak.)

Here is the reverse situation—Argument at the service of Narrative. Fielding's *Joseph Andrews* begins with the following argument:

It is a trite but true observation, that examples work more forcibly on the mind than precepts: and if this be just in what is odious and blameable, it is more strongly so in what is amiable and praiseworthy. Here emulation most effectually operates upon us, and inspires our imitation in an irresistible manner. A good man therefore is a standing lesson to all his acquaintance, and of far greater use in that narrow circle than a good book.

But as it often happens that the best men are but little known, and consequently cannot extend the usefulness of their examples a great way; the writer may be called in aid to spread their history farther, and to present the amiable pictures to those who have not the happiness of knowing the originals; and so, by communicating such valuable patterns to the world, he may perhaps do a more extensive service to mankind than the person whose life originally afforded the pattern.[17]

This argument offers a raison d'être for the narrative immediately to follow. Its rhetorical structure is what we would expect from an eighteenth-century lawyer. The argument is that novels teach virtue more successfully than does ordinary life experience because publication assures a broader audience for moral examples than does straightforward observation of human behavior. It rests in a classical way on a chain of enthymemes. The major premise is a maxim, made palatable by the self-deprecatory "trite but true." Then (since *Joseph Andrews*, unlike *Jonathan Wild*, concerns a virtuous rather than a vicious case) an intermediate premise is offered on a fortiori grounds: who can doubt that a good example influences us more than a bad, since the first we simply imitate, but the second we must take care *not* to imitate? The conclusion of the first enthymeme smoothly concedes the power of the good man's example. The second enthymeme again utilizes a truistic major premise: good men are scarce, and one's chances of learning from their example are limited. The minor premise is as easily granted; indeed, it is true by definition that what is published or broadcast can be enjoyed by more people than what is not. The conclusion—narrower and more arguable than that of the first enthymeme, as it should be—is that the novelist performs a "more extensive service" than the good man whose life he imitates (it is not implied that the novelist is *generally* better than the good man: that would ruin the argument by overreaching).

Argument, of course, may support elements within the story of a narrative rather than its discourse. The following example, also from *Joseph Andrews*, uses an a fortiori argument, blended of supposition, analogy, and hyperbole, to dramatize the impact of a plot event:

> Suppose a stranger, who entered the chambers of a lawyer, being imagined a client, when the lawyer was preparing his palm for the fee, should pull out a writ against him. Suppose an apothecary, at the door of a chariot containing some great doctor of eminent skill, should, instead of directions to a patient, present him with a potion for himself. Suppose a civil companion, or a led captain, should, instead of virtue, and honour, and beauty, and parts, and admiration, thunder vice, and infamy, and ugliness, and folly, and contempt, in his patron's ears. Suppose when a tradesman first carries in his bill, the man of fashion should pay it; or suppose, if he did so, the tradesman should abate what he had overcharged, on the supposition of waiting. In short,—suppose what you will, you never can nor will suppose any thing equal to the astonishment which seized on Trulliber, as soon as Adams had ended his speech.[18]

Naturally, few novels after the time of Fielding go to such argumentative lengths to justify their story or discourse components. In the nineteenth century, Argument, when it occurs at all, is likely to be compressed into a maxim whose premises are so self-evident (the arguer hopes) as to need no logical demonstration. In *The Red and the Black*, for example, the narrator excuses himself for not giving more details of Julien's life at the seminary, on the grounds that "people who have been made to suffer by certain things cannot be reminded of them without a horror which paralyses every other pleasure, even that to be found in reading a story."[19] For all its compactness, this maxim can be seen as the conclusion of an implied argument, on this order:

Major premise: A horrifying experience blocks all pleasure.
Minor premise: Reading a story should be a pleasurable experience.
Conclusion: Reading a story that reminds one of a horrifying experience blocks all possible pleasure.

The argument starts with a generalization about the real world. But its conclusion, the maxim, serves as the major premise of an enthymeme that crosses over into the fictional world or, in this case, metafictional world, since the argument is not about the story but about the discourse:

Major Premise: Reading a story that reminds one of a horrifying experience blocks all possible pleasures.
Minor Premise: The details of Julien's life in the seminary are horrifying.
Conclusion: I am justified in skipping these details so that my reader shall not be deprived of the pleasures of this story.

So far, my examples have been taken from the commentaries of narrators on actions or characters. An argument, of course, can just as easily occur on the lips or in the mind of a character; indeed, his indulgence in Argument can be tellingly characteristic. In *Anna Karenina*, Levin's half-brother, the excessively cerebral Koznyshov, almost abandons his bachelorhood for the charms of Kitty's friend Varenka. But he cannot permit himself simply to fall in love with the woman; he must *argue* his way into it, as if to give himself permission to have feelings:

Why not? he was thinking. If it were a sudden impulse or a passion, if all I felt were this attraction, this mutual attraction (I'm entitled to call it mutual), but felt that it went counter to the entire tenor of my life, if I felt that in surrendering to this attraction I should be betraying my calling and my duty . . . but it's not that. The only thing I can say against it is that when I lost Marie I told myself that I would remain faithful to her memory. . . . However many women and girls he called to mind whom he had known, he could not remember a single girl who combined to such a degree all those qualities, actually all of them, that he, reasoning cold-bloodedly, would like to see in his wife. [Varenka] had all the freshness and charm of youth, but was not a child, and if she loved him she loved him consciously, as a woman ought to: that was one thing. Secondly: not only was she far from being worldly, but she obviously loathed worldliness, while at the same time she was familiar with society and had all the manners of a woman of good society, without which no life's companion would have been conceivable for Koznyshov. Thirdly: she was religious, not naively religious and kindhearted like a child, such as, for instance, Kitty; her life was founded on her religious convictions.[20]

As the plot soon demonstrates, anyone who needs to construct such elaborate arguments about affairs of the heart has strong reasons not to respond to their promptings.

Description

For narratology, Description is the most interesting of the other text-types because its relation to Narrative is the most subtle and complex. It accommodates itself more unobtrusively to an overriding Narrative than does Argument. In the mouth of the narrator, Argument stands out clearly as commentary, more often than not interpreted as "intrusion" of the sort that many modern novelists have striven to eliminate. Think, for example, of the plethora of description but dearth of commentary in a novel such as *Mrs Dalloway*. Not that commentary is intrinsically unnovelistic: there is much evidence of its fruitful revival in many recent novels (quite as Wayne Booth predicted).[21]

The traditional method of introducing Description into a narrative text is to present it at the beginning en bloc, as Dickens does in *Little Dorrit*: "Thirty years ago, Marseilles lay burning in the sun, one day. A blazing sun upon a fierce August day was no greater rarity in southern France then, than at any other time, before or since."[22] More recent fiction takes pains to blend Description with the action. In Genette's pungent phrase, Stendhal, Flaubert, and Proust "pulverize" descriptions, diffusing them along the march of events. Joseph Conrad's and Ford Madox Ford's "distribute" is another term for this effect. A good example is Emma Bovary's survey of her new house at Tostes, in which "the general movement of the text is governed by the step or the gaze of one (or several) character(s), and the unfolding of that movement corresponds exactly to the length of the trip."[23]

Critics promoting the "dramatization" of fiction are less likely to find Description intrusive. Unlike Argument, Description is felt to coexist with Narrative without calling attention to itself. Indeed, some theorists argue (wrongly, as I shall try to demonstrate) that Description is itself intrinsically diegetic.

But we must take care to distinguish between Narrative and Description as text-types, on the one hand, and *sentences* in the surface of a text which are loosely called "narrative" or "descriptive," on the other. There is a strong sociolinguistic imperative to name the persons and things we speak of, and naming is always a minimal kind of description. Furthermore, nouns usually occur in noun phrases, where adjectives and other qualifiers perform further description. But from the textual point of view, this is incidental—not concerted—description, not Description as a text-type.

Of particular dubiety are statements such as Genette's: "To recount an event and to describe an object are two similar operations, which bring into play the same resources of language."[24] It is hard to understand quite what that means: *all* text-types actualized by language use the "same resources," since the resources of language are, ultimately, words. (Similarly, all text-types actualized by drawing or cinematography or whatever are constrained by their media.) But surely "to describe" is different from "to narrate," and if we were asked for the typical verb for representing Description, we would cite the copula (or its equivalent) rather than a more active kind of verb. We would say that the subject *was* so-and-so, not that it *did* so-and-so.

At the surface level a sentence may provide a great deal of description even though its main thrust may be narrative. From *Crime and*

Punishment: "The airlessness, the bustle and the plaster, scaffolding, bricks, and dust all about him, and that special Petersburg stench, so familiar to all who are unable to get out of town in summer—all worked painfully upon the young man's already overwrought nerves."[25] A lot of descriptive evocation is crowded into that sentence, even though the action of its predicate, its "comment" or syntactic focus (as opposed to its "topic") remains an "act," the abrasion of Raskolnikov's nerves by the environment.

It is just as easy for narrative sentences to serve a description as for descriptive phrases to fill out a narrative. Consider this excerpt from Peter Quennell's *Byron in Italy*, which is included in Brooks and Warren's *Understanding Fiction* as an example of a "character sketch"— that is, a description which is not a narrative:

> Marguerite Blessington was an adventurous and amusing personage. The daughter of a petty landowner in County Waterford, at the age of fifteen she had been forced into a miserable marriage with a certain Captain St. Leger Farmer of the 47th Foot. After three months, Mrs. Farmer had left her husband; Lawrence had painted her portrait in 1807; and she next re-emerges as the mistress of a Captain Jenkins with whom for several years she had lived in placid domestic retirement. From Captain Jenkins' arms Marguerite Farmer had moved to those of the plutocratic, extravagant, fashionable Lord Mountjoy, and from Stidmanton in Hampshire to a house in Manchester Square. By falling while he was drunk out of the window of a debtor's jail, Captain Farmer had removed the last obstacle to his wife's good fortune, and from that moment she had swept onward with superb assurance. Lord Blessington, an indistinct but kindly figure, was as lavish as he was rich, and as complaisant or unsuspicious as he was devoted. With the Blessingtons travelled that dazzling ephebus Count Alfred d'Orsay, paragon of elegance and model of manly grace, whom the world regarded, no doubt correctly, as Lady Blessington's lover. At thirty-five, with her shining dark hair, neatly parted down the middle of the scalp and drawn back from the smooth white forehead, her delicate skin, noble brow, and lustrous expressive eyes, Marguerite Blessington retained all her power of pleasing. To good looks she added a brisk intelligence, and to vivacity and curiosity some touches of literary aptitude. Naturally, she was eager to visit Byron.[26]

Though the copula in the first sentence suggests that a description will follow, the next four sentences present a narrative, marked by verbs denoting a sequence of events: "had been forced into," "had left her husband," "had lived in . . . retirement," "had moved." But it is a narrative that operates clearly at the service of the description; in particular, it illustrates how Lady Blessington was "adventurous" and "amusing." Thus, active verbs subserve an overriding descriptive purpose. Notice too the verb in "she next re-emerges": though active, at grammatical face value, "re-emerges" bears descriptive rather than narrative force, suggesting not the *story* of her "re-emerging" but a series of tableaux presenting Lady Blessington's person in timed stages. Elsewhere, too, much of the description is conveyed by sentences that are active or "eventful," but only on the surface. Description is communicated also by adjectives modifying nouns in superficially event-marking sentences: "Marguerite Farmer had moved to [the arms] of the plutocratic, extravagant, fashionable Lord Mountjoy"; "With the Blessingtons travelled that dazzling ephebus Count Alfred d'Orsay." Though active, these sentences have no overriding narrative force. No narrative event is cited by the verb "added" in "To good looks she added a brisk intelligence, and to vivacity and curiosity some touches of literary aptitude." This is simply a more elegant way of saying "She was good-looking, intelligent, vivacious, curious, and modestly apt in literature."

Of course, just as Description is here the overriding text-type, the excerpt itself is overridden by the larger narrative, Byron's biography. But (like Brooks and Warren) I have been discussing the excerpt only. It muddies theoretical waters to argue that Description is always ancillary to Narrative and that it cannot occur autonomously, to say with Genette that "description might be conceived independently of narration, but in fact it is never found in a so to speak free state. . . . Description is quite naturally *ancilla narrationis*, the ever-necessary, ever-submissive, never-emancipated slave."[27] That assertion ignores well-established self-contained Descriptive genres such as the "Character." Consider one of Sir Thomas Overbury's efforts, quoted here in toto:

A Pedant

Hee treades in a rule, and one hand scannes verses, and the other holds his scepter. Hee dares not thinke a thought, that the nominative case governs not the verbe; and he never had meaning in his life, for he travelled only for words. His ambition is *criticisme,* and his example *Tully.* Hee values phrases, and elects them by the sound, and the eight parts of speech are his servants. To bee briefe, he is a heteroclite, for hee wants the plurall number, having onely the single quality of words.[28]

Surely this is not a narrative about a pedant but a description of one. Here again, such event-marking active verbs as "treads" and "scans" are only surface phenomena; the text is basically descriptive. What is stressed is the existence and traits of a kind of person, not a history of that person's actions. Unlike the description of Lady Blessington, the descriptive function in "A Pedant" is marked by the simple present indicative (instead of the preterite or the progressive present). But tense is a surface feature of no *necessary* textual consequence. For the purposes of the text-type, these verbs are structurally equivalent to "to be": they are simply another tool for describing the pedant.

Even when the entire surface representation seems narrative, the text as a whole may be working as a description. Consider, for example, the following passage from the *Guide bleu*:

> One begins his visit of Rouen at the quais, where, from the Boiel-
> dieu Bridge, one has a beautiful view of the entire city and port. It
> was from the Mathilde Bridge, which occupied the site of the
> present Boieldieu Bridge, that the ashes of Joan of Arc were thrown
> into the Seine. Upriver, Lacroix Island is connected to the city and
> the suburb [sic] Saint Sever by the new Corneille Bridge. Down-
> river, the quai de la Bourse borders reconstructed neighborhoods
> which form a vast quadrilateral extending to the cathedral. . . . By
> going downriver from the quai de la Bourse, one finds to the right
> the rue Jeanne-d'Arc, a wide modern thoroughfare connecting the
> quais to the Rive-Droite train station. At the end of this street
> appears the new theater (1962), then, going back up the street, one
> sees, to the left, ruins of Saint-Vincent church, 15th and 16th cen-
> turies, of which there remain only the transept and the portal. A
> little further along, on the same side, is located the Tour Saint-
> André-aux-Fèbvres church.[29]

Clearly, the task of such writing is to describe both what there is and what the tourist should see. This "should," of course, implies touches of Argument; a travel guide is concerned not only to describe but to persuade you that you should see x, y if you have extra time, and z not at all. Now the order of presentation of the *Sehenswür-digkeiten*—the "things worth seeing"—is temporal. The temporality *could* suggest a small narrative (with same such title as "Your Trip to Rouen"), but the motive for temporality is clearly quite different. Whereas narrative time ordering creates typical effects—suspense and surprise, the sense of a completed world in a certain era, and the like—the time-ordering principle of a travel guide is simply the convenience of the tourist. You are instructed to start at the Boieldieu Bridge because it provides an excellent overview of the city, a good thing to experience before investigating the sights close up. The sequence in which the *Sehenswürdigkeiten* should be seen may result simply from their contiguity; hence, temporal ordering relates to convenience, to consideration for the tourist's time and energy. In short, as Wallace Martin has put it, "There is a clear difference between the *writer* determining the order of presentation and *events* determining it."[30]

Films, at least documentaries, can also be predominantly descriptive, though subservient moments may follow a narrative line. As David Bordwell and Kristin Thompson demonstrate, the second part of Leni Riefenstahl's documentary on the 1936 Olympics is largely descriptive ("categorical," in their term).[31] Though the progress of individual events is narrated, the film as a whole describes the Games by these categories:

1. Nature and the Olympians: morning exercise and swimming
2. Gymnastics
3. Yacht races
4. Pentathlon
5. Women exercising
6. Decathlon
7. Field games: field hockey, polo, soccer
8. Bicycle race
9. Cross-country riding
10. Crewing
11. Diving and swimming.

Thus, the narrative of each event subserves the descriptive purport of the film as a whole.

So compelling is our need to recognize an overriding text-type that we may see it in a collection of sentences "more appropriate" to a totally different text-type. For example, the surface of a written narrative may contain an inordinate number of "descriptive" sentences. Alain Robbe-Grillet's *La jalousie*, most critics agree, is a narrative (or anti-narrative), even though almost every sentence is descriptive in form:

> On the opposite wall, the centipede is there, in its tell-tale spot, right in the middle of the panel.
> It has stopped, a tiny oblique line two inches long at eye level, halfway between the baseboard (at the hall doorway) and the corner of the ceiling. The creature is motionless. Only its antennae rise and fall one after the other in an alternating, slow, but continuous movement.
> At its posterior extremity. . . . [etc.].[32]

Genette recognizes this fact, but draws an inappropriate conclusion: "The work of Robbe-Grillet appears . . . as an effort to constitute a narrative (a *story*) almost exclusively by means of descriptions imperceptibly modified from one page to the next, which can be regarded both as a spectacular promotion of the descriptive function and as a striking confirmation of its irreducible narrative finality."[33] On the contrary: what is demonstrated is not Description's "irreducible narrative finality" but rather the actualization of one kind of textual function, narrative, by sentences typical of another.

It is not Description's fate, comments Martin, to be irreducibly narrative "simply because it is, perforce, textually sequential."[34] We understand it as subservient to Narrative when the text makes more overall sense and rewards us more richly as a narrative than as a description. None of the text-types has any special privilege in the universe of textuality. Overriding structures are not necessarily reflected in the surface form of individual sentences (or other signifiers). Texts are hierarchical, and we should acknowledge differences in hierarchy with such words as "overriding" and "at the service of."

CHAPTER 2 /

Description Is No
Textual Handmaiden

OUR LEADING narratologist, Gérard Genette, has written:

It would appear . . . that description, as a mode of literary representation, does not distinguish itself sufficiently clearly from narration,
either by the autonomy of its ends, or by the originality of its
means, for it to be necessary to break the narrative-descriptive
(chiefly narrative) unity that Plato and Aristotle have called narrative. If description marks one of the frontiers of narrative, it is
certainly an internal frontier, and really a rather vague one: it will do
no harm, therefore, if we embrace within the notion of narrative all
forms of literary representation and consider description not as one
of its modes (which would imply a specificity of language), but,
more modestly, as one of its aspects—if, from a certain point of
view, the most attractive.[1]

Genette repeated this view in *Narrative Discourse*: "What is distinctive about these [narrator's commentaries or interventions] is that
they are not strictly speaking narrative. Descriptions, on the other
hand, as constituents of the spatio-temporal universe of the story, are
diegetic."[2]

Genette's assimilation of Description to Narration reflects a prejudice of long historical standing. We owe to Philippe Hamon a rich
account of that history, from classical rhetoric (with its elaborate
taxonomy of subtypes: chronography, topography, prosopography,

22

ethopoeia, prosopopoeia, portrait, parallel, tableau, and so on) down to the *nouveau roman*.[3]

The tradition considers Description secondary or derivative—not just at the service of but positively inferior to Narrative (which usually gets elevated to "epic" in the discussion). This prejudice, Hamon speculates, probably grew out of Description's association with humdrum, utilitarian tasks—stock inventories, travel guides, sets of instructions, and so on. "To describe," writes Hamon, has always been "to describe for." Rhetoricians and critics have perhaps felt that "service" (in the technical sense in which I use the term) is itself a mark of superficiality. Or, because Description is the text-type most favored by lyric poems (seen as a "purer" form of poetry than epics), perhaps its use in Narrative is deprecated because it tempts the author to interrupt the narrative line with extended purple passages for their own sake. Whatever the reason, Description is, to the tradition, "discourse ornament's ornament, a sort of superlative process whose excess must be controlled carefully."[4]

Hamon gives a long and distinguished list of rhetoricians and critics who have mistrusted Description: Marmontel, author of the article on Description in the *Encyclopédie*, Blair, Larousse, Boileau, and even Valéry, who wrote: "If this latitude [of describing] and the habit of facility which goes with it, become the dominating factor, it gradually dissuades writers from employing their ability for abstraction, just as it reduces to nothing the slightest necessity for concentration on the reader's part."[5] "Classical theoreticians," Hamon notes "seem to have seen in Description only a risky 'drift' from detail to detail—a process which, above all else, threatens the homogeneity, the cohesion and the dignity of the [narrative] work."[6]

To the traditionalist, Hamon continues, Description poses a "triple danger": it favors the "foreign vocabulary" or jargon of the *métiers* from which it derives; it becomes "an end and no longer a means" and thus takes over the text-type that it is supposed to subserve; and finally, by its "uncontrollable freedom" it loosens the text's control of "the reader's reactions." So (the tradition proclaims),

description . . . should never constitute the aim of discourse, but must remain a "subordinate means" (the expression is Lukács' in ["Narrate or Describe?"], a text which is surprisingly close to Marmontel's in many ways). Let this subordination be at the service of

23

instances external to the discourse (any practical aim, an auditor to convince, a scholarly text to constitute), or of instances internal to the discourse (a coherence, a hierarchy, an anaphoric chain, a "logic," a narrative *lisibilité* to insure). In short, description must not be digression, "hors-d'oeuvre". . . . Description must . . . remain subordinate to the highest hierarchical instances of discourse, to the narration [*récit*] on one hand, and on the other to the highest existing subject, *the* Subject, the human being.[7]

Like many blanket critical proscriptions, this one ignores the complexity of the discourse situation. It assumes that textual "service" can go in only one direction—from lowly Description to lofty Narrative. But as we saw in the preceding chapter, in many works whose overriding text-type is Description, the "service" is performed by a contained Narrative, not the other way around.

Neither is Description's putative "drift" from detail to detail aimless. Description has a logic of its own, and it is unreasonable to belittle it because it does not resemble the chrono-logic of Narration. Hamon has characterized this logic as metonymic: the description of a garden, for example, presupposes "almost necessarily the enumeration of diverse flowers, paths, parterres, trees, tools, etc. which constitute the garden."[8] The metonymic structure may entail the relation of objects to each other as they occur in the world or in the imagination, but also the relation of objects to their own qualities, where "quality" is to be understood in the broadest sense.

Metonymy, of course, rests on the principle of contiguity (as metaphor rests on that of similarity). And contiguity operates in Description in every dimension—not only the spatial but the abstract, the intellectual, the moral, and so on. Meir Sternberg has written well about the complexities of the relationship between contiguity and other ordering principles that support, modify, or subvert it.[9] These are extremely varied, extending from "hierarchy" (for instance, the seating order in a scene in *Vanity Fair*) to such purely formal connecting devices as rhyme and alliteration ("Of shoes—and ships—and sealing wax— / Of cabbages and kings"). In standard descriptions (like that of Hamon's garden) the contiguity corresponds to "ordinary experience": gardens typically contain such and such objects, the relation container-contained being one of metonymy's subclasses of ordering. Sternberg would say that in such cases a strong ordering principle drives the contents of the descripta.

On the other hand, where the contiguity is weak—that is, where a description conjoins barely related or even unrelated ("discontiguous") particulars—we seek cohesion in other conventions. For example, as Stephen Dedalus walks toward the university, we read this description of Stephen's Green:

> The trees in Stephen's Green were fragrant of rain and the rainsodden earth gave forth its mortal odour, a faint incense rising upward through the mould from many hearts. The soul of the gallant venal city which his elders had told him of had shrunk with time to a faint mortal odour rising from the earth.[10]

"Gallant" and "venal" are hardly contiguous, but we accept their juxtaposition under another convention, namely, that of realism or verisimilitude, based here on some such topos as "the heterogeneity of the modern metropolis" or the "complexity of the poet's mind." Other novelists, Hemingway among them, yoke discontiguous elements but for other thematic reasons. Barthes's *effet de réel* theoretically explains this phenomenon: the unmotivated yet stubborn presence of some incongruent existent or quality is precisely what guarantees the "realism" of its presence.[11]

The same appeal to supporting conventions is implicit in complex descriptions of characters. Here is Dostoevsky's narrator's description of Peter Verkhovensky upon his first appearance in *The Possessed* (or *The Devils*):

> He was a young man of about twenty-seven, slightly above medium height, with rather long, thin fair hair and with a wispy, barely discernible, moustache and beard. He was dressed decently, even fashionably, but not smartly; at the first glance he looked a little round-shouldered and awkward, though in fact he was not round-shouldered at all, and rather free-and-easy in his manners. He seemed to be a sort of eccentric, and yet afterwards we all found his manners extremely agreeable and his conversation always to the point.
>
> No one could say that he was not good-looking, but no one liked his face. His head was elongated at the back and somewhat flattened at the sides, so that his face looked rather sharp. His forehead was high and narrow, but his features rather small; his eyes were sharp, his nose small and pointed, his lips long and thin. He looked a little ill, but only seemed so.[12]

There follows a whole series of contradictions: Peter is complacent but not aware of it; he talks rapidly and hurriedly but self-confidently and with amazingly clear articulation. It is clearly an ambiguous portrait, yet we accept the contradictions—indeed we praise them as high art—because of two conventions we have learned so well: that of the "round" character, and that of the uncertain or ambivalent reporter. Peter is not just a villain; he is an *interesting* villain. Complex self-contradiction is "recuperable" as a source of both "roundness" and narratorial uncertainty, and hence of modern "psychological" interest.

In short, Description has a logic of its own, which is no less explicable—in terms of operant conventions—than that of Narrative or Argument. Further, rhetorical conservatives to the contrary notwithstanding, there is no need to determine its "value" with respect to the other text-types. Value is an issue only to the critic concerned with the relative success of a given work.

Genette is not the only theorist or critic who finds Description somehow ancillary and hence, by implication, inferior to Narrative. The attitudes of Georg Lukács, which inhabit an ideologically different world, are also worth examining. Lukács frames his argument by a comparison between parallel episodes in two novels, Zola's *Nana* and Tolstoy's *Anna Karenina*. The subject of each is a horse race. In Zola, the "race is *described* from the standpoint of an observer; in Tolstoy it is narrated from the standpoint of a participant." The first is "merely descriptive," the second is "epic." Why? Because the first occurs by "mere chance," while the second is "inevitable." Inevitability can arise only "out of the relationship of characters to objects and events, a dynamic interaction in which the characters act and suffer."[13]

One does not need to become a defender of Zola to question the reasoning here. These are clearly sectarian critical pronouncements, not theoretical observations. It is, of course, true that set pieces of description went out of fashion with the Modernist novel. But even "pulverized" or "distributed" description is only one alternative style. We should beware of confusing stylistic preference, whether of an individual or an era, with narrative theory.

Implicit in Lukács's view is a rejection of the Barthesian notion of verisimilitude—that it is precisely the fortuitousness of a *descriptum* that guarantees its realism. Lukács concedes the possibility of the "irrelevantly real," though with some reluctance: "The objective factors in a man's environment are not always and inevitably so intimately linked to his fate [as they are in Balzac and Tolstoy]. They can provide instruments for his activity and for his career and even, as in Balzac, turning points in his fortunes. But they may also simply provide the setting for his activity and for his career."[14]

Lukács goes on to praise Flaubert—faintly—for this effect, acknowledging the merits of the *comices agricoles* episode in *Madame Bovary*. But he praises it only to the extent that it ultimately collaborates in some higher "symbolic" level:

Flaubert presents only a "setting." For him the fair is merely background for the decisive love scene between Rudolf [*sic*] and Emma Bovary. The setting is incidental, merely "setting." Flaubert underscores its incidental character; by interweaving and counterposing official speeches with fragments of love dialogue, he offers an ironic juxtaposition of the public and private banality of the petty bourgeoisie, accomplishing this parallel with consistency and artistry.

But there remains an unresolved contradiction: this incidental setting, this accidental occasion for a love scene, is simultaneously an important event in the world of the novel; the minute description of this setting is absolutely essential to Flaubert's purpose, that is, to the comprehensive exposition of the social milieu. The ironic juxtaposition does not exhaust the significance of the description. The "setting" has an independent existence as an element in the representation of the environment. The characters, however, are nothing but observers of this setting. To the reader they seem undifferentiated, additional elements of the environment Flaubert is describing. They become dabs of colour in a painting which rises above a lifeless level only insofar as it is elevated to an ironic symbol of philistinism. The painting assumes an importance which does not arise out of the subjective importance of the events, to which it is scarcely related, but from the artifice of the formal stylization.

Flaubert achieves his symbolic content through irony and consequently on a considerable level of artistry and to some extent with genuine artistic means. But when, as in the case of Zola, the symbol is supposed to embody social monumentality and is supposed to imbue episodes, otherwise meaningless, with great social significance, true art is abandoned.[15]

27

In this view, Flaubert's artistic means are genuine only "to some extent." "Setting" is to be deprecated *as a general principle*: it is "mere" or "incidental" unless integrated with an "important event in the world of the novel." By "world," Lukács seems to mean the novel's ultimate, total meaning, with all its thematic banners flying. Humdrum setting and characters made humdrum by their presence therein ("they seem undifferentiated, additional elements of the environment") find relevance only as an "ironic symbol of philistinism." So description itself is not what achieves Flaubert's "considerable level of artistry." Only irony gives him that award. To Marxist as to bourgeois literary theory, them, Description's sole value is to subserve some other textual purpose.

Surely a text theory unencumbered by prescriptivism or ideological projects can furnish a better understanding of the differences between the text-types, since it does not need to rank them in order of nobility. Whether a description serves a narrative *well* seems not a theoretical but a critical problem, to be determined by the analysis and evaluation of the individual text. But the notion of subservience itself is not mysterious. It is simply a term naming how it is that text-types sometimes work explicitly and sometimes implicitly. Why they do so well or badly in given cases is the critic's task to explain.

We can distinguish at least three ways in which Description may be rendered by a text's surface:

(1) Assertions. Here the surface representation corresponds directly to what we might call the standard text-type form: "Simon is simple."

(2) Nonassertive mentions or inclusions: "Simple Simon met a pie-man going to the fair." Here, the depiction of Simon as "simple" is, by the syntax, oblique or "casual," that is, not the ostensible purpose of the sentence. Still, the word occurs in the surface representation.

(3) Elliptical implications: "A passerby asked Simon for a shilling, and Simon gave it to him. The passerby laughed and ran off." Here, the reader must infer Simon's simplicity by interpreting the juxtaposition of the two events: Simon's giving money to a total stranger without demanding a reason, and the stranger's gleeful running off. The reader does so according to codes she believes to be operative in this context: for example, the (capitalist) code that

says that giving money away for no reason is foolish. (An opposite inference, of course, might be drawn in a culture not governed by this code, or even in our own culture where a competing code like "Christian charity" countervailed.)

It has been hard for even sophisticated theorists to stay clear on the distinction between surface representations and the overriding (or "deep") structure of a text. Wallace Martin, for instance, argues that Description and Narrative "fuse" into an indistinguishable whole and that any boundary between the two must be artificial:

> Separating description from the dynamics of action and character . . . suggests that it is a fixed element of the text, added to provide emotional coloring or decor, and thus of secondary importance. The conventional distinction between narration and description has reinforced the artificial boundary between the two . . .
>
> When Tolstoy describes a battle, or Huck a thunderstorm, should we call the passages descriptions or actions? "Action" and "narration" tend to be applied only to accounts of what human beings do; other kinds of change may be called events or happenings. But this contrast between the living/changing and inanimate/static is blurred when one realizes that if an event is defined as a transition from one state of affairs to another, it must entail static description of one or both states . . . Furthermore, changes within the mind may be marked by verbs implying dynamism, yet not involve external change.[16]

But, I would stipulate, Description and Narration are "fused" only at the level of sentences, not at that of underlying structure. The term "fusion" blurs the distinction between Narrative (or indeed any text-type) and its actualization in a medium. Obviously, many sentences in a novel, most shots in a movie, and all postures and movements in a narrative ballet or mime show concurrently present actions (events) and characters and settings (existents) in a seamless unity. "The sleepy cat sat on the fancy mat" at once narrates ("recounts") the action of the cat's sitting on the mat and describes ("depicts") the cat as sleepy and the mat as fancy. As Alexander Gelley observes, "Action does not stop so that description may take over. Settings are involved in the action from the start."[17] The seamlessness of a sentence (film shot, balletic movement) at a text's surface should not blind us to the diverse textual functions it may perform at more abstract levels.

In short, the notion of "fusion" raises more problems than it solves. It is not that the text-types fuse; rather, one comes in to assist the other. "Fusion"—if we must use the term—occurs only at the surface level of the actualized text. It is part of the representational capacity of media to do two or more things at once: a given sentence can include elements that narrate but also describe and/or argue. Heterogeneous functions in the discourse get woven together into a homogeneously rendered surface.

Narratology, like text study in general, needs to abstract textual elements from the (theoretically) "accidental" way in which they appear in texts. Only if we keep clear on the differences between surface representation and underlying structure can we know when we are speaking about the *text-type* Description and when, rather, about a descriptive *passage* on the text's surface (note lowercase letter), one that utilizes the copula or its equivalent to assert the qualities of some object. The passage, of course, may subserve any of the text-types. For example, in the following sentence the actualized surface signifier (which could be conveyed in other ways—say, by a camera movement or a stylized drawing) is at one with the descriptive underlying structure: "The cat raced through the house. It was a black streak of lightning." The first sentence overtly represents action, while the second overtly conveys the qualities attributed to a story-object. Consider the different connotations of "John entered the dark room," versus "The room was dark. John opened the door and entered." In the latter, "The room was dark" constitutes an assertion of sorts, calling the darkness of the room to special attention. In the former, the descriptive information seems incidental, slipped in, as it were.

A similar distinction routinely operates in film. Say a film opens with a panoramic shot of a landscape, and we gather that the movement is "descriptive." Since the usual institutional setting of movie-going presupposes narrative films unless otherwise stated, (see Chapter 4), we infer that story time has not yet begun. On the other hand, if a movie opens in the middle of what is obviously a plot-relevant action, it is left to our secondary attention to absorb descriptive details as we can.

However the information is introduced at the level of the actualized text, the distinction between Narration and Description at the discourse level is not artificial but quite real. The two render the world in fundamentally different ways. As has been argued from the earliest days of narratology, Narrative entails two time dimensions, an inner- or story-duration and an outer- or discourse-duration, whereas Description has no inner time dimension, however much time its actual transmission in a medium may require. In the example of the introductory landscape shot, nothing of narrative significance has yet happened.

Nor does *movement* necessarily mark the end of description and the beginning of narrative. A moving object in a film's establishing shot—say, a flying pigeon—does not necessarily represent a first narrative event. The shot remains descriptive unless or until it turns out that the pigeon's movement connects, chrono-logically, with a plot sequence—either *as* an event (the pigeon carries vital news strapped to its leg) or as part of the setting for the first event (the bird flies through the country air as the hero and heroine kiss). This is not merely the difference between animals and human beings; the pigeon may in fact be a narrative agent or even, as in a children's book, a hero. But in any case, the pigeon's movement must operate not only in time but in *story* time; otherwise, its flight, though "dynamic," serves no plot function and remains a descriptive detail.[18]

That is the appropriate answer, I think, to the problem of how to treat the background battles and thunderstorms in *War and Peace* and *Huckleberry Finn*. "Dynamism" is not the issue. If we get no sense that plot time is advanced by an action, no sense that the battle or thunderstorm is tied to the event chain but is simply *there* (and would, presumably, continue to be there even if no plot were unfolding), then we infer that its function is simply descriptive, not narrative.

A related way of looking at the distinction between Description and Narrative has been elegantly argued by Jeffrey Kittay.[19] Asking the question "In what sense can 'description' be truly free of action?" Kittay notes that paintings and other artifacts that traditionally form models for Description have only *surfaces*; therefore, perceiving them is necessarily restricted in a certain way. In contemplating a painting, the percipient cannot go "through" or "behind" the artifact. ("Going through" is obviously essential to Narrative: it is part of its very definition.) A percipient can move anywhere in the room in which the painting hangs but will still perceive it as a timeless and spatially fixed whole. The objects represented in the painting, despite the percipient's changing angle (whose only restriction is that it must be less than 180 degrees), will remain essentially the same. The painting is closed on itself (another way of saying that it is eventless). Even artifacts like sculptures that require a *parcours*—a circumambulation by the percipient—contain parts that necessarily remain fixed and closed; no story is entailed, because nothing can change except the position of the percipient, which is irrelevant. The same thing is true of verbally rendered descriptions. The verbal descriptum, like the painting, has only one surface: there is, essentially, no "behind." This is clearly the case in the opening chapter of *Père Goriot* and in the "establishing" sequence of the classical Hollywood movie.

But once there is uncertainty, once there is openness and "risk," the circumambulation may begin to feel like Narrative. Kittay contrasts the contemplation of a painting with a visit to a haunted house or a labyrinth. For the labyrinth to be truly labyrinthine, the *actions* of the percipient become relevant: he becomes, in a way, the protagonist of a self-created narrative. "He has lost that relationship to what is before him that had guaranteed him harmless witness status. . . . Here is not just sequence, but consequence and irreversibility, as Barthes surely understood it."[20] Choice, risk, consequence, irreversibility: these are the operant conventions of the labyrinth—and of Narrative.

Narrative at the service of Description amounts to the *tableau*, to use Kittay's term. In the tableau, act is "consecrated, memorialized and monumentalized, endowed with power. It is offered up with the varnish of surface. . . . Rather than action putting description 'in its place,' it is action that is taken from its dis-place and put, one might say nailed, in its place. It is action that has become an asyndetic act, like the stages of the passion of Christ, the representation of any of which (as when depicted on a stained-glass window) can singly and independently show his martyrdom. The tableau draws a frame around the act, to ask that meaning be ascribed to it."[21]

The "asyndetism" entailed in the incorporation of a battle or thunderstorm into a narrative as a purely descriptive element is its disconnection from any of its *own* temporal consequences. The tableau effect forms the basis of the Homeric "dramatized" descriptions so admired by Lessing: "Even where [Homer] has to do with nothing but the picture, he will distribute this picture in a sort of story of the object, in order to let its parts, which we see side by side in Nature, follow his painting after each other and as it were keep step with the flow of the narrative."[22]

Consider the oft cited passage in *The Iliad* which "dramatically" describes Agamemnon's armor. As Hamon paraphrases Lessing's point, "instead of listing immediately the different parts of a warrior's armament, the author introduces us to this warrior as he gathers his equipment before leaving to fight—thereby successively putting on the different parts of his armament, that is, dressing himself in the 'natural' order (the shoulder belt for example would come *after* the breast-plate)."[23] This mini-narrative, the process of dressing, works at the service of the description of Agamemnon's armor; the process of dressing itself, Lessing might say, is a kind of pretext for describing what the armor was like. This description itself, in turn, subserves the overriding narrative of the *Iliad*.

An even more complex example is the description of Achilles' shield in Book 13, a passage often discussed and, in the prescriptive tradition, praised as the *only* way to describe something in an overridingly narrative text. What has not generally been recognized, however, is that it presents *two* series of events, only one of which can be called dramatized description.[24] Hephaistos's actual fabrication of the shield is a story event, not a description—precisely, that event which comes between Thetis's request for the armor for Achilles and her "shooting like a falcon from snowy Olympus" to deliver it to her son. After all, a Barthesian "risk" was entailed: Hephaistos might have refused her request. Not that the event is terribly interesting in its surface representation: it is highly iterative, recounting simply a series of Hephaistos's "fashionings," "placings," "puttings," "makings," "workings," and the like, each one attached to the formulaic "Upon it . . ." Still, the actions constitute an important story event, not a description.

The dramatized description occurs, rather, in the representations of what is to be seen in each of the concentric circles. Just outside the innermost circle of the boss (a simple cosmic still life of Earth, Sky, Sea, Sun and thus a descriptive piece in its own right), the second circle is described in a dramatized way:

Upon it he fashioned two cities of mortal men, and fine ones. In the first was wedding and feasting; they were leading brides from their chambers along the streets under the light of blazing torches, and singing the bridal song. There were dancing boys twirling about, pipes and harps made a merry noise; the women stood at their doors and watched. A crowd was in the market-place, where a dispute was going on. Two men disputed over the blood-price of a man who had been killed: one said he had offered all, and told his tale before the people, the other refused to accept anything; but both were willing to appeal to an umpire for the decision. The crowd cheered one or other as they took sides, and the heralds kept them in order.[25]

Here again is a multiple layering of "service." The narrative of the dispute of the two men over a dead man's blood price is at the service of the description of the shield; the description of the shield is, in turn, at the service of the larger plot, in particular that portion of it that encompasses the series "request-manufacture-delivery."

"Service" names a structural, not a critical concept; I do not mean to suggest value implications by the term. There are many texts whose connoted descriptive elements emerge as aesthetically more important than their denoted narrative elements. The narrative elements are there, it seems, only to justify the description. Not that the lines between Description and Narrative are always clear or unambiguous: postmodern fiction regularly problematizes the relations between the text-types. All the more reason for the utility of the notion of text-type "service." Consider, for example, the problematic relations between Description and Narration in Alain Robbe-Grillet's *Instantanés* (snapshots), especially "The Secret Room."[26] Given Robbe-Grillet's express rejection of narrative convention, one must approach this text with due temerity. Our usual expectation of textual coherence prompts us to ask, for example, whether the text is a description of a bloody scene served by a narrative, or a narrative of a grisly murder served by a description. Cleanth Brooks and Robert Penn Warren opt for the second interpretation, calling the text a "story." But they find it a rather imperfect one, complaining that it "does not have a plot in the ordinary sense" and that it "implies an intention for its manipulation of time that it does not fulfill."[27] Clearly, the value judgment masks some uneasiness about what kind of a text "The Secret Room" is. In the text theory I am proposing, it is not possible to say, as Brooks and Warren do, that "the story *describes* a painting" (my emphasis). For if all that happens is a describing, then the text cannot be a story; it must be a description. Is it a description or is it a story?

Identifying the overriding text-type of "The Secret Room" entails questions like these:

(1) Are the descriptions—of the blood, the woman's mutilated body, the killer in his cape, the stairway, the pillars, the incense burner and so on—at the service of a narrative whose central event is that of a man stabbing a nude sacrificial victim?

(2) Or are the events, minimal as they are—the stabbing itself and the escape of the man up the stairs and out the door—at the service of a description of a painting, only clearly identified as such in the last word of the text? If so, what is the nature and purpose of that description, and how precisely do the recounted events serve it?

(3) What is the significance of deciding on a reversed chronologic that moves the killer back down the steps from the door to the woman's side and then, after another reversal (in paragraph 18) back up the stairway, in a more "normal" order of causation?

On the surface, the descriptive *sentences* seem not at all the sort that an omniscient narrator would use to establish a scene. Many of them, including the first, read not as statements of hard information but as representations or, rather, as *struggles* to represent something dimly perceived, as attempts to determine how the components fit into a visual scene. But the struggle is not attributed to any human being within or without the scene. It occurs from the outset in an impersonal way, often in the passive voice: "the first thing to be seen is a red stain"; "the whole stands out against a smooth, pale surface"; "another identical round form . . . is seen at almost the same angle of view"; "the haloed point . . . is . . . quite recognizable"; "a black silhouette is seen"; "it is a uniformly colored velvet of dark purple, or which seems so in this lighting"; "the dimensions of this room are difficult to determine exactly"; "it is the left foot, and its chain, that are the most minutely depicted." All these impersonal observations are explicated by the final phrase "toward the top of the canvas." Brooks and Warren call it a "surprise ending," but it is hardly that in the O. Henry sense of the term. There is no plot reversal but rather a text-type reversal. What we were hypothesizing as a narrative turns in an instant into a description. Or does it? Is the text simply a description of an oil painting? Why are the identity and even the existence of the describer left problematic? What is the import of his or her struggle to make out the painting's contents?

The other problem concerns the events. Brooks and Warren wonder about the time order; but there is a more fundamental question: How can "events" be said to occur on a painted canvas? The killer's movements are first presented by ambiguous passives—"a black silhouette is seen fleeing"—but ultimately they are expressed by active verbs: "the man has already moved several steps back"; "the man . . . leans farther over"; "the [woman's] head turns from side to side, struggling." We can reject a trivial hypothesis out of hand: we have no reason to assume that the painting is like a cartoon, separating the stages of the grisly event into panels. But how then, in a single canvas, can a killer ascend stairs, a victim pant, smoke rise, and so on?

Several hypotheses seem open to us: perhaps the text is a fantasy or dream in which the ordinary rules of nature are suspended; or perhaps the movements are in some sense metaphoric or symbolic; or perhaps they represent something in the *observer's* mind. For me, the most interesting possibility is the third. Assume, for instance, that an art museum visitor is mentally reconstructing a "before" and an "after" of the critical moment of murder depicted on a painting. That interpretation would provide a kind of answer to two questions: what the painting depicts, and why the chrono-logic of events is skewed.[28]

In this hypothesis, the movement backward and forward does not narrate the stages of the sacrificial murder, anachronically, but rather represents the speculations of a person standing in front of the painting about what led up to and away from the gruesome event. That would certainly better explain the relevance of the title "Snapshots" to this particular text. This hypothesis leads us back to an interpretation of the text as a narrative. Perhaps the narrative is not of the murder (the ostensible story) but of the impact of the painting of the murder on some unknown contemplator. In other words, what we had first assumed to be the discourse—sparse as it is—is now recognized as the story. I do not offer this as a foolproof interpretation of "The Secret Room," but it does seem to me more coherent than what we get from other interpretations. More important for the present discussion, it demonstrates the elaborate ambiguities and tensions open to the postmodernist manipulator of text-type conventions.

To sum up, text theory in general and narratology in particular could hardly do better than to follow Hamon's recommendation: "To map out a theory of the descriptive would be . . . to avoid localising it as an *anterior* practice (the 'documents collected before writing') or reducing it to its transitivity by labelling it in such a way as to put it perpetually *at the service* of hierarchically superior instances of narration."[29] No, not "perpetually," only sometimes—and with the recognition that the service may sometimes go the other way.

If the foregoing discussion has any validity, one point needs to be reiterated: namely, that we should avoid such sloppy expressions as "the narrator *describes* such and such a narrative event." Objects and characters may be described, but actions are "described" only if they function as part of the described setting rather than as links in the event chain. Story-relevant events are only "narrated," not described. The function of an action, whatever its inner constitution, is not narrative if it is not in the chrono-logic—not keyed, that is, to the ongoing march of story events.

CHAPTER *3* /

What Is Description
in the Cinema?

TEXT THEORY NEEDS to distinguish between express or *explicit* Description and *tacit* Description. Sentences that explicitly describe are cast so as to focus on or even assert the properties of whatever they describe. Sentences that tactitly describe, on the other hand, direct our primary attention to something else—in the case of Narrative, to the story events; the properties of characters, objects, or ideas are communicated secondarily. Most sentences contain tacit descripta; even the name of a person or object is in some sense descriptive.

Though each text-type can be actualized in any communicative medium (texts can be written, drawn, mimed, acted, sung, danced, painted on canvas, projected as shadows on movie screens, illuminated by pixils on television sets, and so on), each medium privileges certain ways of doing so. Films, obviously, are more visually specific than novels, and filmmakers traditionally prefer visual representations to verbal ones. In other words, the medium privileges tacit Description. The choice of certain actors, costumes, and sets and their rendition under certain conditions of lighting, framing, angling, and so on all constitute what Aristotle called *opsis* or spectacle. The choices are, of course, made by the set designer, costumer, and the like, but from our text-immanent perspective we attribute them to the inventional principle (or implied author), who furnishes them to the cinematic narrator[1] for immediate presentation.[2]

Still, some film critics claim flatly, with Claude Ollier, that "the

38

idea of description . . . has no equivalent in the cinema."[3] Though Ollier does not elaborate, we can imagine at least two reasons for this claim. The first derives from the explicit-tacit distinction and from the plenitude of the visual image. Because narrative film keeps characters and props persistently before our eyes and ears with virtually limitless sensory particularity, there seems no *need* for films to describe; it is their nature to show—and to show continuously—a cornucopia of visual details. But to say that such showing *excludes* Description implies a questionable definition of the term. Ollier perhaps feels that Description proper requires a *selection* among visual or other details for the purpose of evoking some kind of picture of persons and objects. That is true enough for literary descriptions; even the most elaborate provide only a relatively small number of details, leaving to the reader the task of filling in the total picture.

Consider the first description of the protagonist of the novel *The French Lieutenant's Woman*: Charles Smithson, as he walks along the quay at Lyme Regis, dressed "impeccably in a light gray, with his top hat held in his free hand, had severely reduced his dundrearies."[4] "Dundrearies" are long flowing side-whiskers, named after the character Lord Dundreary in the play *Our American Cousin*. Compared with the rich visual evocation of the film, these details of Charles's appearance are relatively sparse—though precise, because *named*. The film offers a multitude of visual details, more than any viewer could mentally specify; the specification would be in words, and we do not name every detail we see. Further, these details appear simultaneously in the first instant of the sequence. We see not only Charles's sideburns in their full glory but along with them the exact contour and color of his hat, the curl of its brim, the angle of his spread collar and Windsor tie, the precise color and texture of his overcoat and suit coat, his vest and trousers in matching tweed, his darker brown gloves, and so on. Indeed, the film image, as a sign or group of signs of Charles's appearance, *exhausts* the total potential of visible descriptive details. There is no "hole": the image is complete, of a single piece. But for all this plenitude, we still do not know (short of being experts in Victorian fashion) that Charles's sideburns are "dundrearies."

Film gives us plenitude without specificity. Its descriptive offerings are at once visually rich and verbally impoverished. Unless supplemented by redundancies in dialogue or voice-over narration, cinematic images cannot guarantee our ability to name bits of descriptive information. Contrarily, literary narrative *can* be precise, but always within a relatively narrow scope. Even if a dozen more details were added to the novel's description of Charles's clothes, they would still constitute only a selection among the vast number that could be cited. There would always be "holes" left. Verbal description could, but never does, encompass the multitude of detail available in a photograph.

Why should "description" be limited to the discrete, discontinuous, heterogeneous citation of details characteristic of literature? For a general text theory, I see no reason for such a limitation. Just because the camera gives the "complete" picture, with no holes, why should it be said to be incapable of rendering description? In a sense, the very cinematic projection of images entails Description. It is not that cinema cannot describe; on the contrary, it cannot *help* describing, though usually it does so only tacitly. Its evocation of details is incessantly rich. Every screen "noun" is already, by virtue of the medium, totally saturated with visual "adjectives." The screen image cannot avoid them; it cannot present a minimal verbal account like "A woman entered the room." Rather, it must provide an exhaustive set of visual details, transcribable by a potentially unlimited verbal paraphrase: "A woman with a Roman nose, high cheekbones, and blond hair piled elaborately on her head (etc., etc.) flounced ostentatiously into an ornate ballroom lit by a hundred candles in a glass candelabra (etc., etc.)." The *effet de réel* is intrinsic to the medium: film cannot avoid a cornucopia of visual details, some of which are inevitably "irrelevant" from the strict plot point of view.

Literary narratives, on the other hand, though they may employ many adjectives, cannot *dictate* mental images; they can only stimulate them. Everyone watching the film version of *Gone with the Wind* must agree about Rhett Butler's appearance: he is the spitting image of Clark Gable. But readers of the novel, if they have not seen the film, will probably disagree about the exact details of Rhett's appearance. Indeed, some may resent having to form a mental picture of him at all. It is well known that readers differ in their capacity or desire to construct mental imagery out of words. And even the most enthusiastic imager probably does not keep an unchanging mental portrait in constant focus as he plows through a novel.

Conversely, literary narrative has a kind of power over visual details that is not enjoyed by the cinema. That is the power of noncommitment. A novel can say simply, "He went walking," leaving unspecified the appearance of "he," the vigor and speed of his stride, the environment through which he walked. A film rendition would *have* to add descriptive details: the film's "he" would be of a certain height and weight and age, wear certain clothes, and so on; the environment would be urban or rural; even a time of day would be chosen by the camera and lighting crews.[5]

Let us consider again the two versions of *The French Lieutenant's Woman*. In the novel, the characters Charles and Ernestina are not identified until the second chapter; the first refers to them simply as a "pair" walking down the quay. Because we understand the text to be a novel, and convention tells us that a novel is about characters, we are likely to identify the "pair" as human beings, as potential characters. But the word itself means only "two of something." And the indeterminacy is sustained through similarly vague words—"strangers," "people," "them"—until the last paragraph of the chapter, when we learn that this pair is a couple, a man and a woman.

Of course, a literary narrative could go on indefinitely at this level of vagueness (think of Samuel Beckett). Readers can be kept in the dark, for as long as the implied author wishes, about the reason for a character's physical indeterminacy—whether, for example, it is intended to evoke a sense of distance, or to sustain curiosity, or to stress her spiritual over her bodily self. We accept indeterminacy as a convention of literary narrative. Indeed, we are generally unconscious of it. We have learned to believe that vague words have some raison d'être. The author will either replace them with more specific words or demonstrate why a hazy image is appropriate. But film cannot be vague, at least not visually vague. There is no way of conveying, photographically, a "pair" and nothing else. Of course, two objects could be photographed in such poor light (dusk, fog) that it would be impossible to determine what they were. But the image would still not be synonymous with "pair"; the word alone offers no explanation of the illuminational cause of indeterminacy, whereas the image would contain elements of self-explanation—in the lighting, in the distance of the two objects from the camera, in atmospheric conditions.

A second reason for Ollier's denial of the possibility of Description in cinema might be the temporal demands of the medium. Because screen time moves inexorably forward, carrying the spectator with it, films permit none of the "lingering" that we associate with Description in literary Narrative. Descriptive details in cinema, it might be argued, can occur only as a byproduct of plot action; they do not have a separate existence. Film, Ollier might say, tolerates no "pause," in Genette's technical sense; a film's discourse time cannot continue in the abeyance of story time, because the film—and hence the forward movement of the story—cannot be arrested. In film, the traits of characters and features of setting must be picked up on the run.

But even if we credit these arguments, we must, I think, still recognize Description in the cinema. Again, it is simply that cinematic Description tends to be tacit rather than explicit. Christian Metz includes the "descriptive" as one of his large articulative syntagmas; it is that kind of editing in which the relation of shots is one of simultaneity, not consecutiveness. A landscape may be described, for example, by "a tree, followed by a shot of a stream running next the tree, followed by a view of a hill in the distance, etc."[6] Even though these views appear consecutively on the screen, the point is not that the shots are diegetically simultaneous but that story time has temporarily been suspended. The shot sequence forms a narrative pause. The sign of the pause is precisely the temporally unmotivated shifting from tree to stream to hill. On the other hand, exactly the same sequence of shots *would* be narrative if they preceded or followed shots indicating the eye movements of a character looking or something ("first he looked at the tree, then at the stream, then at the hills").

Professional transcriptions of what has transpired on the screen, called "cutting continuities," often indicate the film's intention to describe. Here is a published transcription of the first shot of Michelangelo Antonioni's *L'Avventura*:

> Long shot. A sunny summer day. Anna, a twenty-five-year-old brunette, walks through the courtyard in front of a stately villa and comes through an archway at the entrance to the courtyard. She stops, looks around and hearing her father's voice, moves toward him.[7]

"Sunny summer day," "a twenty-five-year-old brunette" and "stately villa" specify in words what film can only tacitly show in images of the set—including the villa under certain lighting conditions—and of an actress whom the costumer has dressed, the lighting technician lit, the cinematographer photographed, and the sound engineer recorded in a certain way. The film cannot guarantee—as a novel could—that everyone in the audience understands the character to be exactly twenty-five and the villa stately.

Or consider the first appearance of Quinlan, the detective (played by Welles himself) in Orson Welles's *Touch of Evil* (1958), as he struggles to get out of a car. He could have appeared in any number of ways, but the act of squeezing through the car door visually emphasizes his bulk. In describing the shot in prose, the published cutting continuity emphasizes the importance of the descriptum by making it syntactically prominent in an absolute noun phrase:

Very low angle M[edium]S[hot] of Quinlan slowly thrusting open the car door: a grossly corpulent figure in an overcoat, a huge cigar in the middle of his puffy face.[8]

The phrase after the colon explicitly describes Quinlan (a less assertive word order would be "A grossly corpulent figure in an overcoat, a huge cigar in the middle of his puffy face, thrusts open the car door"). But it is the continuity transcriber who has drawn the *conclusion* that Quinlan is "grossly corpulent." The film shows only features; it is up to the audience to interpret them—that is, to assign them adjectival names. As Ernest Callenbach puts it, this inconclusiveness "is the magic of cinema, its aesthetic 'purity' or perhaps its inherent capacity for discretion and indirection."[9]

Certainly, the standard cinematic way of dealing with descriptive details is to submerge them in ongoing action. They are not featured but presented by the bye, as items for contingent attention. In *Touch of Evil*, Quinlan's corpulence is registered tacitly, not explicitly; the camera does not prowl about or dwell unduly on folds of fat in his face.[10] But it *could* prowl in just such a way and in other films does so, often for descriptive purposes. Such prowling, I would argue, qualifies as the filmic equivalent of explicit Description, which prose might express through such copular sentences as "Quinlan was grossly corpulent." Camera movements that have no other motive (like communicating a character's perception of a scene) are often purely descriptive. They highlight properties, rather than actions, for the viewer's attention.

I do not mean to suggest that the camera's description-by-prowling approximates literature's precise *fixing* of description. Only words can fix descriptions conclusively. The cinematic narrator of *Touch of Evil* has no way of ensuring that every viewer finds Quinlan "grossly corpulent." One person's "grossly corpulent" may be another's "sort of fat," and a third's "rather stout." Film can only hope that you get something like the idea.

Then there is the question of agency. A description in fiction may be produced by the narrator or by a character. Balzac's *Père Goriot* begins with the narrator's description, long before we even meet the first character: "The front of the lodging-house gives on a little garden and it is placed at right-angles to the Rue-Neuve-Sainte-Geneviève from which you can see it, as it were, in sections".[11] Here explicit description comes from without, from the extradiegetic narrator, who is depicting the appearance of the Maison Vauquer long after Père Goriot has died. The date and duration of the description bear no relation to the story time; the place is presented, as it were, atemporally.

Description may also be expressed in dialogue by a character. For example, in Rudyard Kipling's "Man Who Would Be King," Dan Dravot describes himself and his sidekick to the narrator in these terms: "The less said about our professions the better, for we have been most things in our time. Soldier, sailor, compositor, photographer, proofreader, street preacher, and correspondents of the *Backwoodsman* when we thought the paper wanted one. Carnehan is sober, and so am I. Look at us first and see that's sure."[12] Or the description may occur within the character's mind, as in this example from *Madame Bovary*:

> Léon walked meditatively, keeping near the walls. Never had life seemed so good. Any minute now she would appear, charming, all aquiver, turning around to see whether anyone was looking—with her flounced dress, her gold eyeglass, her dainty shoes, all kinds of feminine elegances he had never had a taste of, and all the ineffable allurement of virtue on the point of yielding. The church was like a gigantic boudoir, suffused by her image: the vaults curved dimly down to breathe in the avowal of her love; the windows were ablaze to cast their splendor on her face; and even the incense burners were lighted, to welcome her like an angel amid clouds of perfume.[13]

Léon's lustful expectations are presented in descriptive terms that are clearly his own. As the *Encyclopédie* would have it, his mind is "rendering [Emma] visible by the animated and vivid exposition of her most interesting properties and circumstances"—properties and circumstances that the ironic narrator would probably not express in such terms.[14]

These two kinds of explicit Description in fiction have different narratological consequences. When a narrator describes, story time may pause (though it need not). But when a character describes, whether in dialogue or in the privacy of his own mind, story time necessarily continues, since the describing activity itself constitutes a significant event in the plot. Léon walks along the walls; Léon thinks that life has never seemed so good; Léon describes to himself the imminent appearance of Emma, charming, agitated, in her flounced dress and dainty shoes. Aside from their descriptive function, these thoughts and activities form important links in the chain of events of *Madame Bovary*. These examples demonstrate the need to distinguish "atemporal" descriptions by an extradiegetic narrator (or by an intra-diegetic narrator after the fact) from "temporal" descriptions by a character in the heat of the action, which are thus governed by story chrono-logic.

When we consider how this distinction might operate in cinema, two questions arise: (1) can the cinematic narrator explicitly describe, independently of any character's filter ("point of view")? and (2) can story time be stopped to allow a description to take place?

The answer to the first question is clearly yes. Hundreds of examples could be cited. A familiar one is the opening sequence of Alfred Hitchcock's *Rear Window* (1954).[15] The film begins with a view (under the titles) of the rear of some Manhattan apartment buildings as seen through an open window across a courtyard. The camera remains fixed while three blinds roll themselves up. On the sound track we hear lively Gershwinian music. When the titles end, the camera moves out through the window to scan the scene. We do not yet know whether we are to understand that the camera is showing us the stage upon which story events will transpire, or that we are seeing these rear windows through the eyes of some as yet unidentified character (though the magically self-rolling blinds strongly suggest the former). To contribute to the puzzle, the camera does not seem clear about what it wants to show. It acts as if it is simply moving about, looking for something of interest. It follows a cat climbing some steps, but the cat disappears off-frame. Then the camera tilts up as if to explore various apartments. On one balcony stands a husband putting on a tie, his wife hovering behind him, but they are too far away for us to make out their faces or conversation. In another film these figures might have come forward as characters; a closer shot would reveal their features. But here they are passed over quickly, and we infer that they are irrelevant to the plot; we hypothesize that they are not characters but walk-ons—mere furniture in the tableau of "Early Morning in a Manhattan Courtyard." The camera next tilts down a bit, revealing a passageway between the buildings and the street beyond, and finally it comes back into the window from which it set forth.

If the film were to continue only in this way, it could end up as a descriptive documentary about life in a Manhattan courtyard. However, immersed as we are in the elaborate institutional context of "seeing a Hollywood movie" (the theater marquee, after all, is alight with the names of James Stewart, Grace Kelly, and Alfred Hitchcock), we reject that conclusion. We are virtually certain—we were certain before we bought our tickets—that the film will present a story.

Inside the apartment, a close-up of James Stewart's face slides into view; but since he is facing away from the window with his eyes closed in sleep, we understand that the camera's meandering look at the courtyard has been its own descriptive act. The description has taken place in "real" time; however; there has been no pause. What was shown was not a frozen moment but one filled with actions. Story time has passed, even if nothing of great significance has happened. A verbal paraphrase might read (retrospectively), "While Jeff sleeps, the courtyard comes to life: cats prowl, husbands put on ties," and so on. Hence, it is reasonable to say that a cinematic describer—the cinematic narrator *as* describer—explicitly presents the opening sequence of *Rear Window*.

Descriptive sequences can also *reestablish* locale. Metz cites an example in *Adieu Philippine* (1962): as the film cuts from Paris to Corsica, "five consecutive shots articulate a descriptive syntagma . . . of life at the *Club Méditerranée*: men and women in bathing suits, *pareos*, and leis are sunbathing, sitting at the bar, walking around or dancing to aggressive music."[16] The reestablishing sequence is very common in classical Hollywood cinema; an example in *Notorious* is the aerial view of Rio just before the Ingrid Bergman character arrives to infiltrate the German spy ring.

It is harder to answer the second question: can films *stop* story time for Description? Let us recall the literary situation, in which explicit descriptions typically occur during moments of pause. The march of the plot stops for the depiction of properties of persons and objects in the story world. Even the most compelling action can be interrupted without seriously jeopardizing verisimilitude. The interruption is a convention that readers accept without ado (their reward is a fuller sense of the story world). Indeed, the pause can be used to heighten suspense and tension: " 'Hold your noise!' cried [Magwitch's] terrible voice 'or I'll cut your throat.' " Then the narrator of *Great Expectations*, the adult Pip, interrupts the action to describe the convict: "A fearful man, all in coarse grey, with a great iron on his leg. A man with no hat, and with broken shoes, and with an old rag tied round his head. A man who had been soaked in water, and smothered in mud."[17] And so on—the leisurely description could have interrupted the action for several pages if that had suited the implied author's purpose. The convention tacitly asks the reader to suspend the story until the descriptive moment ends and the action resumes. If the description is properly paced, we do not reject the invitation to be patient.

Can such pauses occur in the cinema? A few films seem to provide clear-cut examples. There is one in Joseph Manckiewicz's *All About Eve* (1950)[18] at the end of a larger sequence of the more usual "in-story-time" description, whose context is achieved by narratorial voice-over. Unlike *Rear Window* with its purely visual approach, *All About Eve* begins with a verbal description and interpretation supplied by a voice-over that supplements what we see on the visual track. The first shot is a close-up of an elaborate trophy for the "Sarah Siddons Award for Distinguished Achievement in the Theater." The voice, recognizable to Hollywood film fans as that of George Sanders (regularly typecast as an "attractive, supercilious cad" or "witty rake"),[19] explains the award. It addresses us in condescending tones (the prize is a "questionable award," the chairman presenting it is an "old actor," and "it is not important that you [we narratees] hear what he says"). Then the voice-over identifies the banquet room, gives a brief history of the award, and says a word about each of a group of characters associated with the award recipient, Eve Harrington. Egoist that he is, the speaker introduces himself first. Over a shot of Sanders, looking bored as usual, the voice says, "My name is

Addison De Witt." The camera pans right and pauses on his neighbor, whom he introduces as Karen Richards (Celeste Holm); then on her husband, Lloyd Richards (Hugh Marlowe), author of the play in which Eve stars; on Max Fabian (Gregory Ratoff), the producer; and on Margo Channing (Bette Davis), another famous actress. De Witt's voice-over explicitly describes and judges these characters as each face fills the screen in close-up: Karen belongs to the theater only by marriage; Fabian is not dedicated to art and is interested only in "making a buck"; but "Margo is a "truly great star."

At the same time, the camera is providing its own tacit but independent description. As De Witt speaks of Max's devotion to the buck, the camera gives evidence of Max's dyspepsia (he pours antacid powder into his glass of water) and boorishness (he falls asleep at the table). As De Witt recounts Margo's first stage appearance, as a child, in *A Midsummer Night's Dream*, the camera shows her smoking and drinking heavily (she disdainfully brushes aside soda water, preferring her whiskey straight). The sequence illustrates how richly the camera can interact with the voice-over's specifications, anchoring them but also potentially undermining them (for example, Karen proves to be more sympathetic than Addison suggests).

So far De Witt has given us only explicit description *in* story time—the chairman is up on the dais throughout, endlessly recounting the history of the society. This sequence structurally resembles first person or homodiegetic literary narration: a person who is both narrator and character is explicitly describing other characters preliminary to the story proper. But unlike literary narration, with its distinction between the discourse moment's "now" and the story moment's "back then," here—as in cinema regularly—the story time continues its march contemporaneously with De Witt's descriptive discourse.

Once De Witt's voice-over ceases and the voice of the chairman comes on the sound track, the text becomes totally shown, no longer (partly) told. The cinematic narrator has taken over the showing, and the two tracks are conventionally synchronized. As the old actor sings Eve's praise, the camera registers the reactions of De Witt and Margo: De Witt smirks derisively, Margo seems no less cynical. The chairman finishes his encomium, bravos fill the hall (but Karen and Margo do not applaud, and De Witt does so tepidly), news photographers crowd the dais for pictures, and at last we see Eve (Anne

Baxter). She walks toward the chairman and is about to take the award when the image freezes, the trophy just inches from her hand. De Witt's voice resumes, but now against the frozen image:

> Eve. Eve, the Golden Girl. The Cover Girl. The Girl Next Door. The Girl on the Moon. Time has been good to Eve. . . . You all know all about Eve. What can there be to know that you don't know?

Clearly, this is an invitation to watch and listen to the untold story that is about to begin.

That brief moment when De Witt picks up the description of Eve over the freeze-frame showing her on the podium seems to be what we have been looking for: a cinematic description that is not only explicit but occurs during a pause in the story. All events—even trivial events—have ceased; no one in the story world is speaking or moving. Only the narrator's voice comments, and it does so out in the discourse, not in the story. It is not a common moment in Hollywood cinema, but it is certainly a legitimate and easily readable one.

At least, in the case of the frozen image, then, description outside of story time does seem possible in commercial cinema. The use of actual pause is unusual, whether because filmmakers feel that the medium intrinsically favors constant action or because, for a whole battery of institutional reasons, the industry caters to or cultivates a taste for it. In any case, the prevailing fashion is that everything, including descriptive details, should simply appear as part of the events graphically happening before us. Characters and sets are not often dwelt upon for their own sake.

But there is another kind of pause, one in which description is visual rather than auditory, and the camera itself—not an interjected voice-over—renders the description. In this effect, it is not that story time actually pauses but that its progress no longer seems to matter. How is this achieved? The camera can photograph objects for a shorter or longer period of time; it can rest on them or sweep past them, slowly or rapidly; it can represent them in whole or in part, in long or close shot. And that's about all. Narratively, its ability is to show, not tell. How then can it demonstrate that its own concern has switched, for a time, from the onward flow of actions to that activity

49

which the *Encyclopédie* calls the "simple indication of objects"? How can it seem to pause to "contemplate" these objects: that is, to provide a "vivid and animated exposition of their most interesting properties and circumstances" for themselves alone, and not merely as byproducts of the action? This kind of cinematic description would seem to occur only when persons or objects appear on the screen not primarily to serve plot needs but to reveal their own properties.

My impression is that something like this effect occurs in films deviating from predictable rhythms. In general, narrative films set up a rhythm correlated to the action, a rhythm that is followed more or less relentlessly. Great efforts are made in classic Hollywood films to adjust the pace of editing to the mood: the cuts in a suspense thriller are taut and rapid, those in a moody melodrama languorous and slow, with the dissolve much favored over the straight cut.[20] These rhythms set up conventional expectations. And the basic convention is the "literal" correspondence of discourse time to story time, Genette's "scenic" mode.[21]

Once established, this becomes the norm, a kind of zero-degree temporal order that is understood by the spectator to correspond to the duration of the events themselves. To change this conventional disposition—to give a sense that events are being summarized, for example—the cinematic narrator must use some artifice. Sometimes the device is all too artificial: the peeling calendar and moving clock hands of early films or, with more artistry, the swish-pan sequence at the breakfast table in *Citizen Kane* to show the gradual breaking up of a marriage.

But my concern is the opposite of summary; it is pause, which occurs when story time stops, though the discursive statement continues. Pause is most frequent at the beginnings of films, many of which presuppose a kind of diegetic zero. There is no movement and hence no suggestion that story time has begun. The opening shot may be a still-like photo from a great distance of a buttercup-covered field or the Manhattan skyline. The film has started but not yet the story. Moving in from a height corresponds to the omnipresent narrator's panoramic view over the story world which begins many nineteenth-century novels. The industry calls these "establishing" shots; the very word is a sign of their institutionally conventional character. In such films as *The Lady Vanishes* (1928) and *Psycho* (1960), the camera moves down from a bird's-eye view of an unmoving landscape—a snowed-in chalet in Ruritania, a seedy hotel room in Phoenix. Since the characters have not yet appeared and the action has not yet begun, it makes sense to say that there is not yet a story-time, or *now*.[22]

The effect resembles the conventional descriptive openings of many novels, even recent ones. Malcolm Lowry's *Under the Volcano* begins: "Two mountain chains traverse the republic roughly from north to south, forming between them a number of valleys and plateaus. Overlooking one of these valleys, which is dominated by two volcanoes, lies six thousand feet above sea level the town of Quauhnahuac."[23] Shots taken from a helicopter or of a model could begin a movie version in the same way (though John Huston's film version does not). But these are relatively privileged and usually brief moments. Once the plot begins, it usually dominates; indeed, the general rule of classical cinema is to get the story clock going as quickly as possible, and the audience expects that convention. Once the plot is under way, we are not much disposed to entertain descriptive pauses. If the film shows an actor, then cuts to a sequence of objects—a tree, a stream, a distant hill—we do not assume that the cinematic narrator has stopped the action to describe the landscape but rather that the character is performing the story-relevant act of scanning the landscape. It requires something rather special, like the freezing of a frame, to suggest the actual arrest of story time.

In recent years, establishing shots have become rather old hat. The pressure to begin the action as early as possible has made it fashionable to start story time behind the titles, or even before they appear. Contemporary audiences expect the plot to start with the very first frame. We are encouraged by the codes of film narrative to understand that a camera's movement is plot directed, not merely contemplative or establishing, and that the appropriate diegetic object will appear at the end of the shot: in other words, that the camera is moving resolutely *toward that object*. A classic example opens *Citizen Kane*: the camera climbs a fence with a sign reading "No Trespassing," moves through the bizarre grounds of "Xanadu," and ends up witnessing (with an attendant nurse) the death of Charles Foster Kane. (Interestingly enough, something like this camera movement is repeated a few minutes later with explicitly descriptive purport: part of the newsreel obituary of Kane's death is devoted to a travelogue-like survey of the grounds at Xanadu, but this time the descriptive intent is made clear by the "official" voice of the newsreel commentator.)

Ordinarily, camera movements occur simply to expose the action; horse and rider race to the scene of the battle with the Indians, and the camera naturally follows along. Or the panning camera functions as the surrogate of the moving eyes of the protagonist, in a manner analogous to that in which description by a character functions in the nineteenth-century novel. To show that she scans the horizon, the camera also does so. We infer that characterial point of view (or filter) is the purpose of the shot because the character is standing nearby, and we identify with her interests.

Now one way for the filmmaker to interrupt story time and to render description explicit is to deviate from such conventions as cutting rhythm and eyeline match. Interesting deviations occur in the work of Michelangelo Antonioni, whose films explicitly describe the story world both by camera movement and by camera stasis. For instance, the beginning of *The Passenger* (1975)[24] provides descriptions of the Sahara by unpredictable movements of the camera. Rather than standing in for the protagonist, David Locke, the camera seems to be wandering on its own (in an interview at the time of the film's appearance, Antonioni said that he no longer believed in the subjective camera). The effect is one of spatial disorientation. First the camera shows Locke scanning the horizon; then it begins a broad pan, as if it were looking for something with him. But its movement proves not to correspond to that of his gaze because it ends up "finding" *him*, too, almost accidentally, in a completely unexpected spot. In shot A he's on the left side of the frame looking right; in shot B the camera moves across the landscape from left to right as if continuing his glance; but in this movement it discovers him over on the *right*, not at all where we expect to see him (there is no evidence of a 360-degree turnabout). So we understand, though only retrospectively, that the movement is not an extension of his glance at all but an independent view. The camera seems to be conducting its own inquiry. We conjecture that it is concerned with the desert not as the place where the plot events are occurring (the movement of rebel troops in the mountains of Chad) but as an object of independent, perhaps "painterly" interest. In Antonioni's desert our conventional sense of the character-eyeline match is consistently undermined; we cannot assume that the images are there to illustrate a character's perspective.

Or Antonioni's camera may establish itself as an independent describer by disrupting the viewer's sense of scale. When Locke meets his guide, the first shot effects a mismatch in which, as Noël Burch explains, "the real dimensions [and hence distance] of whatever is visible on the empty screen are impossible to determine until the appearance of a human figure makes the scale obvious."[25] The camera scans a broken desert horizon whose distance is indeterminate. Are they small hills close up or tall mountains far away? Then, still in the same shot, the scanning camera suddenly finds the Chadian guide at a close-medium distance. We are jolted, having assumed that if anyone appeared, it would be in a long shot, at a distance appropriate to Locke's point of view, which is the only one we have been following. But here is the object of his search suddenly under our very noses. The "faraway" hills—they have seemed far away because we have assumed that they were being scanned by Locke—now become much closer and hence much smaller than we had thought. And, to our surprise, there is Locke's tiny figure standing far below on the desert floor. Struggling to regain our bearings, we try to explain the new scale through the *guide's* point of view in the shot of him that follows, looking back. Reliable eyeline matching seems established at last, much to our perceptual relief. We hope that according to conventional rhythms the next shot, another pan of the desert, will resume Locke's point of view. Wrong again, for at the end of the pan Locke is discovered once more at a completely arbitrary middle distance, accompanied by the guide; both are laden with equipment and are struggling up another (or the same?) mountain. Again the camera asserts its independence of the protagonist's perceptual filter. It does so, I believe, to show that it finds the desert an object of independent visual interest and wants to communicate that interest to us in much the same spirit as does a literary narrator who (for whatever reason) presents an independent description of the scene rather than its perception by a character.

Another kind of explicit description occurs in Antonioni's film *Red Desert* (1964).[26] This time the sense of description is effected not by a deviant camera movement but by an unaccountable *lingering* of the camera for several seconds beyond what would seem a reasonable duration. Here is the context: the heroine, Giuliana (Monica Vitti), the unhappy and neurotic wife of an engineer, has taken a brief trip with her husband's friend Corrado (Richard Harris) in search of workers whom he hopes to hire for a business venture in Patagonia. They meet a technician, and Giuliana leaves the two men to discuss their business. When she rejoins Corrado—only to learn that the technician has refused the offer—both characters walk off-screen. But instead of cutting away with them to the next shot, the camera lingers on the background, making *it* for several seconds the main subject: an antenna tower and a dull, vague old building.[27] The lines of the orange tower extend from top left to lower center of the frame; the dark gray oblong of the building stretches vertically off-center right, the portion at the far right carrying the eye off-frame at a very shallow angle. Tying the two together is a cable forming a counterangle from top right to bottom left. The composition is that of an abstract painting, made so by the geometric simplicity of the objects, which are rendered even simpler by the flattening effect of the telephoto lens. The shot ends the scene. The next scene begins elsewhere and at a later story moment.

For a few seconds, story time "dies," to adopt the term French critics were quick to apply to the technique—*temps mort*. It dies presumably because the film loses interest in the story's relentless need to flow. The effect is so intrusive that if it were not for its recurrence (and its beauty), we might write it off as a slip in the editing or an anomaly of the print. What is the intention? We can imagine the cinematic narrator responding: "I find the composition interesting, so I choose to linger on it. That is, I *describe* it." This momentary halt in the story is an invocation of something timeless, not necessarily "eternal" in the poetic sense but temporally indifferent. As such, it conflicts with our desire to have the story move ahead. This momentary frustration of the viewer's hunger for diegetic resolution seems one more instance of that self-conscious meditation on its own structures that figures so prominently in Modernist and Postmodernist art.

Antonioni's *temps mort* is a descriptive subversion of cinema's relentless narrative drive, a drive that leads E. M. Forster to lament "Yes—oh dear yes—the novel tells a story. That is the fundamental aspect without which it could not exist. That is the highest factor common to all novels, and I wish that it was not so, that it could be something different—melody, or perception of the truth, not this low atavistic form."[28] Antonioni maneuvers us through the cracks of diegetic convention—narrative's "low atavistic form"—out of the domain of story time and into that of the Descriptive mode, into the timelessness of a painting, into a place where things shine more purely because their surfaces have been cleansed of story pressures, even if only momentarily.

CHAPTER 4

Argumentation in Film:
Mon oncle d'Amérique

Aᴿɢᴜᴍᴇɴᴛꜱ ᴀᴛ ᴛʜᴇ service of or in the guise of narrative fiction
are highly familiar to readers of the various literary genres: parables,
fables, allegories, *romans à clef*, and heavily moralizing novels. Adaptation of these genres into films is not uncommon: early movies were
heavily moralistic and often spelled their messages out in dialogue or
even in commentative titles, and there have been films based on
fables (for instance, the delightful animated adaptation of James
Thurber's "Unicorn in the Garden," from *Fables of Our Times*) and on
allegories (such as George Orwell's *Animal Farm*). Most commonly
of all, arguments were embedded in hundreds of Hollywood "message" films, from *Public Enemy* (James Cagney, dying in the gutter,
gasping out for the edification of potential lawbreakers that he ain't
so tough) to that classic tribute to sexism, *Mildred Pierce* (Joan Crawford confessing that she would have been better off not abandoning
her housewifely tasks for financial success in the restaurant business).

Explicit argumentation, however, is not an easy or usual property
of commercial films. Unlike the narrators of novels—especially
those in traditional novels, who break off the story at any moment
and engage in relatively explicit argumentation—argumentative
commentators do not ordinarily intrude into narrative films. Even
rarer are films whose whole structure—visual as well as verbal—
constitutes an argument in the usual rhetorical sense, complete with
premises and proofs. But there are some. As David Bordwell points
out, Soviet films of 1925 to 1933 are "frankly didactic and persua-

sive," with arguments working "by appeal to example" (in the technical rhetorical sense of the word): "The fabula world stands for a set of abstract propositions whose validity the film at once presupposes and reasserts." And Bordwell and Kristen Thompson have demonstrated the argumentative structure of Pare Lorenz's documentary *The River*.[1]

The latter is not surprising; it is a common belief that argument occurs in explicit form only in documentary films, that somehow it is incompatible with narrative films. Christian Metz even proclaims: "Remove 'drama,' and there is no fiction, no diegesis, and therefore no film. Or only a documentary, a 'film exposé' "[2]—as if documentary were doomed to an inferior place in the hierarchy of cinematic genres (perhaps just as Description is thought to be inferior to Narrative). But that seems to take too narrow a view of the possibilities of Argument in cinema. It may go against the grain of the medium to deal in formal syllogistic or enthymemic structures, but certainly many fiction films entail argument of an informal sort.

Cinema evolved, of course, as a medium for popular narrative fictions—"feature films," as the trade calls them.[3] Though it may be true in theory, at least, that the visual media are textually neutral, the appeal of cinema as an institution has been primarily narrative-fictional, and it was the public's clamor for stories that spawned the vast industry we call "the movies." Still, especially from the 1920s through the 1950s, many Hollywood films delivered or at least implied messages that we can think of as "arguments" in a weak sense of the term; some still do. It is not hard to understand, after seeing *The Birth of a Nation*, an "argument" against carpetbaggers and freed slaves; or, after *Intolerance*, an "argument" against intolerance. Similarly, *Public Enemy* "argues" that crime doesn't pay; *It's a Wonderful Life*, that the world would be a far worse place if even one of us had never been born; *Star Wars*, that we should trust in the Force; and *Country*, that the FHA should not evict farmers, no matter how broke they are.

But these arguments are generally conveyed implicitly by the narrative. The more sophisticated films become, the less often do characters or voice-over narrators explicitly argue a film's thesis. The exceptions are often of a spoofing or parodic cast, like the moralizing of the voice-over narrator at the beginning of the film *Tom Jones*. Only early and more primitive films seriously inserted morals

("Crime does not pay!") in so many words at the end. The big Hollywood studios have rarely found any profit in explicit and formal argumentation.[4] Nor can the narrative preference be explained away simply as one more capitalist plot: though Sergei Eisenstein dreamed of a film version of *Das Kapital*, all his films are narrative. Films are expensive to make, and socialist no less than capitalist societies have devoted the lion's share of their production to films that will appeal to large audiences—narrative-fiction films.

Nevertheless, the industry's historical devotion to Narrative is not a good reason for theoreticians to ignore the other textual possibilities latent in film. One fruitful sort of inquiry—which I shall not pursue—would be to outline or taxonomize the technical means by which film *could* argue in ways correspondent to formal verbal arguments. It would consider such questions as the relations between shot juxtaposition and the argumentative proofs traditionally distinguished by rhetoric: deduction, induction, analogy, and the like. Perhaps one could devise a scheme for argumentative film parallel to the Metzian *grande syntagmatique* of narrative articulations. This chapter, however, is concerned, not with the general question of what *might* be done but rather with what *has* been done. The cinema, at least in the hands of some directors, has already shown unique potentials for introducing Argument into the textual mix, a potential that arises in part from film's multichannel capacity. Unlike a written text, a film can utilize different channels for different text-types, presenting, say, Narrative in the visual channel and Argument in the auditory, or vice versa. The results are uniquely its own.

Although early feature films contained a good deal of didacticism and moralism, American and European cinema, in keeping with the growing sophistication of the audience, have generally either avoided "messages" or presented them very obliquely. Though contemporary filmmakers remain preoccupied, if not obsessed, with social issues, they are leery of using narrative at the service of argument in any obvious or simplistic way. Hence the multichannel capacity for mixing text-types is not often used. Arguments may be presented by characters, but then they remain within the story. Few contemporary films use the discourse—for example, through a narrator expressing himself in titles or voice-over—to argue explicitly.[5] Films, of course, are notoriously ridden with ideology, and ideology announces itself in all kinds of ways. But those ways are mostly dramatic and implied; indeed, when an explicitly argued film does come along, the general public and the critics are likely to be puzzled and even angry.

One such film is Alain Resnais's *Mon oncle d'Amérique* (1980), which exemplified a broader and more complex approach to text-type actualization than the commercial cinema had yet seen. Though the film was generally praised in America (its scenarist, Jean Gruault, won the 1980 Oscar for best foreign screenplay), it has been little discussed since the initial reviews.[6] That is a pity. Beyond its artistic merits—which are considerable—it illustrates the power of explicit argumentation inherent in film, a power that remains to be developed by adventurous filmmakers. Of particular interest is the textual interplay of Argument and Narrative. Most critics failed to see that source of the film's textual appeal and condemned it for intentions which, on my reading at least, it does not have. I want to discuss the film in considerable detail for two reasons: first, it introduces explicit argumentation in an innovative way; and second, it problematizes the relationship between narrative and argument in ways unusual to the cinema (though not to literature).

A stylized red heart appears on the screen. It "beats," appearing and disappearing. A voice-over says, "La seule raison d'être d'un être—c'est d'être" (The only reason for a being to be—is to be). From that moment on, the film both tells a story and explicitly argues a thesis. But unlike the Hollywood "message" film, the product is less a fusion than a problematization of both texts. The "service" is there, but it gets confused and blurred. The film crosscuts between a story about three fictional characters and the argument of a real biologist named Henri Laborit. Laborit argues his case in person, sometimes on-screen, sometimes "over" the story. The film intercuts the fictional struggles of the characters—Jean Le Gall (played by Roger-Pierre), Janine Garnier (Nicole Garcia), and René Ragueneau (Gérard Depardieu)—with the nonfictional problems of other members of the animal kingdom: tortoises, crabs, boars, and laboratory rats. As the intercutting proceeds, the viewer is faced with a question that never seems answered: Is this an argumentative essay serviced by a narrative, or a narrative whose story line is explicated by argumentative commentary?[7]

Many reviewers assumed the latter, leading some to condemn the film—not for its own sins but as if *any* explicit argumentation in the cinema were ipso facto a bad thing. The critic for *Le Monde*, for example, accused the film of "profitlessly inverting the relations of knowledge and fiction" by using the fiction to illustrate the argument; this, he asserted made it "the worst of didactic films."[8] "Didacticism" here seems to be another name for explicit argumentation, and some find that *in itself* antifilmic.

Others saw the film as belonging to the fiction, with Laborit simply there to elucidate. That interpretation also misses the point. On a more sophisticated reading, it seems precisely the tension between the text-types, their struggle for control, that makes the film interesting and even tantalizing. Which dominates, the argument or the narrative? ("Dominates" is a suggestive word here, since the film's overall preoccupation is domination in animal and human behavior.)

Laborit's opening argument is accompanied by a collage of photographs, each momentarily illuminated by a light moving in a counterclockwise direction. The light seems to embody the process of scientific inquiry; it is like a microscope trying to find order in an apparent chaos of images. The sound track plays a cacophony of fragments of dialogue, out of which the voices of the three protagonists finally become discrete. The resolution of sounds and images seems almost a matter of chance, as if these particular human subjects were selected randomly out of a general population, implying that we would see the same patterns in other randomly chosen individuals of the species. New images appear which look abstract at first, then become recognizable as small shore plants. The scientist's voice-over tells us that plants can stay alive without moving around, acquiring their sustenance by photosynthesis, but that animals need a space, a feeding ground.

Cut to close-ups of a teaspoon, a doorknob, an ink bottle, a pair of scissors, a bicycle chain—old-fashioned household artifacts, souvenirs of childhood—as the voices of the off-screen protagonists detail their place and manner of birth, but only in sentence fragments: "Brittany," "Paris," "les Mauges," "in a hospital," "on an island," "Avenue de la République," "it was a neighbor." Though the switching back and forth among the voices slows down enough to make the characters distinguishable, the principle of piecemeal narration extends throughout the film. At this stage the crosscutting seems to facilitate Laborit's disquisition (Narrative at the service of Argument) on the proposition that science deals not with individuals but with species and that species are best described through random samples. The randomness disappears as the story comes into its own, as these characters become very much involved in each other's lives. That is one of the sources of textual tension.

The three first appear visually in medallion inserts, telling their life stories not dramatically but in testimonials. So far, they are subjects of scientific inquiry rather than characters. They address the audience directly and dryly, as if from some place outside the story. The presentation is formal, emotionless; these are not fictional confessions but clinical discourses.

Over shots of a trudging tortoise, then a frog, then a goldfish, Laborit explains that the need of animals to search for food inevitably gives rise to a sense of territoriality. The intercutting makes it increasingly clear that the plants and animals are presented not as metaphors or symbols for the characters but rather as their biological peers; both images and commentary remind us that we all inhabit the same ark.

There follow vital statistics about each of the three case studies, read by the colorless, bureaucratic voice of a *speakerine* (a French neologism for a female voice over). Born to a visibly affluent family, first trained and employed as a teacher, then appointed news director for French National Radio and fired in eighteen months, Jean Le Gall has written a best seller attacking the National Radio and is now running for political office. Janine Garnier's background is urban proletarian. She is the daughter of a blue-collar father and a mother who deplored her interest in the theater. Despite initial success as a stage actress, she has drifted into the sterile profession of fashion consultant and troubleshooter for an industrial conglomerate. René Ragueneau is of peasant origin; by correspondence course and against his father's wishes, he has risen through the ranks to become manager of a textile plant. The very diversity of the characters' backgrounds, highlighted by the crosscutting, reaffirms a random— hence "scientific"—approach quite indifferent to such human concerns as social class.

Separating these sketches are brief speeches by Laborit outlining his general theory, often over images of the struggles of other animals to survive—a disoriented puppy, a wild boar rooting for food. The disquisition of Laborit, the bureaucratic voice, and the visual images are not mechanically matched. For example, when the speakerine mentions Le Gall's appointment as news director, the accompanying shot is of a small boy gawking at a crab; as she says that he suffers from kidney stones, we see a picture of a toy duck floating in a pond; as she tells us about his being fired, we see him being tenderly hugged by his mother. But neither are these juxtapositions random. They provide not "exposition" in the traditional Balzacian sense but evidence for the film's central argument: namely, that territorial habits determine success or failure, happiness or frustration in human as in animal lives. It was precisely Le Gall's upbringing as a little prince, with dominion over his own island, that formed his style of coping with the problems of life. The discontinuity of sound and visual image seems to accomplish two things: to stress the independent objectivity of Laborit's argument, and to force us to puzzle out the application of that argument to the fictional story. The puzzle is one neither of plot nor of scientific argument but a somewhat uneasy mixture of both.

Central to Laborit's theory is his view of human behavior as a species of animal behavior. He presents this point directly, either looking straight into the camera or speaking over clearly illustrative images. All animals, he argues, manifest four kinds of behavior: a behavior of consumption; a behavior of gratification (animals will repeat what is pleasurable and avoid what is painful), a behavior of flight or fight (when confronted with a potentially painful experience, they have only two recourses—fleeing or, if that fails, fighting); and, in situations where it is impossible either to flee or to fight, a behavior of inhibition—which in humans goes by the special name of "anguish." To minimize our problems, we and the other animals strive to acquire territory. Inside our territory we exercise our impulses to dominate. All animals need to dominate, and there is in nature an inevitable hierarchy of dominance, of victors and vanquished.

To illustrate some of the kinds of behavior, the film shows a rat in an experimental situation. The floor of a cage is electrified. When a buzzer sounds, the rat has four seconds to get into an adjacent, safe cage. As long as the door between the two cages remains open, the fleeing behavior works well: the rat stays healthy by simply moving back and forth at the sound of the buzzer. Then the door is closed; the rat hears the buzzer but can do nothing to prevent getting shocked. Once it has become a victim of inhibition, its health is quickly impaired. (We assume that this experiment occurs not inside the story world, the world of Le Gall, Garnier, and Ragueneau, but out in Laborit's argumentative discourse.) Another experiment demonstrates fight behavior: a second rat is introduced into the electrified cage and the door is kept closed. Despite the repeated shocks to both, the rats remain healthy—simply because they vent their frustration about their inability to escape by fighting each other.

In humans, however, these behaviors and the drive for territorial domination are not innate. There are no proprietary or dominating instincts as such; rather, domination is a behavior learned in the first two or three years of life. Laborit considers the newborn human nervous system pretty much a *tabula rasa*. The need to dominate is imprinted on our consciousnesses by significant others; indeed, he says, "we are nothing *but* the others." The human brain is divided into three layers—the "reptilian" (concerned only with food and reproduction), the "affective" (concerned with remembering what is pleasurable and what painful), and the associative cortex, which rationalizes—that is, provides "alibis" for—the drives of the other two. The cortex's crowning achievement, the institution of language, exists, biologically speaking, only to rationalize our more primitive needs and behaviors.

Laborit metaphorically characterizes the unconscious as a sea and language as its mere foam, a foam that masks the true undercurrents of our behavior. The behavior of the fictional characters illustrates the point. Beneath their all too familiar personal peccadilloes and domestic and business battles, we can see the broader biological economy driving their (and our) behavior.

After explaining the four behaviors, Laborit describes the limitations placed on men and women by their situation in society. Human culture, whose purpose is to secure the cohesion of the group, stringently controls the degree to which we can either flee or fight. This control subjects human beings to a level of inhibition far beyond that experienced by other animals. Because our aggressions tend to be interiorized, we are more susceptible than the other animals to psychosomatic illness. Because overt physical struggle, like that between rats, usually won't do in "civilized" society, many humans "somatize" their frustrations, "directing their aggression against their own stomachs where it makes an ulcer." They may even perform the ultimate self-aggression of committing suicide.

That is the gist of Laborit's speech, a speech that accomplishes one of two functions, depending on our textual perspective. If we read the film as an argument, his commentary is obviously the major device for its presentation. Shots of Laborit in his laboratory constitute a visual representation of a man arguing a certain case. Shots of the rats' reactions are simply illustrative evidence, and so is the behavior of the human beings. If we read the film as a narrative, however, Laborit becomes a commentator in the discourse. But he is an unusual kind of commentator: he is not an interpreter of the fictional story. He never mentions the fiction, neither the characters nor their actions. The uniqueness of the film turns on the fact that the implied author has divided up the discourse functions, parceling out to different agents tasks that would, in the traditional novel, be performed by the narrator alone. (For a literary counterpart, imagine two different discourse agents in *Tom Jones*: one who only tells the events of the story, and another who only makes philosophical, moral, and social comments without any direct reference to the story.) From the narrative perspective, the laboratory, the rats in the cage, and so on, are part of a discourse that is parallel to but not somehow inclusive of the fictional story.[9]

Still, as each text-type follows its own course, our moviegoer's need for coherence prompts us to make connections. It is we who will read the child Jean's search for crabs as an example of consumption behavior; René's lecture to a young worker on how to succeed in business as an example of gratification behavior; and the adult Jean's refusal to confront his friend's complicity in his dismissal from his job as an example of fleeing behavior. When Le Gall cannot get away quickly enough from the unpleasantness and the blunter Janine attacks Michel on his behalf, we interpret Jean's resultant kidney-stone attack as an example of inhibition behavior.

Though Laborit's argumentative discourse makes no reference to the story, the narrative discourse brings in elements of the argument—sometimes in a humorous way. In a reprise of the scene in which he leaves his wife Arlette for Janine, Jean's body is crowned with a rat's head. Later, symmetrically, a real rat is let out of a miniature replica of the Le Gall apartment and into one of Janine's apartment. To reinforce the fight instinct felt by René when his rival, Veestrate, encroaches on his territory, there is a shot of the two of them, also wearing rat heads, wrestling on the desks of the cramped office they share.

The story as such is presented in parallel, crosscut tiers: each stage of life—childhood, breaking out of the family, early success, mature distress—occurs concurrently "across" the characters. In the childhood stage, Jean hides in a tree so that he can read pulp novels, in particular *Le Roi d'or*, a French Horatio Alger or legendary "American uncle" story; Janine gets strokes from her family by standing up at festive dinners and reciting Communist paeans; René studies accounting by the light of a bare bulb hanging from the ceiling of his bedroom. At the adolescent stage, Jean is dissuaded from going to Paris by his girlfriend's imperious need for an early marriage. Janine breaks from her family in the middle of the night after her mother tries to thwart her activity in amateur theater. René, disgusted with his father's petty and outmoded farming methods, leaves with his fiancée Thérèse in the middle of a family dinner. At the adult stage, Jean becomes a radio news director, Janine wins a role in a small theater production, then leaves it to become an executive in a fashion conglomerate; René rises to assistant manager of a textile factory in Lille.

Then the troubles begin: Jean falls for Janine at a performance of her play; he moves in with her, over his wife's hysterical protests. Then he is fired from his radio job, for obscure reasons. René's firm merges with another, and he sees his job taken away by a tougher and wilier rival, Veestrate. Janine, tricked into believing that Jean's wife is dying, pretends to quarrel with Jean and sends him back home. The wife does not die but manipulates the malleable Jean into returning to her. René is transferred to another factory, hundreds of miles from his family, but he cannot keep up with the technical and commercial demands. His boss proposes that he go into one of the conglomerate's new lines—packaged gourmet foods. Though cuisine is his hobby, René is humiliated and enraged by the proposal and tries to kill himself. Fortunately, he is rescued; the last we see of him is in a hospital bed, where he has just come to and is not yet aware that he is out of a job.

The relation between Janine and Jean also ends on a desultory note. Two years after their breakup she rows to his island, which he never invited her to visit. By chance he also rows there, to get some papers concerning his legal claim to the island (territory again). They meet and reminisce, but he shows no sign of wanting to resume their affair. Janine goes on to her business meeting. Unnerved by René's attempted suicide, she returns to Brittany to tell Jean that she only provoked their breakup to let him return to solace his wife in her "last days." She finds Jean hunting boar with a neighbor (exercising territorial dominion in good *haut-bourgeois* style). She confronts him with the truth. To her dismay, Jean's wife has already confessed, but Jean admires his wife's "marvelous" courage in telling such a lie, and Janine's "marvelous" self-sacrifice in giving him up. Pushed beyond endurance, Janine assaults him, and the story ends with the two in a clumsy fistfight.

So the three characters who seemed randomly picked as biological samples at the beginning of the film become intimately involved in the fictional plot. But the copresence of Laborit's argument restrains us from indulging too fully in the narrative code for its own pleasures. Rather, we are invited to seek in the fiction illustrations of Laborit's argument. And indeed, Laborit's discourse *seems* to account for the behavior of the characters. When he speaks of an infant's reaction to the mother's caresses as an example of gratification behavior, or of the actor basking eagerly in the applause of the audience, we see shots of Jean being hugged by his mother and Janine being praised by her family after reciting at the dinner table.

Other visuals illustrate the argument more subtly. For example, when a framed photograph of Janine's grandparents accompanies Laborit's discussion of inhibition, we infer that the old and traditional are by definition conservative and hence inhibitory. Or, as Laborit's voice-over explains that "language only contributes to hiding the cause of dominance," we watch René follow a beautiful secretary through the overwhelmingly grand lobby of the conglomerate's headquarters. Here "language" obviously means *all* sign behavior: the décor serves the double function of impressing the clients and intimidating the employees.

The film ultimately trains us to see past "linguistic alibis" on our own, to break our usual habit of reading events empathically through fictional characters' eyes and instead to interpret them through Laborit's argument. Though Laborit never mentions the fiction—in fact, seems unaware that he is sharing textual space with it—we find ourselves eager to apply his laboratory findings to its interpretation. We are not taken in by Jean's "reasons" for going back to his wife, though he obviously prefers Janine; or by Janine's explanation of why she abandoned the theater for the colorless world of business ("I've always liked a change of skin. I've always liked to drive, to go to foreign countries"). We even speculate that the final event, the fist-fight between Janine and Jean, is not as horrendous as it might seem: Nature prompts the ex-lovers (like the frustrated rats) to engage in physical conflict perhaps, to stay in good fettle.

And yet the story is sufficiently affecting to keep us from writing these people off as mere clinical examples. And the argument is not so powerful as to explain all the eventualities of the fiction. As we watch Grandpa teach Jean how to catch and eat crabs, we remember that we are not supposed to sentimentalize; this is, after all, an example of how young *homo sapiens* is taught to dominate the lesser beasts. But it *is* a cozy scene, and it is hard not to think of parallel moments with our own grandfathers. We interpret a shot of Jean being scolded by his father for turning a tortoise over on its back as an example of how human culture gives children mixed messages, teaching it sometimes to dominate and other times to be "nice" and "good" and not to torment the poor beasts. In Jean's case, the order to be good leads to adult inhibitions, particularly to the inability to fight for his rights. In a similar way, by giving René's competitor a Flemish name, "Veestrate," the implied author suggests the impera-tive of broader territorial domination as it becomes institutionalized at the economic and political level. There is a long history of eco-nomic struggle between the French and the Flemish; the latter have a reputation for commercial shrewdness and a penchant for encroach-ing on French markets. Another kind of domination, or *droit du seigneur*, is the power to "advise" an underling to do what you want him to do "for his own good." The sign of René's dominion, of having "arrived," is that he can advise a young worker not to work nights and to study instead. But the modern world turns quickly, and we soon see René reluctantly listening to advice from *his* boss, offered in the same "kindly" paternalistic spirit. Nor does it help his already wounded self-esteem to discover that this suave Parisian is visibly younger than he is.

I have gone into detail in characterizing this film because of its effective demonstration of how cinema can tell a story and *explicitly* argue a relatively complex case at the same time. A familiar truism about films is that they contain nothing corresponding to the linguis-tic word;[10] their smallest unit is already something like the sentence. A shot of an umbrella does not mean simply "umbrella" but, at the very least, "Here is an umbrella." Of course, most photographed objects are not asserted baldly by a close-up but inserted *in medias res*, as already justified by the context. The medium requires the audience to do a lot of inferring. Filmmakers prefer to present information visually, through eyeline matches, close-ups, and other techniques. Even unsophisticated audiences have learned to draw conclusions from relatively small bits of visual information. Our skill in doing so is especially developed for narrative films, since they are the kind that we most often see. The task is made easier by the narrative context. We constantly test our interpretations against some story line, and most commercial films, as is often pointed out, are "transparently edited": they strive to join visuals and familiar plot and character types seamlessly. (Most of what counts as "new" in the commercial cinema is visual embroidery—odder camera angles, more daring cutting and composition, more blatant lighting and color effects— while themes, plots, and characters remain pretty much the same.)

But films like *Mon oncle d'Amérique* require us to interpret against a less familiar context. Many of its shots constitute evidence for intellectual propositions. Consider the prominently focused childhood playthings—plastic duck, toy locomotive, doll. Though we might first interpret them narratively, as sentimental souvenirs, they take on new meaning as we become familiar with Laborit's argument. We come to see them as "dominated objects." Toys, in the biologist's perspective, are the culture's means of training children to possess things and hence to dominate others. Similarly, the competition between René and Veestrate is captured in its earliest stages by sheer visuals, for example, by René's baleful looks (Dépardieu has a prodigious capacity to project feelings through facial expression) and by finely chosen details of body language. Though René's factory is hosting Veestrate, and though French rules of politeness demand a host to follow, not lead, his guest through the door ("après vous, Alphonse"), each man struggles to get ahead of the other as they tour the plant. These movements anticipate such later tussles as who should first reach the telephone when the boss calls.[11] Similarly, when Jean discovers that his island has been "invaded" by Janine, the camera captures him in a posture quite like that of a cornered animal, and these shots are explicitly intercut with those of the laboratory rat: Jean moving from left to right among the bushes—cut to the rat moving from left to right through its cage; Jean guardedly looking out for the owner of the strange boat—cut to the rat attentive, ready to flee.

What makes *Mon oncle d'Amérique* a fascinating departure in film history is the tension, the "discrepancies," to be found between the two text-types that inform it. The story often stretches out beyond the requirements of the argument, taking on its own buzzing interest. In doing so, it revels in what Laborit's science dismisses as "alibi," precisely the lived detail that makes realistic narrative fictions persuasive. It is not always clear whether the narrative elaboration is a part of this particular text's intention or a consequence of the medium in which it is transmitted. To tell a story at all in the cinema, even one that illustrates some other kind of text, may be precisely to introduce "excess," to open floodgates of "distracting" but absorbing story material. "Excess" is clearly an effect of verisimilitude, of Barthes's *effet de réel*, but it fits in nicely with the correspondent argument. Janine's "nobility" in giving Jean back to his wife, for example, might be explainable in Laborit's theory as biological gratification: she is trying to replicate the gratification she got from her father for being "fair" or "comradely." "Excess" also names the audience's vicarious gratification—its fulfillment of its own biological agenda—in experiencing the human gratifications of others, even of fictional characters. Despite the training in biology that we get from Laborit, we desire to know more about the *story*, even as we sense that its presence in the film is more than a little whimsical.[12]

It is easy to get caught up in narrative "excess." Critic Jan Dawson marveled at the beauty of the photographed natural settings; the mere fact of this beauty, she implied, put the lie to Laborit's purely functional view of nature.[13] But just as everything in Laborit's argument can be used to explicate the narrative, everything in the narrative can be used to illustrate the argument. The "beauty" of nature also has a biological explanation. Man chooses among territories, migrates to *certain* places on this earth which he finds desirable; their desirability is understood by the biologist in terms of survival value. "Beauty" is only the name given to that desirability. A race that evolved on Mars would doubtless find its red dust more beautiful than our verdant forests. Because the audience of *Mon oncle d'Amérque* is torn between a traditional conception of beauty and a new functional definition, the story element of the film seems stretched between two poles, at once in service of the argument and fiercely autonomous.

In one way, diegetic "excess" is a consequence of narrative elaboration itself. It is in the nature of realistic narrative, whether invented for illustration or for its own sake, to create details of independent interest, *effets de réel*. Cinema enhances this interest by favoring richly detailed sets, elaborate acting business, and the like. For example, it isn't enough—narratively speaking—for René to express his anguish by trying to kill himself. The cinematic imperative requires a complicated photogenic method: he tries both to strangle himself (on the window handle, not from the chandelier) and to take an overdose of barbiturates. The purely visual representation of his determination combined with clumsy ineptitude endows the sequence with such an air of *particular* reality as to make us almost forget that it is introduced to "illustrate" the Laboritian "anguish."

In more uniformly narrative texts, we look for explanations of problematic details in hypothetical extensions of the story. But in this film we must decide—and that is the textual strain—whether the explanations lie in the fictive world or in biological theory. Events of psychoanalytic import, we conclude, can be incorporated under a more general biological principle. Jean's oedipal complex—exemplified by shots of him being hugged by his mother and trying to shoot his father with a toy arrow—is simply one more kind of territorial stakeout. Human beings are love "objects"—but now in the context of the theory of territorialism. They are like pieces of real estate rather than, say, gold bars. Gender matters little here: dominatrixes are as common as dominators. His wife gets Jean in the first place by staking her claim loudly and persistently (Jean in his initial medallion appearance says, "Of all my girlfriends, the most decided was Arlette"), then keeps him by cunning, feigning illness. With our newly acquired biological insight, we interpret feigning as a form of fighting.

Psychological inheritance too can be explained in Laboritian terms. René reacts, by fight and flight, against his father's outmoded production techniques, but it is his fate to watch himself displaced in turn by Veestrate—on the same grounds. "Nous ne sommes que les autres"—"we're nothing more than those around us." He accuses his father of provincial small-mindedness and paranoia, but when he gets "kicked upstairs" to head a new factory, he asks, like the veriest rube, "But is it a trap?" And if the requisite traits do not emerge in a character's own behavior, he manages to marry someone who can

70

furnish them at the critical moment. Confronted with his wife's refusal to leave their home in Lille for the new job, René says that she reminds him of his father.

The film even ramifies aspects of Laborit's theory in a wheels-within-wheels kind of structure. Jean "flees" into illness rather than accuse his "friend" Michel of betrayal. Then confinement to bed with sore kidneys legitimizes the aggressiveness his illness was designed to mask, and so he turns on Janine, imperiously and furiously ordering her about in the name of his pain.

But—and here's the textual novelty again—within the story issues and behaviors arise that seem inexplicable in the Laboritian scheme of things (the text-types are clearly being played with). Peacemaking, love, and compassion are such issues. For all the talk about biological gratification, it is hard to duck the question, how can these emotions be explained in strictly and coldly biological terms? How can the biologist account for Thérèse's gentle attempt to make peace between her husband and his enemy Veestrate? or for the nunlike compassion in her face when she sees René—a failure even at suicide—in his hospital bed? Where are the parallel behaviors among the lower animals? The fictional fine print makes it hard to accept the principle that territorialism, fight and flight, and the like are sufficient to explain every event.

Nor can they fully explain the *intricacy* of some behaviors: for example, when Janine *pretends* to be angry and to fight with Jean in order to return him to his wife. Some animals, of course, can sham, but the film shows nothing in the animal world that corresponds to acting a false role for altruistic reasons.[14] Nor does the biological argument, though it defines children's play as training in territorialism, account for the difference between vocation and avocation: why is it that René loves to cook on his days off but resents the suggestion that he should manage the conglomerate's new catering project? Laborit's theory would have equal difficulty explaining other instances of peculiarly human behaviors, such as "pride," "dignity," and "manhood." I am not arguing that examples (and hence explanations) of these behaviors may not indeed occur in the animal world but only that the instruction we receive from the film's argument does not enable us to account for them.

Appropriately enough, the tension between text-types is keenest in the final event of the story, the fistfight between Jean and Janine.

The narrative text ends in a quite unromantic and even distasteful debacle. But the argumentative text tells us something quite different, that though such struggles are absolutely useless for resolving frustrations, they do have a purpose: human beings, like rats, *need* to fight. It keeps their eyes clear and their skin rosy as nothing else can. Still, Jean and Janine do not look very happy or healthy. Is there some disanalogy between the external surfaces of aggressors—clear eyes and rosy skin—and their inner surfaces? Here again, the biological argument is silent.

The final story event does not end the film. There are reprises: the humble domestic objects, the spectacle of René and Veestrate battling for the telephone, Jean shouting "Vite, vite" for his hot compresses, the turtle on its back, and finally Laborit in his office giving us *his* final message, which is inconclusive: as long as the need to dominate moves human beings to crucial action, as it does the animals, there is little chance that anything will change. Cut to a traveling shot of an abandoned slum that looks very much like the South Bronx. Following Laborit's last words, these images might seem to illustrate his point: the slumlords dominated the tenants, and (presumably) the tenants, when it became more than they could bear, abandoned the neighborhood to seek another territory. But the camera comes to rest finally on the outside wall of a building upon which someone has painted a forest. It approaches the image of a single large tree, then a part of the tree, then closer still until all we can see are traces of paint on a few bricks. The effect is like that in Antonioni's *Blow-Up*: the closer one observes something, the more amorphous it becomes, until its original outline vanishes.[15]

What are we to make of this ending? Clearly, it is as much figurative as literal, since the neighborhood and the building do not at all share the story world of Le Gall, Garnier, and Ragueneau. On the other hand, they do not particularly support Laborit's discourse. The cinematic narrator could well be imagined to be saying, "Thanks, Dr. Laborit, but all your scientific theorizing leaves us no clearer than we were before. How do you account for the inhabitants' longing for nature's beauty in this urban squalor? Nor does your science help us solve the political and moral and economic problems that have led to this desolation. And what can we make of your message? It's all very well to say that as long as we want to dominate others, nothing will change. But if that's the way our *brains* are constructed, how can we hope to do anything about it? How do you propose we change our brains?"

There seems to be nothing in the film to help answer these questions. A final quandary haunts us as we leave the theater, resulting directly from the unresolvable struggle between the text-types, Narrative and Argument, for control of the film.

CHAPTER 5

In Defense of
the Implied Author

THOUGH THE NOTION of an "implied author" has enjoyed widespread currency since Wayne Booth published *The Rhetoric of Fiction*,
(1961) narratologists do not agree about its precise meaning or even
its raison d'être.[1] Few reject the distinction between real author and
narrator,[2] but some wonder why a third, seemingly "ghostly" being
should be situated between the two.

I believe that narratology—and text theory generally—needs the
implied author (and its counterpart, the implied reader) to account
for features that would otherwise remain unexplained, or unsatisfac-
torily explained. The implied author is the agency within the narrative fiction itself which guides any reading of it. Every fiction contains such an agency. It is the source—on each reading—of the
work's invention. It is also the locus of the work's *intent*. Following
W. K. Wimsatt and Monroe Beardsley, I use "intent," rather than
"intention," to refer to a work's "whole" or "overall" meaning,
including its connotations, implications, unspoken messages.[3] The
concept of an implied author ensures against simplifying the real
reader's relations with the text and reducing them, as some contextualist theories would, to one more instance of ordinary conversa-
tional interchange. I believe that each reading of a narrative fiction
reconstructs its intent and principle of invention—*reconstructs*, not
constructs, because the text's construction preexists any individual act
of reading. Though reader-response and other constructivist theories
correctly insist on the active quality of the reader's share, seeing it as

74

an energetic and creative act, the reader can constitute only one-half of that actualization.[4] There must already exist a text for her to activate. It is odd that so self-evident a principle needs reaffirmation, but the current climate of opinion suggests that it does. Given the plenitude of studies of implied readers, I shall concentrate my attention on the implied author, and assume that the former is the mirror image of the latter.

My defense is strictly pragmatic, not ontological: the question is not whether the implied author *exists* but what we *get* from positing such a concept.[5] What we get is a way of naming and analyzing the textual intent of narrative fictions under a single term but without recourse to biographism. This is particularly important for texts that state one thing and imply another. That can also be done, of course, in ordinary conversation: I can say "I admire you" in a tone of voice that conveys precisely the opposite sentiment. Since I am the source of both ostensible and real message, my interlocutor understands me to be a single speaker delivering a duplex message. But suppose I tell a first person anecdote in a voice that is obviously not my own, and it becomes clear that the story is ironic, that the "I" ultimately responsible for the story does not endorse it but is rather making fun of it and of its ostensible narrator—an "I" whom the real I am mimicking. In that instance there are clearly two narrative agents: I, who invented it, and the narrator "I," whose voice I am imitating. Yes (you might agree), there are two agents, but one of them is quite real, not implied. Exactly, but published fictions are more complex than oral anecdotes: the real author retires from the text as soon as the book is printed and sold (the film released, the play staged). Yet the principles of invention and intent *remain* in the text. Reconstructed by the audience in each reading, projection, or performance, they inform and control the narrator's message. And they occupy a different order or plane of existence than the does the narrator, even when there is no contentual disparity between text's intent and narrator's intention. Though there is no reason to believe that the implied author disagrees with the narrator of, say, *Hard Times*, there is good reason in theory to keep invention and transmission separate as text principles.

The source of a narrative text's whole structure of meaning—not only of its assertion and denotation but also of its implication, connotation, and ideological nexus—is the implied author. The act of reading a text, though ultimately an exchange between real human beings, entails two intermediate constructs: one in the text, which invents it upon each reading (the implied author), and one outside the text, which construes it upon each reading (the implied reader). Further, the implied author is not the "voice": that is, the immediate source of the text's transmission. "Voice" belongs uniquely to the narrator. (The implied author of Ring Lardner's "Haircut" is clearly not the morally obtuse narrator of the story, Whitey the barber.) We find a parallel distinction in other text-types, in Argument, for example. In Swift's "Modest Proposal," the implied author is clearly not the arguer. We cannot imagine the tract's implied author endorsing the resolution of economic problems by cannibalism. And we would make the same assumption even if the text were anonymous: that is, had no identifiable real author. But the need for "implied author" is not limited to ironic texts: even where there is no discrepancy between the implied author's intent and the narrator's or other speaker's intention, the theoretical distinction is worth preserving because the two terms account for different levels and sources of information.

Positing an implied author inhibits the overhasty assumption that the reader has direct access through the fictional text to the real author's intentions and ideology. It does not deny the existence of important connections between the text's and the real author's views, but it does deny the simplistic assumption that somehow the reader is in direct communication with (1) the real author (with all the troublesome questions that idea raises) or with (2) the fictional speaker, for how then could we separate the denotation (what the speaker says) from the connotation (what the text means), especially where these differ? However attractive it may be in theory, reading the text as the speech act of the real author is too simplistic to account for the semantic complexity of many texts. Despite the important influence of speech-act theory on text analysis, we cannot successfully analyze published fictions in terms designed to explain ordinary conversation. Fictions are more complex than such utterances as "Can you reach the salt?" (whose illocutionary force varies according to its use: a request in one context, a question about the speaker's physical state in another). In conversation, the auditor can request feedback in order to pinpoint the speech act, by asking, for example, "Does that mean you want the salt, or are you asking me how far I can stretch?" But the reader cannot query the author about the fiction's meaning or force. As Roland Barthes put it, published fictions are "hardened."[6]

Indeed, there are many instances where a real author's pronouncements about his text's meaning have struck critics as misleading or downright wrong. The meaning of a text is necessarily and forever subject to interpretation. As we have learned repeatedly in this most hermeneutic age, the question of what the text means (not just what it "says") varies radically from reader to reader, from interpretive community to interpretive community. Indeed, we might better speak of the "inferred" than of the "implied" author.[7]

The Hermeneutic Background

The concept of implied authorship arose in the debate about the relevance of authorial intention to interpretation. Though it started many years ago, this debate is not over; there is even something of a revival of claims about the real author's centrality in the textual complex. Any defense of implied authorship depends on an understanding of the two polar positions. Intentionalists in the tradition of Goethe, Carlyle, Croce, and J. E. Spingarn argue that interpretations can be supported by appeal to the real authors' intentions. In the primitive version, "intention" refers to the author's *plans* at the moment of composition, what she had *in mind* to do. More sophisticated intentionalists such as E. D. Hirsch change the sense of "intend" to mean not the author's psychic acts but the "process of consciousness"; still, the intention of the real author remains the sole source of "objective interpretation." Without its authorial moorings, the intentionalist fears, a text would drift among the capricious winds of critical styles and personal preferences. Using Gottlob Frege's terms, Hirsch argues that any semantic value other than what the real author intended is not the text's "meaning" (*Sinn*) but its "significance" (*Bedeutung*).[8]

An even more ardent intentionalist, P. D. Juhl, uses this argument to reject the concept of the implied author:

> How we view the story, the situation, or events presented in a work, or what we take to be expressed or suggested by it, is determined not by our picture of the so-called implied author, but rather by our picture of the real, historical person. If a literary work conveys or expresses certain propositions, then—or so I shall argue—the real author is committed to the truth of those proposi-

tions and to the corresponding beliefs; that is, the propositions a work expresses or conveys are expressed or conveyed by, and hence attributable to, not the "implied author," but rather the real, historical author.[9]

Anti-intentionalists such as Monroe Beardsley reject the relevance of original authorial intention, arguing that an interpretation should derive only or at least principally from the text itself.[10] Beardsley's remains the best discussion of literary intention. He questions the interpretive relevance of the "psychological states or events in [the artist's] mind: what he wanted to do, how he imagined or projected the work before he began to make it and while he was in the process of making it." At best, biographical material provides only indirect evidence of what the object is, and indirect evidence is obviously secondary to the evidence of a "direct inspection of the object."[11]

Anti-intentionalism does not argue that the study of conventions and meanings that prevailed during the artist's lifetime are irrelevant or that the critic is misguided to search for them; to interpret Bach well, one should know as much as possible about how music sounded in his time. To interpret Milton well, one should know as much as possible about seventeenth-century Christianity. Nor do the anti-intentionalists suggest that the artist's statements of intention should be discounted in interpretation. They argue only against the relevance of the sounds Bach might have heard in his own *head*, or what Milton was *planning* as he composed *Paradise Lost*—and only against the *interpreter's* considering them: there is no suggestion that biographers and historians may not do so.

The anti-intentionalist insists on distinguishing between what words mean and what people mean. Texts obviously continue to mean, long after their authors are dead. Authors sometimes mean one thing but their texts another. Beardsley cites the case of a poem by A. E. Housman called "1887": Frank Harris interpreted the poem as ironically critical of Queen Victoria's easy dispatch of young men to die in wars—a not unreasonable interpretation, given the content of some of Housman's other poems. But Housman himself rejected an ironic reading of "1887." Similarly, Saul Bellow recently complained that some readers have misunderstood the comic intent of *Herzog* "to show how little strength 'higher education' had to offer a troubled man."[12] The intentionalist would have to argue that "1887" is not ironic and that *Herzog* is comic, because their authors say so. The anti-intentionalist would counter that Housman and Bellow may have misconstrued the meanings of their own work, that their unconscious may have guided their pens more than they knew, or that they simply did not achieve their intention. Whatever the reason, concludes Beardsley, "if [a poet's] report of what the poem is intended to mean conflicts with the evidence of the poem itself, we cannot allow him to *make* the poem mean what he wants it to mean, just by fiat."[13]

Beardsley faults criticism whose language unnecessarily stresses the author's intention when it only wants to describe what the text says or does. He questions the validity of such pronouncements as "According to Jane Austen, Emma is overbearing but basically well-intentioned," and "In *Rear Window*, Hitchcock implicates the viewer in the protagonist's voyeurism," as opposed to the simple statements "The novel *Emma* presents an overbearing but well-intentioned heroine," and "*Rear Window* implicates the viewer in the protagonist's voyeurism." The former make *unnecessarily* intentionalistic claims; the latter claim only that the primary evidence for judgments about the heroine's character or the viewer's complicity inhere in the text itself.[14]

In more technical language, the anti-intentionalist distinguishes between (in William Tolhurst's terms) "utterer's meaning," "utterance meaning," and "word-sequence meaning."[15] "Utterer's meaning" is what the author had in mind when creating the text. "Word-sequence meaning" is what the words or other signs signify by linguistic and semiotic convention; in speech-act terms, it is the bare "locution." "Utterance meaning" is word-sequence meaning plus a context, the locution plus its illocutionary force. In other words, word-sequence meaning is only the semantic potential of well-formed speech acts. Meaning as a practical matter cannot arise until the text is "uttered" in respect to some perceivable or inferable state of affairs. It must be interpreted by someone who understands the semantic and syntactic rules by which the sentences or other semiotic structures cohere *and* the context into which they plausibly fit. The anti-intentionalist argues that what is chiefly relevant to interpretation is utterance meaning, not utterer's meaning. The reader makes out the word-sequence meaning and tries to divine a context appropriate to the text. "This is not to say that utterer's meaning is irrelevant to a determination of textual meaning," concludes Tolhurst. "It is just to say that it is not identical with it."[16]

The anti-intentionalist position, no matter how venerable, has not been successfully refuted. In an era when skepticism prevails about the very possibility of knowledge, communication, and interpretation, it seems worthwhile to recall the sensible views of philosophers such as Beardsley.

Booth's Argument for the Implied Author

The intentionalist debate helps clarify the question of the "implied author." Let us consider five definitions of the term proposed by Wayne Booth in *The Rhetoric of Fiction*.[17] (These definitions are resurrected only as a point of departure: I do not mean to suggest that Booth still conceives of the implied author in these ways. His later work refines the concept considerably).

First, *the neutral (or objective or ideal) person that the real author wants to be in order to create an objective account.* Booth notes that novelists often use some such term to describe their own process of composing: Jessamyn West writes of an "official scribe" who discovers or creates her appropriate stance to the story; Edward Dowden and Kathleen Tillotson refer to the author's "second self." The real author, says Booth, wants to avoid pouring "his untransformed biases into the work," so he creates a neutral representative or surrogate author.[18]

But this "second self" or "official scribe" suggests a definition of intention that not even sophisticated intentionalists would defend: namely, something *planned* by the author prior to the moment of composition, some alter ego that real authors take on to help them establish a desired state of objectivity.[19] Real authorial behavior is a subject for literary biography, not text theory. If the overcoming or "transforming" of biases in the act of creation is all that "implied author" means, why would we need the term? Wouldn't "real but bias-free author" do the trick? What text theory wants to know is how and whether "implied author" names something essential to and derivable from the text itself.

Second, *the different aspects of themselves that authors show in different works.* Since this definition refers to a process by which the real author decides which of several assumable personae shall inform her text, it, too, refers to subjective compositional intentions or plans and thus seems unusable by text theory.[20]

Third, *the creator as opposed to his creatures*—including the narrator, describer, or other agent transmitting the discourse, who, after all, is no less a constructed object than the characters in the story. Booth demonstrates vividly that the narrative voice may be separated from the implied author "by large ironies." The standard case here is the "unreliable narrator." Though everyone grants the possibility of such ironies, not all theorists agree that they should be explained by the notion of an implied author. The question is whether the real author and the narrator *between them* account for all the distinctions we sense in actual texts. If we posit some third entity immanent to the text, does that mean we must assume that all three sources are human? To anticipate: my answer to both questions is no.

Fourth, *the "choosing, evaluating person" who produces the work* (so that we do not think of the work "as a self-existing thing"). This definition straddles the fence of "intentionality," half accepting and half rejecting its relevance to textual structure. On the one hand, Booth disallows the intention of the real author, but on the other, he wishes to avoid calling texts "self-existing things."

I stick by the anti-intentionalist view that a published text *is* in fact a self-existing thing. Invention, originally an activity in the real author's mind, becomes, upon publication, a principle recorded in the text. That principle is the residue of the real author's labor. It is now a textual artifact. The text is itself the implied author. As Roger Fowler puts it:

> In its cryptic way, "the text speaks" finds the correct source for the voice of narrative discourse: in the public conventions of language, in relation to which the author is a facilitating medium—the text, once written, liberates itself from his act of writing and "goes public." Language, transcending the individual, imprints the text with the community's values. And, without contradiction, the reader is the producer of meaning, since he, as much as the writer, is a repository of the culture's linguistically coded values, and has the power to release them from the text.[21]

Upon publication, the implied author supersedes the real author. Unlike the oral anecdote, whose real author continues to stand in immediate relation to it and thus in open communication with his audience, a written text is closed until read, though it contains, latently, its principles of invention and intent. Those principles are available to and activated by each reader upon each reading. Intention ceases being a private authorial matter: it becomes the work's intent.[22] We must distinguish between a real author's activity and the *product* of that activity: the text before us. It makes perfect sense to speak of intent—what R. W. Stallman calls "actual" intention—as a property of the text, as "the effect which the work aims to evoke, the organizing principle informing the whole, or the meaning which the work manifests or suggests."[23] Or, in W. K. Wimsatt's phrase, we learn the author's "*effective* intention or *operative* mind as it appears in the work itself."[24]

One problem with Booth's use of "implied author" to recall that the work is the product of "a choosing evaluating person" is that many texts do not evoke such a person. Some texts, such as portions of the Bible or traditional ballads, were created by anonymous authors working through many generations. Others, such as films churned out by Hollywood, are made by a consortium of writers, producers, actors, directors, cinematographers, distribution executives (who may not have totally agreed on the final product). Still, the books (or certain sequences of books) of the Bible and traditional ballads and Hollywood films *seem* to have been created by a single author. That is because they are governed by the unified invention and intent of the text: that is, their implied authors. Rather than calling attention to the work as the product of a choosing, evaluating person, I see the work as a repository of choices—of already *made* choices, which can be considered as alternatives to other choices that might have been made but were not.

Perhaps some of the resistance to the term might dissipate if we stop thinking of the implied author as a human surrogate or image of the real author. Hatching a third human being is unnecessary. Little is gained by assuming an "image" of Mark Twain which is in any important respect different from the real Twain,[25] but much is to be gained from recognizing the differences between the implied author and the narrator Huck Finn.

Fifth, what I call the *recorded invention of the text*, which is in Booth's words *based on a "core of norms and choices" that inform* it. For this construct, Booth prefers the term "implied author" over such possibilities as "theme," "meaning," "symbolic significance," "theology," or "ontology"—terms he finds misleading because they "come to seem like purposes for which the works exist." I would add that such terms tend to obscure the commonsense notion that a narrative text (like any text) contains within itself, explicitly or implicitly, information about how to read it. A real reader comes to a novel or film presupposing the existence of such information. If she has difficulty finding it, she will either reject the text out of hand or learn to cope with its novelty (thus extending her repertoire of orientational topoi). Even if she goes to someone else's explication of the text, that other person has found in the text itself the requisite tools for interpretation.

The Record of Textual Invention

This fifth sense of "implied author" is, I believe, essential to narratology and to text theory in general, though I would qualify Booth's "norms and choices" and speak instead of codes and conventions, both of literature and of life. "Value," in English (as opposed to *valeur* in French), connotes ethical (and, to a lesser extent, esthetic) merit, precisely the subject that Booth has gone on to discuss in great depth in *The Company We Keep*. But from another perspective, text theory chooses to talk about the whole range or network of means by which we understand the diegetic world and the discourse presenting it.

The real author's engagements with codes and conventions leaves a mark on the text, the record of an invention. This recorded invention differs from the real author's act of creating the text. The actual composition of the work by the real author in the real world was a series of nonreplicable events—meditations, the making of disconnected notes, drafts, revisions—events "spread out in time," says Wallace Martin, "that have come together in a fixed form that cannot be equated with any [single or isolatable] moment of 'intention' in the past."[26] But the record of that invention reposes in the text and is recuperable at any moment by an audience. Why distinguish the two? Simply because the *act* of a producer, a real author, obviously differs from the *product* of that act, the text. As an inscribed principle of invention and intent, the implied author is the reader's source of instruction about how to read the text and how to account for the selection and ordering of its components. It is these principles that readers reconstitute, not the real author's original activity.

Of course, we may bring in other information, other contexts (in the root sense of the morpheme: texts *around* or associated *with* the text). Among such contexts is what we remember of other works by the real author. The information about how to read the text is thus "emergent." Though different readers may construct different implied readers, the process itself is common to us all. And that is why it makes sense to call the construct of invention "implied" or "inferred": it remains only latent or "virtual" in the text until it is actualized by our act of reading. Readers infer a self-consistent textual intent, rather than guessing directly at the real author's state of mind. We recuperate the intentions of a "Dickens," not those of the man Charles Dickens.

Even as he established these vital distinctions, Booth did not himself escape the potential confusion between the implied author, as source or "instance" of narrative invention, and the narrator, as the "utterer" or "enunciator." Occasionally, *The Rhetoric of Fiction* refers to the real author when it seems to mean the implied author, that is, to Dickens and not to "Dickens." Given the groundbreaking quality of Booth's work, it is easy to forgive him this lapse, but we should take pains not to replicate it. For example, Booth argues that the implied authors of *Tom Jones* and *Joseph Andrews* exhibit a certain facetiousness and insouciance quite unknown in Fielding's other novels, whereas the implied author of *Amelia* seems uncharacteristically sententious and solemn.[27] But Booth's formulation can be interpreted in a clearer and more useful way, I think, if we distinguish between who speaks the text and who (or the principle which) has invented it. In this model the implied author is the inventor, and the narrator is the "utterer": that is, the one who articulates the words assigned to him by the implied author. Consider the narrator's meditation on Joseph Andrews's ancestry:

Suppose, for argument's sake, we should admit that he had no ancestors at all, but had sprung up, according to the modern phrase, out of a dunghill, as the Athenians pretended they themselves did from the earth, would not this autokopros have been justly entitled to all the praise arising from his own virtues? Would it not be hard that a man who had no ancestors should therefore be rendered incapable of acquiring honour; when we see so many who have no virtues enjoying the honour of their fore-fathers?[28]

This passage safely qualifies, I imagine, as facetious. And we assume that a narrator, in speaking this way about ancestry—ordinarily a serious matter to eighteenth-century Englishmen—intends to be facetious. But what does it mean to say that the narrator intends these words? Clearly, the "narrator," no less a constructed object than the characters and events he speaks about, is no more capable of intending or "choosing" his words than is Joseph Andrews. The power of selection and ordering is the (real) author's, and its record is the novel itself, governed by its own invention and intent, its own implied author. The narrator "comes by" his words because they are assigned to him. To believe otherwise would be to fall victim to the very illusion we are struggling to explain. Ultimately, of course, it was the real Henry Fielding (1707–54) who chose the words for the narrator to "speak." But narratology wants to say that it is something in the text itself, some principle of design, which creates anew, for each reading, a narrator who tells and shows these things in these ways. Whether the text itself—that is, its implied author—intends facetiousness or sententiousness is inferred not only from what the narrator says and how he says it in this or that passage but from the whole effect of the novel. To say that in a given "speech" the narrator of *Joseph Andrews* sounds facetious is one thing; to call *Joseph Andrews the novel* facetious is another. The one characterization does not necessarily entail the other.

In my view, it makes sense to attribute to every narrative fiction an agency that does not personally tell or show but puts into the narrator's mouth the language that tells or shows. The implied author has no "voice." The implied author only empowers others to "speak."[29] The implied author (unlike the delegated speaker, the narrator) is a silent source of information. The implied author "says" nothing.[30] Insofar as the implied author (the text itself) communicates something different from what the narrator says, that meaning must occur between the lines. Any narrator, whether authorial, camera-eye, or dramatized, is a tool of the invention. As inventor, the implied author is by definition distinguishable from the narrators, who are invented. It is the implied author, for example, that dictates the elaborate network of tellings and tellings-within-tellings of *The Nigger of the*

Narcissus. The choice of narrators in that novel, as in other narratives, is basically a rhetorical one (see Chapter 11). Conrad's novel assumes that the most suasive presentation of the narrative would entail a series of imbricated frame stories, thereby distancing its strange import from the workaday world.

For readers who feel uncomfortable about using the term "implied author" to refer to this concept, I am perfectly willing to substitute the phrase "text implication" or "text instance" or "text design" or even simply "text intent"—always on the understanding that "intent" is used to mean not what was in the mind of the real author bent over a desk but what is *in* the text that we hold in our hands, or see on the stage or the screen or the comic strip. It is a sense of purpose reconstructable from the text that we read, watch, and/or hear.

Thus, my position lies halfway between that of some poststructuralists, who would deny the existence of *any* agent—who would acknowledge only our encounter with *écriture*—and that of Booth, who has spoken of the implied author as "friend and guide." For me the implied author is neither. It is nothing other than the text itself in its inventional aspect.

Some narratologists have suggested that the implied author is a marginal concept, useful only where the text's intent is clearly distinct from the narrator's intention. The term they use to describe this supposed marginality, a term taken from linguistics, is "marked": in English, some nouns ("man," "woman") are marked for gender; others ("voter," "driver") are not. For the unmarked word "voter," the "degree" of gender is "zero." But "marked" and "unmarked" are not useful terms if they downplay a distinction unless it has some immediately practical consequence, such as unreliable narration. The proponents of this view argue that in most cases the implied author and the narrator are indistinguishable and that dramatized narrators are therefore special, "marked," and somehow deviant cases. This too easily becomes the argument that since the narrator usually reflects the implied author's view of things, we might just as well go back to saying that the two are identical, that it is the implied author who tells or shows the story—or, conversely, that there is no longer any need for the notion of implied author at all. But such an argument is like saying that because the third person plural English pronoun is unmarked for gender, the gender of individuals referred to as "they" is inconsequential. It may be irrelevant in some contexts, but obviously the gender distinction remains importantly implicit, in the language as in life.

Recognizing the logical distinction between real author, implied author, and narrator sensitizes us to interpretational prospects that we might otherwise miss.[31] The narrator's relation to the implied author is not to be presumed but to be uncovered. Even more important, the theory recognizes the copresence of implied author and narrator in every text, even those where no irony or double meaning exists, even where the implied ideology of the text is consonant with that expressed by the narrator or, indeed, with that of the real author. Refusal to acknowledge this copresence will prevent us from accounting *in advance* for possibilities that we already know to exist. That not all narratives have unreliable narrators (like *The Turn of the Screw*) or nested levels of narration (like *The Nigger of the Narcissus*), that most were written not by a gaggle of coauthors but by well-known individuals whose actual views resemble strongly those of their fictions—none of these facts *negates* the viability and importance of the text principle that we call the implied author.

The narrator, and she or he alone, is the only subject, the only "voice" of narrative discourse. The inventor of that speech, as of the speech of the characters, is the implied author. That inventor is no person, no substance, no object: it is, rather, the patterns in the text which the reader negotiates.

The Career Author

Even a reader sympathetic with the views expressed above might still be prompted to ask, Doesn't our understanding of a text's invention and intent rest in important ways on our knowledge that it was written by a certain real author? Doesn't the name "Henry James" on the spine of a book provide important clues about the novel we are preparing to read even before we read it? And doesn't that fact belie any argument for the autonomy of textual invention and hence of implied authorship? With his customary acumen, Wayne Booth has recognized the problem and has offered a solution: the concept of the "career-author."

Criticism has no name for these sustained characters who somehow are the sum of the invented creators implied by all of the writer's particular works. For lack of a good name, I shall call such a sustained character (still different, of course, from the writer, with his quotidian concerns, his dandruff, his diverticulosis, her nightmares, her battles with the publisher) the career-author. [This is] the sustained creative center implied by a sequence of implied authors. Implied authors may remain fairly constant from one work to another by the same author (as in Jane Austen's novels), or they may vary greatly, as in the extreme case of J. I. M. Stewart, a scholar whose detective stories require an "author" with an entirely different name: Michael Innes.[32]

Again, Booth has identified an important convention. But again—and at the risk of seeming ungrateful—I must suggest a slight modification of his language. Do we really want to say that the career-author, this "sustained creative center," is a "character?" Let us once more resist the anthropomorphic trap. We can comfortably define the career-author as the subset of features shared by all the implied authors (that is, all the individual intents) of the narrative texts bearing the name of the same real author. The real author's name, then, can be understood as the signifier of a certain constancy or common denominator of method among the implied authors of the various works. Its signified is the known subset of features, carried over from other, similarly signed texts, which provides readers with narratively significant information as they make their way through the new text. It is what permits us to put *Gravity's Rainbow* in the context of "Thomas Pynchon" if we have already read *The Crying of Lot 49* and *V* but know nothing about the life and opinions of the real Thomas Pynchon.

It is a narratological (and not merely a biographical) fact that a text is signed by a "Pynchon" or a "Hemingway" or a "James" (quotation marks to stress these as signifiers, not signifieds). The reader will certainly utilize such information. However, what is relevant to narratology (as opposed to other kinds of literary study) is not the history of the real author's career but rather the necessary constraint on possible contents and styles implicit in his or her signature on the text.

The notion of the career-author enables us to acknowledge narratively significant information implicit in the author's name without confusing the issue with biography. That a story is by "Hemingway" circumscribes it in some ways; that it is by "James" circumscribes it in others. Imagine an event that might occur in a novel by either author—say, the protagonist's remaining silent in response to a direct question. A reader may interpret this refusal to speak within the novel's own context, but she may also remember that such a refusal crops up in other texts by the same career author. Perhaps she remembers that other instances of reticence in "Hemingway's" fiction are associated with heroic stoicism. Within this larger context, she may well hypothesize that the reticence here has the same motive.

What is gained by speaking of the career-authors "Hemingway" and "James" instead of the real authors straight out? The same theoretical clarity and consistency that derives from "implied author." What the term keeps us focused on is texts per se, rather than real authors. It also permits us to understand such concepts as "narrative style" (as opposed to prose style): that is, the kinds of narrative choices typical of a given real author.

CHAPTER 6

The Implied Author
at Work

WITHOUT THE implied author, narratology and literary criticism lose an important distinction. The test case here is the possibility of unreliable or "discrepant" narration. The narrator alone tells or shows the text, and if we cannot accept his account, we must infer that it belongs to someone (or something) else. If all meanings—implicit as well as explicit—are the products of the text's activity, and if this activity always presupposes agency, then we have to posit some such text principle or agent as the implied author. Thus, it is the implied authors of Ford Madox Ford's *Good Soldier*, of Ring Lardner's "Haircut," and of all the other "suspicious" novels and stories in Booth's "gallery"[1] who are the sources of the "true" stories.

But we need to recognize the implied author also in texts that do *not* overtly undermine the narrator's account. There are many texts which, though narrated with total reliability, are difficult to characterize as the creation of some single real author. Yet each of these clearly coheres as a unity, seemingly the product of a unified agency. Again the term "implied author" is very useful to name this agency. The wide (and wild) diversity of the following examples demonstrates the broad relevance of implied authorship.

Authorship by Committee:
The Bible and Hollywood Films

The implied author names the convention by which we naturalize the reading experience as a personal encounter with some single, historically identifiable author addressing the public, even if we know nothing about that person's life. But the convention also clearly operates where no such address was intended. Consider, for example, personal diaries, like that of Anne Frank, which were never meant to be seen by anyone other than their authors. We could hardly say that the "real Anne Frank" speaks to the "real us." Clearly, she intended only to speak to herself; still we read the diary as if it addresses us. Narratologically, then, it can only be the implied author of the *Diary* who addresses us.[2]

The illusion of a single author addressing us is sustained even when no individual "authority" can be demonstrated, as in the case of collaboration. Multiple authorship is a common phenomenon in literary history. And often, some of the "authors" are humble sorts indeed. W. K. Wimsatt, Jr., notes

> how much some literary works actually owe to editors and other agents of transmission and even to such chance activity as that of a compositor, who may by mistake introduce a word that conceivably is better than the author's. . . . Frequently . . . a . . . designed work is the design of more than one head. . . . Editors . . . in assessing and adopting the accidental intrusion . . . [are] the very junior collaborators in the original author's designed and intended work. . . . In our frequent focus on the history of modern literature . . . with its heavy personal underpainting, its vigorous cult of personal authentication, let us not forget the massive foundations of the world's literature—-the Book of Genesis, the *Iliad*, the *Odyssey*, the works of Virgil, Dante, Chaucer, Shakespear—which survive for us either anonymously or with the merest wisps or shadows of biography attached.[3]

Many texts were created by collaboration, often anonymously, with the details of their authorship difficult or impossible to determine. The collective authors never knew or forgot or lied about who did what. Details of the authorship of many of our most precious texts are forever lost in the mists of history. Narratives have been produced by people at odds with each other, none of them satisfied with the end product. Still, readers conventionally impute, at each reading, a unifying agent. That agent can only be the implied author.

Consider the obvious case of the Bible. For centuries scholars have recognized that the Pentateuch was not written by Moses or, indeed, by any single person. E.A. Speiser, for example, draws a sharp line between the authorship of Deuteronomy (*D*), on the one hand, and that of the four preceding books, the Tetrateuch; and within the Tetrateuch, between the so-called Priestly source (*P*) and the outright narrative material. The latter, in turn, came to be attributed to two groups of authors, according to which name they assigned to God. These are called by Biblical scholars *J* (Yahwist) and *E* (Elohist). Further, *P* probably "was not an individual, or even a group of like-minded contemporaries, but a school with an unbroken history reaching back to early Israelite times, and continuing until the Exile and beyond." Biblical scholars postulate an additional group *R* of redactors and compilers. Though there have been various other proposals about the authorship of the Pentateuch, most scholars agree "that the Pentateuch was in reality a composite work, the product of many hands and periods." Further, though many parts are confidently ascribed to one or another source, some are "so fused that they may never be pried apart."[4] Still, many readers think of these books of the Bible as a unified narrative and have little difficulty speaking of their "implied author."

Turning from ancient Israel to our modern Babylon, we hear the loud voice of Louis B. Mayer invoking the Holy Book (nothing less) to defend the studio system of film authorship: "If a writer complains about his stuff being changed," commented Arthur Freed, Mayer "always says, 'The Number One book of the ages was written by a committee, and it was called the Bible.'"[5] Though a familiar phenomenon, the collective creations of Hollywood films are likely to be overlooked by narratologists who dwell too exclusively on literary narratives. One well-documented case is *The Red Badge of Courage* (1951), adapted from Stephen Crane's novel and directed by John Huston for MGM. The checkered authorship of this film is particularly interesting, given Huston's usual inclusion in the "pantheon" of *auteurs*.[6]

When *The Red Badge of Courage* opened in New York on August 31, 1951, reviewers treated it as Huston's exclusive achievement. The *New York Tribune* wrote that "Stephen Crane's 'The Red Badge of Courage' has been transformed by John Huston"; the *Morning Telegraph*, that the novel "has been brought to the screen by the brilliant John Huston as an offbeat motion picture"; and the *World-Telegram & Sun*, that "John Huston has written and directed a stirring film in an understanding and close reproduction of the novel." No other person was mentioned in connection with the making of the film; reviewers universally assumed that Huston was solely responsible. In fact, the *New York Post* critic was so innocent of the film's history (and Hollywood production practices in general) that he attributed the film's failure to Huston's "lethargy:" "It is as if, somewhere between shooting and final version, the light of inspiration had died. Huston got tired of it, or became discouraged, or decided that it wasn't going to come off. . . . Mr. Huston's product is that of a splendid director who had lost interest, who was no longer striving for that final touch of perfection, who had missed the cumulative passion and commentary on human beings that mark his best pictures."[7] Apparently, film critics no less than ordinary readers need to believe in individual and personal, not collective and anonymous, authorship.

That fantasy was dispelled by Lillian Ross's eyewitness account of the making of the film, which appeared in five installments in the *New Yorker* and later as a book titled *Picture*. The facts, as Ross revealed them in pungent detail, were quite otherwise. For one thing, Huston did not have "final cut" or, indeed, any hand in the editing at all. In Hollywood in 1951 it was still customary for directors to give over raw footage to another department of the studio, run by resident editors. This film was edited by Ben Lewis and Margaret Booth, in collaboration with producer Gottfried Reinhardt, after Huston went off to Africa to shoot *The African Queen*. "Editing" in the cinema, it must be remembered, is not merely cutting out excesses but literally assembling the film (as the French say, it is a *montage*). In classical Hollywood production, it is often the editor who decides on such compositional matters as the order of the shots. Imagine a hypothetical literary parallel: one person writes the sentences, and another prunes and arranges them.

Music too was often added to studio films independently of the director's control. Bronislau Kaper, the studio composer who wrote the music for *The Red Badge of Courage*, considered himself not merely a collaborator but a kind of therapist: "Every picture is sick. . . . That is my premise. We must make it well and healthy." Here is the medication he prescribed for *The Red Badge of Courage*: "After the Youth's regiment wins the first battle, the solders act happy. . . . But I come along, and I tell the audience, with sad music, what is so good about this? I make a little ridiculous the whole idea of one American killing another American. Sometimes I bring phony emotions into the picture to wake the audience up."[8] Many others— some less self-impressed about their importance—also contributed to the making of the film, with or without direct instruction from Huston: lighting technicians, set designers, costumers, makeup artists, and the like.

Nor did collaboration end there. To the consternation of MGM, the film inspired negative comments from a sneak-preview audience. Many viewers expressed indifference to the film's antiwar intention, and there was laughter in the wrong places. Fearing a commercial failure, Reinhardt added a voice-over sententiously proclaiming that the film was based on a literary classic, implying that it therefore deserved respect. The voice (that of James Whitmore) was also assigned the task of conveying the protagonist's thoughts, despite Huston's express wish that those thoughts remain implicit in the visuals. Even before shooting started, Reinhardt had asked Huston, "The book is about the *thoughts* of the Youth. Will we show what really goes on inside the boy?" Huston had responded confidently: "Audie Murphy [the actor who plays the Youth] will show it, Gottfried."[9] But Reinhardt questioned Huston's artistic intuition, and his doubts prevailed; the voice-over periodically intones, in Crane's very prose, what is passing through the protagonist's mind.

The effect is quite bad, as a critic for the *New York Times* pointed out: "The picture could not convey the reactions of Crane's hero to war, for Crane had conveyed them 'in almost stream-of-consciousness descriptions, which is a technique that works best with words.' "[10] Actually, that is not what Crane did, and the problem is as much the novel's as it is the film's. The Youth's thoughts are precisely *not* presented in stream-of-consciousness style, nor even in indirect free style, but rather in what Dorrit Cohn calls "psychonarration":[11] that is, paraphrases in the narrator's own prose, which tends to intense purple. The novel is flawed by the a discrepancy between this well-spoken, self-consciously literary representation of the Youth's thoughts and that of his actual uneducated speech. Whereas the Youth *says* such things as

I got shot. In th' head. I never see sech fightin'. Awful time. I don't see how I could 'a' got separated from th'reg'ment.

the novel's narrator represents his thinking in sentences like this:

He told himself that, despite his unprecedented suffering, he had never lost his greed for a victory, yet, he said, in a half-apologetic manner to his conscience, he could not but know that a defeat for the army this time might mean many favorable things for him. The blows of the enemy would splinter regiments into fragments. Thus, many men of courage, he considered, would be obliged to desert the colors and scurry like chickens.[12]

Reinhardt decided that this sort of effete language should be given to a heterodiegetic voice-over narrator rather than to Audie Murphy's characterial voice-over. The best that can be said is that the latter solution would have been definitely worse than the former.

But even voice-over pronouncements of the literary merit of the novel were not enough for Dore Schary, head of production at MGM; he made substantive additional cuts. Like Crane's, Huston's concern for the Civil War was mostly a pretext for a psychological study of soldiers ignorant of the cause for which they risked their lives. As Garbicz and Klinowski explain: "Huston said that he did not want the war as shown in his film to be understood only as the war between the North and the South, but a war which shows the uselessness of the courage of the protagonist—who in the film's finale storms a piece of crumbling wall. This was seen as a blasphemy against the history of the United States: MGM [read, Schary] re-edited the material so as to show how a soldier can defeat fear and become a hero."[13] Schary cut the film's original seventy-eight minutes to sixty-nine and rearranged several of its events. As a result, according to Lillian Ross, "the battle sequences added up to an entirely different war from the one that had been fought and photographed at Huston's ranch in the San Fernando Valley." When the audience at the next sneak preview seemed friendlier, however, Schary was confident "that the picture was now a doll. 'Everything is better now, sweetie,' he said to Reinhardt. 'The audience understands this boy now.'"[14]

So, by conservative count, the list of the "real authors" of *The Red Badge of Courage* includes Crane, Huston, Reinhardt, Lewis, Booth, Kaper, and Schary—not to speak of the actors, cinematographer Harold Rosson, designers Cedric Gibbons and Hans Peters, and other production people who made choices about how things should look or sound, with or without Huston's knowledge—plus several hundred Los Angeles moviegoers, to the extent that Dore Schary interpreted their input. These viewers were not some theoretical construct but literal collaborators: their scribbled comments on evaluation cards, collected and nervously interpreted by studio executives, led to a substantial reworking of the film.

Yet despite this motley crew of real authors, the film *The Red Badge of Courage*, for better or worse, gives an impression of unity so strong that reviewers spoke persistently of a single authorial source: it was "Huston's film"; it was Huston who "became discouraged with it," and the like. What they were talking about, of course, was not the real John Huston but the film's implied author.

We are not limited to Hollywood films for examples of uneasy collaboration. There is the famous misunderstanding between Chekhov and Stanislavsky about *The Seagull*: according to Stanislavsky, the play is supposed to be a tragedy, but Chekhov "always referred to it as a comedy." "Practically every producer," says Wimsatt, "in spite of Chekhov's unmistakable intentions [to be found in his letters], regards the play as a tragedy."[15]

The aesthetic problems caused by an excessive commitment to individual "real authors" is no less evident in the study of masterpieces of painting. Consider the fascinating controversy currently raging about Rembrandt. In *The Transfiguration of the Commonplace*, Arthur Danto poses the philosophical question of what happens to our judgment of the value of a painting when we learn that it was not done solely by an established master; his theoretical example is Rembrandt's *Polish Rider*. Reviewing Danto's book, Rosalyn Krauss notes that "at this very moment there is a collective project under way to establish the true, the authentic, the original Rembrandt from within the miasma of fakes, copies, shop pieces, student-produced look-alikes, and all the other forms of 'indiscernibilia' that have clouded our view of the genuine article." Ironically enough, one of the suspected paintings is precisely the *Polish Rider*. Krauss wonders what lesson we can draw from the possibility

> that this "deepest painting" may not be by "one of the deepest artists in the history of the subject." [Danto's words]. . . . Do we shrug our shoulders and decide we were duped: "Oh, so it was not really a moving painting after all"? Or does this become an occasion . . . to rethink the structure of agency, of authorship? . . . The idea of the unique hand of the master begins to appear . . . as a

Romantic prejudice that has very little to do with the actual conditions of artistic practice. Even many of Rembrandt's *self*-portraits, we are now able to realize, were painted by his students.[16]

Isn't it reasonable to ask whether the "Romantic prejudice" of "the unique hand of the master" still dominates literary scholarship and has also made inroads into the infant discipline of cinema scholarship? If so, shouldn't we be looking at narratives with eyes made clearer by such concepts as that of the implied author?

Is Stepan Trofimovitch Verkhovensky Redeemed?

In *The Rhetoric of Fiction*, Booth usefully (if a bit erratically) adds quotation marks to distinguish the implied from the real author. Marianne Torgovnick tells us, however, that "today such devices have largely been dropped.. since it is clear when [one] speak[s] of authors as narrators or as 'implied authors,' and when [one] speak[s] of authors as 'real' men and women."[17] Would that it were so. Take the case of Dostoevsky's novel *The Possessed*. Some critics believe that if any character in this dark novel finds redemption, it is Stepan Trofimovitch Verkhovensky, the liberal aesthete who, after a largely parasitic life, musters the energy and courage to leave his protectress, Varvara Stavrogin. His final pilgrimage, they argue, however quixotic, allows him to recapture some last remnant of dignity and honor. Albert Guerard, for example, writes: "The next to last chapter, 'Stepan Trofimovich's Last Wandering,' brings his Christian redemption, and his redemption too as a comic character long ridiculed for his many weaknesses, but now achieving a kind of mad heroism and magnitude."[18] And Irving Howe asserts that to Stepan, "Dostoevsky is least merciful of all; he stalks him with a deadly aim; he humiliates him, badgers him, taunts him, and finally shatters him— and yet: he loves him." Despite his errancy, dependency on matriarchal Russia, half-heartedness, cowardice, unconscious indulgence of authority, "it is Stepan Trofimovitch who is allowed the most honorable and heroic end. . . . Since for Dostoevsky salvation comes only from extreme suffering, Stepan Trofimovitch begins to rise, to gather to himself the scattered energies of the book."[19]

The editor of the author's notebooks for *The Possessed*, Edward

Wasiolek, sounds a similar though more restrained note: "Stepan Trofimovich begins his last quixotic journey in ignorance and hope. He remains foolish and self-serving, but some spark of recognition and repentance flickers faintly in his soul. It is too much to say, perhaps, that he is redeemed, but he is born before death into responsibility." But then Wasiolek cites an odd and troubling fact: "There is almost nothing in [Dostoevsky's] notes—from beginning to end and throughout variant after variant—to indicate that Dostoevsky meant Stepan Verkhovensky to emerge, no matter how slightly, a better man. He is always the fool, and never the hero. . . . there is no learning from suffering. The best that Dostoevsky can say is that he meant well."[20]

That finding must give pause to those who testify to Stepan Trofimovich's redemption. Something may have happened between notes and completed novel; then again, nothing may have happened. Literary scholars don't often confess the limits of their powers so candidly; Wasiolek's modesty is commendable. Neither his fine-toothed examination of the notebooks nor his equally close reading of the novel enabled him to determine whether Stepan is redeemed or not. On the negative side, he finds every one of Stepan's acts compromised: "Stepan Trofimovich does battle with Peter and the forces of nihilism and radicalism, but in the name of abstract beauty; he confesses his wrong, calls himself the worst sort of swine, but in delirium and sickness; he admits that he has lied to Sophia Matveevna, but perhaps for effect. Stepan Trofimovich says the right things at the end, but the 'right things' abstracted from soul and heart can be the wrong things." Yet, despite all these shrewd observations, Wasiolek concludes: "I am not sure, but the notes may help us to decide."[21]

With all due respect to and, indeed, sympathy for Wasiolek's position, I cannot help reading this as a last gasp of unreconstructed biographism. The text itself is what it is, and we have it on Wasiolek's high authority that Stepan's redemption is ultimately compromised. But in what is almost a denial of that authority, Wasiolek plaintively hopes that the notebooks will somehow prove the case to be otherwise. Perhaps that hope stems from an American reader's ideological bias: we would like to find merit, at long last, in any poor, likable old fellow who loves the arts so much and who, virtually alone in this novel, values human tolerance. It seems almost bad form to insist that our final dealings are not with Dostoevsky, no matter how copious and fascinating his notebooks, but with the implied author "Dostoevsky." The implied author, Wasiolek seems to be saying, does not certify some simple conclusion about Stepan's fate that matches our own ideological longings.

It is popular to argue these days that the text is what the reader constructs, and that a good portion of the reader's share is ideological (more often unconscious than not). Clearly, liberal critics proclaiming Stepan's redemption find what they want to find. Deconstructionists, following their own agenda, probably discover that the encounter between implied author's and reader's ideology ends in a murky standoff. Both recognitions struggle to stay afloat amid the heavy seas of critical fashion, driven as they are by errant ideological blasts. We may wonder whether ideological proficiency helps very much with texts like *The Possessed*. True, Marxists may help us adjust to our loss of innocence about liberals like Stepan. They may even help us understand something about Dostoevsky's own witch's brew of humanism, Pan Slavism and Orthodoxy. But are they any better than their predecessors at accounting for the complexity of Stepan, or of Shatov (Dostoevsky's reactionary spokesman, murdered for his beliefs), or of Pyotr (the monarchist disguised as nihilist), or of Stavrogin (whose negativity furiously resists ideological categorization)? What can ideologues really *do* with texts written by an author who believes (writes Soviet critic Vladimir Tunimanev) that "the essence of things and phenomena is hidden so deeply that not even the subtlest scientific analysis is capable of recovering it with mathematical precision," that "there always remains an 'irrational' and inaccessible residue, in which, perhaps, the solution is also contained?"[22]

An Aleatory Cigarette Advertisement

An advertisement for Benson & Hedges cigarettes raised considerable excitement in the advertising world a few years ago. The ad consists of two panels. The upper panel shows a slim, curly haired young man, attired only in pajama bottoms, standing with a kind of shy impudence at the end of a table littered with the remains of an elegant luncheon. The man is not robust; he is no Marlboro man. His tummy sticks out like a small boy's. Unlike the long cigarettes flaunted by the elaborately smoking ladies, his is short and tucked between the knuckles of his dangling left hand. Two walls are visible: upon each hangs an oil painting. The room is flooded with light. Six diners in business clothes—five attractive young women and a balding middle-aged man—relax over cigarettes. The women seem to be making pleasantries about the man in pajamas; the bald-headed man has turned and raised his wine glass to toast him. In the bottom panel, the young man now stands behind the woman on the bald man's right. He bends over her, his hand on her shoulder; she smiles up at him, her left hand around his neck. The bald man has his right hand on the young man's naked shoulder.

The only caption—the same one that keynotes a whole series of two-panel Benson & Hedges ads—reads "For people who like to smoke . . ." In all other such ads, the narrative is easier to make out. In one, for example, the upper panel shows two smoking couples in sports clothes sitting on colorfully upholstered porch furniture. The man on the left is dealing cards; the other three are laughing. The couple on the right sit in a love seat, the woman leaning intimately against the man, whose head is raised in a hearty chuckle. In the lower panel, only the couple on the right remain. The woman has snuggled up and fallen asleep on the man's side. His cigarette raised aloft in his left hand, his right arm thrown casually along the arm of the love seat, his leg up on the table, he gazes into a bright future with smiling contentment. A simple narrative easily comes to us: "A couple has come over for an evening of lighthearted cards (Yuppies do not take cards seriously). Everybody smokes and has a good time. Afterward, as the hostess sleeps, her head on his lap, the host reflects on the simple pleasures of life."

But the details of the pajama-man story are uncertain in a way that is surprising for a business ordinarily intolerant of uncertainty. It furnishes us an interesting angle on the difference between real and implied author even in the mundane, throwaway world of advertising. This series of ads tries to shape narratees and implied readers who are open, easy, knowing, sociable, tolerant—tolerant, especially, of the idea of cigarettes as facilitators, like drinks, of communal good cheer and, later, as coals in the afterglow. The pajama man would never have appeared if that meaning were not implicit. Whatever else the audience may conjecture about him, they are clearly invited to understand that he can be received by the other diners with unflappable and sophisticated good humor. If the ad did nothing more than promote that attitude, its sponsors would be content. But, clearly, they intended—and in fact achieved—an additional response. Readers, at least those who are interested in such things, found the explanation by urbane tolerance insufficient. They wanted to know what was *happening*. *Newsweek* demanded:

> Just what's going on here? Who is this guy in his jammies? So many people have asked those questions that *Advertising Age* magazine was recently compelled to sponsor a 'What's Going on Here?' contest. Officials at Wells, Rich, Greene, the cigarette's ad agency, say the picture has prompted a flood of calls and letters. The strategy behind the concept? As it turns out, perhaps none at all. Rob Ramsel, the actor who played the pajama man, says the ad was largely the result of a fluke—and the keen eye of photographer Denis Piel. When Ramsel wandered into the picture from a bathroom setting where another B&H ad was being shot, Piel captured the ambiguous scene on film. 'What does the ad mean?' laughs Ramsel. 'It means that Robbie gets a check.'
>
> Call it ad hoc advertising. At a time when many ads are getting safer and more homogenized, some Madison Avenue firms are finding success in old-fashioned spontaneity. On-the-scene inspiration has helped sell everything from oatmeal to antacids—often with astonishing results.[23]

But it seems unlikely that the ad has "no strategy at all," that Benson & Hedges spent a bundle merely to publish some photographer's *objet trouvé*. The two panels don't make an abstract collage. Like their predecessors, and as *Advertising Age* understood, they tell a story, or at least purport to do so. That is, they stimulate the reader to devise a narrative that would explain the odd costume. The advertising novelty here is to invoke one that shall forever remain, in part, untold—however much the audience is teased into speculation. Indeed, that speculation is precisely the desired effect.

Obviously, it is not in the nature of things for us to know who this "guy in his jammies" is and what he's doing there. If we know anything, it is that he and his pajamas are nothing more than a pretext to encourage us to try out stories to account for them. If he were wearing a business suit, there would be little to speculate about: a junior executive stands at the head of the table because he has just been promoted. The bald man and the five women toast him at a luncheon party thrown in honor of the occasion. The paintings, the light, the absence of waiters and other tables suggest that the room is not in a restaurant. It's a staff luncheon, a catered party in the board room.

But the pajamas invite us to wonder what a young man so attired could be doing in such a room. Why is he being toasted? Why all the laying on of hands? People tend to wear pajamas at home. Perhaps the young man is *chez lui*, entertaining this group. But why in dishabille? Perhaps he's an eccentric, some kind of artist: the painting directly behind him has a fashionably abstract look. Maybe he is entertaining the owner and salespeople of the gallery where his successful show has just opened. Or maybe he's a rock star who gets up late and is staring sleepy-eyed at his manager and staff; he has overslept the celebration but remains the apple of every eye. Or perhaps it's a family matter: he's the son of the older man, and the luncheon is taking place not at corporate headquarters but in his father's penthouse apartment. The young man hasn't seen his father in a while. He arrived the night before from out of town, went to sleep not knowing that his father was planning to entertain, heard merriment, and just wandered in. Or perhaps it's the young woman's apartment, one she shares with the man (lover, husband, brother, roommate?), who didn't know that she had invited her colleagues home to celebrate her promotion. And so on. None of these has anything to do with a Robbie from another set. But imagine even, if you like, the metatextual possibility: a group of models hired to do an ad celebrating the pleasures of communal smoking find their Manhattan studio set invaded by a pajama-clad young man on a cigarette break from another shoot. Seeing the hilarity of the situation, they take their own break, lighting up (now they're *really* smoking, rather than merely acting the part of smokers). The older man raises his fruit juice to toast the handsome young interloper. Accepted so jovially by his colleagues, the young man hugs one of the models, in a purely collegial way, and is hugged in return. And so on.

Notice that our speculation has nothing to do with what some real author—the writer or the photographer—did; it concerns only the "identity" (quotation marks for red herring) of the young man as character and the possible reasons he might have for sporting such attire in that room. In other words, we are trying to create a world in which events corresponding to these images are feasible. Our negotiations are not with a photographer or any other real "author" on the advertising team but with a hypothesized narrator—hypothesized at the moment we decided that this page in this magazine constituted a narrative. But behind that narrator there is an implied author who urges us relentlessly to make up *the* story that would account for this unlikely pair of events. And he/she/it continues to do so—that is, continues to exist—as long as we continue to desire to assemble these fragments into a story.

Clearly, however, we shall never know what is "really" happening in this fiction, who these people are, why the young man is wearing pajamas. It is not that kind of text. In this newest of ploys, the advertisers—the real authors—have not created a narrative whose implied author has assigned a definitive story to the narrator to tell. Rather, the text only supplies clues for a *range* of stories. It is safe to say that the real authors don't really care what story we ultimately hit on but are perfectly content to know that we are busy making some up. What could be more heartwarming to an advertiser than to see an audience expending such energy on behalf of its product?

The ad hardly constitutes a narratological innovation. "Aleatory" or random stories are a staple of postmodern literature. This story, of course, is not even all that random: every interpretation that arises is bathed in comforting tobacco smoke. A cozy range of alternatives is offered, each one providing charming answers to potentially troublesome questions. All promote the cause of enjoying oneself and doing so with a cigarette. Whatever else they may mean, the pajamas and the bare tummy connote a graceful tolerance. The ad is aimed neither · at antismokers nor at grim four-pack-a-day addicts but at moderate smokers and at ex-smokers who have forgotten (or remember all too well) the fun of it. The ad jovially accepts, indeed encourages, "reasonable" smoking, convivial smoking—which is to say, a wishy-washy attitude toward cigarettes, obscuring in a magical cloud of good cheer the threat to health that everybody knows they pose. (The magic inspires still another interpretation: who better administers magic than a presiding spirit? The young man is Puck, or Peter Pan,[24] arriving mysteriously and with some slight bewilderment as the tutelary spirit of nicotine, a kindly minor deity, the good genius of the East Side, protecting and reassuring those who wander, innocently seeking pleasure, into his haunts. How *could* he wear street clothes on such an occasion?)

It is interesting to speculate about why a cigarette company should be among the first to present its message in an aleatory narrative. Is it because smoking is—or the manufacturer wants it to seem—a random matter? Is it that the random tale supports the low-energy resistance of smokers in the face of all evidence of the deadliness of their habit? "If you're sufficiently knowing to understand the clever open-endedness of these images, *you* can get away with smoking, no matter what the authorities tell you." Perhaps the company itself takes a random attitude, since it feels it has nothing more to lose. In an era when the surgeon general stamps blunt pronouncements on its ads, Benson & Hedges may feel that it has little choice but to go with innuendo.

Narratologically, then, we have the following structure: The real authors of the narrative are decision-makers at the cigarette company, Benson & Hedges, and the advertising agency, Wells, Rich, and Greene, and their assistants and contractors. Their motive is direct suasion of the public to smoke their product, by whatever means capitalism has invented for such suasion. Their overriding concern is the sale of cigarettes, not narrative innovation. So (we may speculate) they turn to aleatory narratives because such narratives are new, and they are betting that the faddish "enigma" will get people interested in their ads—and their product. If they can do so by introducing the startling (to the mass audience) prospect of an unclear, random narrative, they are willing to take the chance. Thus their motives are quite different from those of the avant-garde novelist whose intention in problematizing the event structure of a narrative is aesthetic. The advertisers do not wish to "make things strange," as the Russian Formalists would put it—that is, to upset our everyday expectations—but only to titillate a bit, to make us all chuckle together and, of course, to light up.

But even so, the ad necessarily implies an author, a textual intention. The implied author is born in our ingrained eagerness to find stories wherever possible. Even the shrewder reader who understands the advertiser's true motives will continue to infer an implied author (on the principle, perhaps, of trying *not* to think of a pink elephant). Regardless of our sophistication, once we interpret the ad *as* a narrative, we cannot but negotiate with its implied author.

The implied author is the textual intent responsible for the choice of characters and decor (including the enigmatic garb of the young man), the decision that the occasion alluded to should remain unspecified (including such details as the reason for the lunch itself, the mysterious appearance of the pajama man, the toast, the embrace), the decision that only a single phrase of commentary ("For people who like to smoke . . .") should be verbalized, and so on. Ideologically, of course, the implied author is no less committed to aggressive capitalist suasion than the real authors. But unlike the real authors, the implied author, by the very logic of the situation, honors the conventions of narrative textuality. And in their very decision to treat the ad as a narrative-to-be-completed, real readers are effectively endowing the implied author with a genuinely narrative intention.

The narrator of the ad has only a minimal task: to present the whole discourse in two photographs and a caption. The presentation of the photographs relies on the common convention of reading strip graphics from left to right or top to bottom, and of assuming that "further left" and "upper" mean "diegetically earlier." Thus, the narrator is, narratologically, innocent and relatively unimportant. What is of interest is the gap between the commercial motives of the real authors, who couldn't care less about the text-type they are promulgating as long as it attracts attention, and the textual motives (as we persist in projecting them) of an implied author.

A Marxist Analysis of *Dog Day Afternoon*

Interestingly enough, Marxist criticism may need the implied author more than any other kind. For example, our most astute Marxist critic, Fredric Jameson, addresses the problem of how the abstract truth of class—the marginalization of petty bourgeois suburban workers, their merging with the inhabitants of the urban ghetto, and the control of this "gray class" by invisible forces of international monopoly capitalism—gets concretized (or "figured," in his term) in popular narrative. How do characters and actions arise in "the tangible medium of daily life," in "that whole area of personal fantasy, collective storytelling, narrative figurability, which is the domain of culture," to effect the sense that class is finally emerging as an issue even to the bourgeois consciousness?[25]

Jameson's example is a successful and popular Hollywood film, *Dog Day Afternoon* (1975), directed by Sidney Lumet. The film is based on an actual event, the attempted robbery of a Chase Manhattan bank in 1972 by one Sonny Wojtowicz and his partner Sal, to raise money for the sex-change operation of Sonny's significant other. Sonny and his partner laid seige to the bank for many hours; he was finally captured and his partner killed by an FBI agent on the way to the airport where a plane out of the country was ready (in exchange for the release of bank employees held as hostages).

What proved remarkable (at least to bourgeois capitalists) was that Sonny became a kind of hero to the crowd of onlookers outside the bank. He sensed the opportunity to play on their sympathies, much to the discomfiture of the police. It was the crowd's recognition of their affiliation with the outlaw that probably stimulated Hollywood to exploit this media event, whose interest to the public was already proven. As Jameson explains: "Social reality and the stereotypes of our experience of everyday social reality are the raw material with which commercial films and television are inevitably forced to work." But in using this material, Jameson feels, the media unknowingly permitted the class message to seep through. He explains the process this way:

The immense costs of commercial films, which inevitably place their production under the control of multinational corporations, make any genuinely political content in them unlikely, and on the contrary ensure commercial film's vocation as a vehicle for ideological manipulation. No doubt this is so, if we remain on the level of the intention of the individual film-maker, who is bound to be limited consciously or unconsciously by his or her objective situation. But it is to fail to reckon with the political content of daily life, with the political logic which is already inherent in the raw material with which the film-maker must work: such political logic will then not manifest itself as an overt political message, nor will it transform the film into an unambiguous political statement. But it will certainly make for the emergence of profound formal contradictions to which the public cannot but be sensitive, whether or not it yet possesses the conceptual instruments to understand what those contradictions mean.[26]

Thus, to Jameson, the personal politics of the film's real authors (Sidney Lumet and his production crew, the producer, the studio, the banking interests behind them) are irrelevant.[27] Rather, in their close, quasi-documentary pursuit of everyday journalistic truth—an exercise sparked by the usual motives of financial profit—the real authors cannot help presenting, "consciously or unconsciously . . . the political content of daily life," which is, for Jameson, the reality of the class struggle. The real authors function as a kind of impersonal conduit or lightning rod for the transmission of history's already formed political message to the actual audience, even if the audience is as yet unable to understand it as such. All that counts is their *sensitivity* to it, a fact which is established by "the manifest sympathy [with Sonny] of the suburban movie-going audience . . . which from within the tract housing of the *societé de consommation* clearly senses the relevance to its own daily life of the re-enactment of this otherwise fairly predictable specimen of urban crime."[28]

In other words, in going about their usual business of recreating or "docudramatizing" a bizarre news events, the filmmakers created an allegory of the actual state of class repression in America and the world. The allegory turns on a struggle among three groups: (1) a new coalition of the proletariat (the marginalized Sonny, Sal, and the ring of urban ghetto dwellers outside the bank who cheer them on) with the "atomized petty bourgeoisie" (the exploited women bank employees, who quickly get over their fear and begin to fraternize with the two robbers); (2) the impotent power structures of the local neighborhoods, represented by the New York City police—in particular, Lieutenant Maretti (Charles Durning), who fails to raise the siege of the bank; and (3) the hitherto invisible power structure, now concretely "figured" in the FBI agent (James Broderick) who takes over from Maretti the attack on Sonny and Sal.

Jameson nowhere argues that the film crew's objective was anything other than verisimilitude: that is, a plausible reconstruction of the event. Theirs was a practical, not an ideological reality; it is doubtful that they were aware of the allegory they were communicating. Though Jameson finds in the actor James Broderick's performance "a narrative answer to the fundamental question: how to imagine authority today, how to conceive imaginatively—that is in non-abstract, non-conceptual form—of a principle of authority that can express the essential impersonality and post-individualistic structure of the power structure of our society while still operating among real people,"[29] it is doubtful that Broderick was aware of any of that. His effort was, presumably, to effect a lifelike representation of the surface appearance and behavior of an FBI agent, at least as Hollywood conceives it. Similarly, the concern of the other actors was to convincingly portray desperate men, transsexuals, bank clerks, New York City police officers, and so on.

The same must be said about the choices of setting. Jameson finds the multinational capitalist power structure figured by "the spatial trajectory of the film itself as it moves from the ghettoised squalour of the bank interior to that eerie and impersonal science fiction landscape of the airport finale: a corporate space without inhabitants, utterly technologised and functional, a place beyond city and country alike,"[30] yet he would hardly argue that the real authors cleared the airport with such phrases ringing in their ears. Their purpose must have been simply to reflect a cleared New York City airport as they imagined it would look.

I am concerned not so much with the power or legitimacy of Jameson's interpretation (though I do find it powerful and legitimate) as with its utilization of a model of narrative in which real authors are said to be unconscious of and, in a way, theoretically irrelevant to a narrative text's broader ideological implications. These implications, at the level of the "political unconscious," become the intention of the work. Any such model necessarily implies a distinction between the original authorial and the textual intention, and the latter, as I have argued, is synonymous with "implied author."

Of course, the notion of the real author as meaning's *unconscious* facilitator—more midwife than mother—is by no means new, or unique to Marxists. It informs such ancient topoi as the inspiration of the poet by his Muse or the Aeolian harp reverberating in the wind. But the Marxist critic provides us with a fascinating new example of how, despite the real authors' unconsciousness of what they are doing, communication is effected by their implied counterpart.

CHAPTER 7 /

The Literary Narrator

In his attempt to develop a viable theory of "distance" in narratology, Gérard Genette called up the authority of Plato's account (*The Republic*, Book 3) of diegesis and mimesis:

> Plato contrasts two narrative modes, according to whether the poet 'himself is the speaker and does not even attempt to suggest to us that anyone but himself is speaking' (this is what Plato calls *pure narrative* [*diegesis*]), or whether, on the other hand, the poet 'delivers a speech as if he were someone else' (as if he were such-and-such a character), if we are dealing with spoken words (this is what Plato properly calls imitation, or *mimesis*).[1]

Genette emphasizes the difference between diegesis and mimesis, but the important recognition here, I think, is that both are *narrative* modes. I want to argue that in important ways drama *is* a kind of narrative, at least in the sense that it is based, like epic, on that component of narrative which we call "story." As Aristotle pointed out, "Whatever parts epic poetry has, these are also found in tragedy."[2] The parts he meant are "plot" (with its "recognition" and "reversal"), "character," "thought," and "diction." The first two of these (plus "setting") are what modern narratology typically calls "story." Only "spectacle" was said to be unique to drama. But spectacle, surely, is an element of the actualization of stories, and not one of the underlying components of narrative structure. The fundamental property of story (in the narratological sense) is that it consists of a series of connected events, and that property is shared by both drama and epic.

Genette, however, identifies narrative with diegesis and drama with mimesis. In *Narrative Discourse* he writes " 'Mimetic' representation [is] borrowed from the theatre,"[3] and in *Narrative Discourse Revisited* he speaks of the "truly insurmountable opposition between dramatic representation and narrative."[4] Certainly at the level of actualization, a play and a novel are quite different. But at the textual level they resemble each other far more than either resembles any other text-type—say, Argument or Description. Indeed, Aristotle wrote that both tragedy and epic "imitate" the "lines of action"; thus, "imitation" is not limited to words alone, but includes larger structures—in particular, structures of plot.[5]

Here, as always, we must be careful about the polysemy of terms. At the very beginning of *Narrative Discourse*, Genette is very clear about the three senses of *récit*. His caution is applicable no less to the polysemy of English "narrative." We must take care to specify which sense is entailed in a given application of the word. Genette has used *narratif* in one sense in the expression "two narrative modes" (deux modes narratifs) and *récit* in another in "truly insurmountable opposition between dramatic representation and narrative" (l'opposition, vraiment incontournable, entre récit et représentation dramatique). In the first, he seems to be referring to the story aspect of narrative; in the second, to its discourse aspect, its manner of being *told*. There is indeed an obvious difference between dramatic representation and epic or novelistic representation. But there is no great difference between the structures of the "what," the *story component* told by epics and enacted by dramas. Both rely on sequences of events, and both present a chronology of events different from the chronology of the discourse. This double chronology is the fundamental property that distinguishes the text-type Narrative from the others. It makes easy sense, for example, to speak of the "story" in Shakespeare's *Hamlet*, whereas we would hardly speak of the "story" in the Declaration of Independence or some other argument.

But it is not even clear that the *discoursive* difference between plays and novels is all that profound. A short story or novel becomes more or less purely "mimetic" when it consists of nothing but the quoted dialogue of the characters. Then it is an "unmixed" case, and only the nontheatrical circumstance of its publication distinguishes it from a drama. Thus, the difference between drama and narrative fiction is not primary but secondary, as the diagram shows.

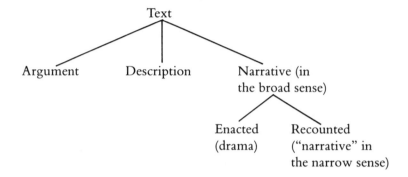

What precisely are the differences between the actualization of stories in drama and in epic or novel? The latter, of course, are communicated by words only, and words are arbitrary or unmotivated signs—or, in C. S. Peirce's term, "symbols." As Genette correctly maintains, words can hardly be said to "imitate" nonverbal events.[6] They can, of course, imitate—or, as Genette now prefers to say, reproduce—the exact speeches of the characters.[7] To the extent that the epic or novel represents nonverbal events in words, it is a mixed diegesis, mixed because of the introduction of mimetic elements. In the theatrical actualization of story, however, there is indeed more or less pure mimesis. The signs that stand for the bodies of the characters are "iconic." That is, they function as signifiers that somehow resemble their signifieds in a nonarbitrary way: Hamlet is played by a young, noble-looking actor; Polonius by an older actor who adopts a pontificating and fuddy-duddy manner. The same is true of the events performed by the actors: Hamlet's slaying of Polonius is represented by an actor's plunging a sword into a drape and the other actor's falling down in a simulation of dying. The staged event looks like what we imagine the "real" event would look like.

So, in a sense, we could say that the distinction between mimesis and diegesis or, to use their rough modern synonyms, "showing" and "telling" is simply the distinction between iconic and non-iconic or symbolic signs. The latter include, for example, all normal (non-onomatopoeic) language. In "told" narratives, such as epics and most novels, the narrating function is assigned to a set of signifiers that are "arbitrary," unanalogous to the actions, characters, or settings they signify. In "shown" stories, such as narrative films, both characters and actions tend to be represented in an iconic or "motivated" fashion. For example, the reader of Joseph Conrad's *Outcast of the Islands* can find little in the names "Willems" or "Lingard" or, indeed, in the descriptive epithets applied to them by the narrator to form a *precise* mental image of these characters. Whatever images we form, they can only be less detailed and determinate than the photographed images in Carol Reed's film version of the novel. To be more precise, the photographed images signify actors named "Trevor Howard" and "Ralph Richardson"; these in turn signify the characters named "Willems" and Lingard." At the most basic level, the signifiers (actors) share with the signifieds (characters) the contours and other visible attributes of "men" (rather than women or elephants). At a more refined level, the actors, through their skill and the director's guidance, create facial and bodily representations—signs—appropriate to the characters: a drifter of devious morality and a courageous but too trusting sea captain.

To say that a play or movie or cartoon is "shown" is to say that its narration is conveyed by a set of signifiers (human beings on stage, photographs of them on film, drawings of them on paper) which are "motivated" or "analogous": that is, they resemble their signifieds in some culturally recognizable way. But the analogy itself contains a certain element of the arbitrary, since the signified can be shown now by this actor and now by that. Hamlet is always a man, but that man may be a Laurence Olivier, a Maurice Evans, a John Barrymore, even a Sarah Bernhardt. All quoted *speeches*, however, are totally mimetic. Whoever the actor, the lines purport to be exactly the words that Hamlet speaks (though their intonation varies, as a function of the performance). This is also true in the print medium, in novels and short stories: though print itself is not analogous to voice, the choice of words, syntax, and the like purport to copy exactly what characters say.

Both noniconic and iconic representations entail a kind of delegation. In diegesis, the (real) author delegates the final shape of the signifers to the editors, typesetters, and other members of the publisher's production team; in mimesis, the author delegates it to the performers, directors, stagehands, photographers, animators, and so on.

If we are to say that *both* telling and showing can transmit stories, and in any combination, we need a term that can refer to either or both indifferently. If "to narrate" is too fraught with vocal overtones, we might adopt "to present" as a useful superordinate. Thus we can say that the implied author presents the story through a tell-er or a show-er or some combination of both. Only the one who tells, then, can be said to have a "voice." This, I think, is the proper answer to theorists skeptical of analogies between the presentation of stories by the performing arts that favor mimesis (stage, cinema) and by the discursive arts that favor diegesis (literature). Film and other performative media often have nothing like a narrative voice, no "tell-er." Even the cinematic voice-over narrator is usually at the service of a larger narrative agent, the cinematic show-er. But that show-er can reasonably be called a presenter (if we want to avoid calling him/her/it a narrator), since "presenter" is not limited to some actual voice telling the action in words. For those who find "narrator" awkward, "presenter" is a good alternative.

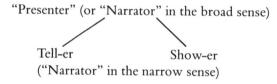

"Presenter" (or "Narrator" in the broad sense)

Tell-er   Show-er
("Narrator" in the narrow sense)

Much is to be said for redefining "narration" to include showing as well as telling and to recognize that it is sometimes totally limited to showing. If we do not do so, we have no way of accounting, in general narratological terms, for performed stories: movies, plays, mime shows, and the like. The argument that narrative fiction films are "non-narrated" has resulted in some rather strained and unnecessary verbal maneuvering (as I illustrate in Chapter 8).

It stands to reason that if shown stories are to be considered narratives, they must be "narrated," and only an overly restrictive definition of "to narrate"—identifying it solely with telling—keeps that observation from being self-evident. To "show" a narrative, I maintain, no less than to "tell" it, is to "present it narratively" or to "narrate" it. Why? To accommodate a general theory of text-types and the primacy of the double chronology over such lesser concerns

as the means of actualizing the narrative. We need a more encompass-
ing term for all those texts we call novels, novellas, short stories,
dramatic lyrics, verse ballads, plays, and so on, one that avoids
confusing them with other kinds of texts. Once we decide that stories
may indeed be totally enacted on the stage or screen, consistency
requires that we label them "narratives." The difference between
telling and showing then comes down simply to the implied author's
choice of signs—analogous or motivated for mimetic narratives,
arbitrary or "symbolic" for diegetic narratives, and a mixture for
mixed narratives.

Of course, the choice of signs is not a cut-and-dried matter. Some
signs chosen to do the "enactment" are not so purely analogous or
arbitrary as theory might suggest. The few squiggles that render
Charlie Brown do not imitate or enact that droll character with the
same full force that the body and behavior of the flesh-and-blood
Laurence Olivier imitated and enacted Hamlet. Though still relatively iconic, the cartoon's spare lines are closer to the "arbitrary"
than the actor's majestic appearance. In the ballet, a signifier such as a
pirouette does not uniquely enact some such signified as "joy" or
"enthusiasm."[8] Nor are many of the hand signals of the language of
the deaf self-evidently iconic. Stories conveyed by such hand signals
seem more properly "told" than "shown."

But despite such blurred, intermediate, and mixed cases, there is
no particular reason why "to narrate" should mean *only* "to tell."
Once we decide to define Narrative as the composite of story and
discourse (on the basis of its unique double chronology), then *logically*, at least, narratives can be said to be actualizable on the stage or
in other iconic media. The burden of disproof falls on theories that
would deny the name Narrative to "performed" texts. They would
need to explain why—having agreed that "mimesis" is a way of
conveying Narrative (even in such nontheatrical texts as dialogue-
only novels)—it should not be called an *act* of narration.

In short, Narrative may be defined in a broader and a narrower
sense. In the broad sense that I have proposed in previous chapters,
Narrative is the text-type distinguished from others by a double
"chrono-logic"—a logic of event sequence, performed by characters, in a setting. In the narrower, traditional sense, Narrative is a text
entailing all the conditions of the broad sense *plus* the diegetic condition: that is, that the text must be *told* by a human narrator. This more

restricted definition obviously provides a narrower base for narratology. To me, the distinction between Narrative and the other text-types is of a higher order than that between the two ways of communicating a narrative, telling and showing. Rather than simply laying out the opposition as

Diegesis   vs.   Mimesis

I propose the hierarchy implicit in this diagram:

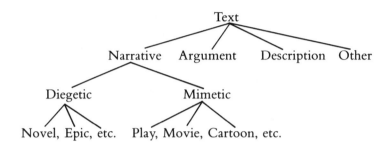

This allows for the recognition of a kind of narration that is not performed by a recognizably human agency. I argue that human personality is not a sine qua non for narratorhood. Some readers may find this rejection of a traditional and nostalgic image of the narrator hard to accept. In novels written a hundred years ago, and still in many today, the narrator is a familiar figure, named and self-characterized, fitted out with opinions, judgments, or generalizations that convey or imply something of his personality. But in the twentieth century, fictions began to minimize their discourse, and the "voice" of the narrator grew fainter. To describe the art of such writers as Hemingway (in "The Killers," for example), many critics invoked a narrator who was not a speaker but a visual recorder, a mere "camera-eye." Some narratologists—I include myself—even claimed that the narrator had disappeared, that certain literary narratives were simply "non-narrated."

But I now believe that that claim is a contradiction in terms. I would argue that every narrative is by definition narrated—that is, narratively presented—and that narration, narrative presentation, entails an agent even when the agent bears no signs of human personality. Agency is marked etymologically by the *-er/-or* suffix attached to the verbs "present" or "narrate." The suffix means either "agent" or "instrument," and neither need be human.

This definition rejects the proposal I made in *Story and Discourse* that heavily mimetic or shown stories—such as "The Killers"—are not communicated by narrators. That view, I now believe, leads to an inadmissible paradox or, at least, a counterintuition: namely, that narratives just appear, unannounced, so to speak—a view that contradicts both logic and common sense.[9] The notion of "non-narrated" narrative arises as a misguided effort to restrict "agency" to human beings, but the restriction will not hold. A presentation argues a presenter, whether human or not, whether vividly dramatized or not. Once we allow the possibility of showing a narrative, we perforce recognize the existence of a show-er, even if not a human one. In this age of mechanical and electronic production and reproduction, of "smart" machines, it would be naive to reject the notion of nonhuman narrative agency. Remember, we are now speaking neither of the original creators of narrative texts, the flesh-and-blood authors, nor of the principle of invention in the text that we call the implied author, but of the someone or something in the text who or which is conceived as presenting (or transmitting) the set of signs that constitute it.[10] "Presentation" is the most neutral word I can find for the narrator's activity. As part of the invention of the text, the implied author assigns to a narrative agent the task of articulating it, of actually offering it to some projected or inscribed audience (the narratee).

As has often been noted, modern novels and short stories tend to be shown rather than told. Some literary fictions purport to be nothing more than mechanically recorded copies of characters' speeches; the pure dialogue short story is a common form. Clearly, it is better to say that these are "shown" by a silent, extradiegetic narrator than that they are "told" or "spoken" by her.

My difficulty in *Story and Discourse* was implicit in the question I asked at the very outset: "Is the [narrative] statement directly presented to the audience or is it mediated by someone—the someone we call the narrator?"[11] But the narrator need not be a "someone." Every narrative statement is presented by a narrator, and the narrator may be not a someone but a something. The agent of presentation need not be human to merit the name "narrator."

Let me repeat the senses in which I think the terms "narrative," "drama," "mimesis," and "diegesis" best operate in narratology. The question is one of priority: Is the distinction between diegesis and mimesis, telling and showing, of greater consequence (higher in the structural hierarchy) than that between Narrative and the other text-types? I find no reason to assume so. To me, any text that presents a story—a sequence of events performed or experienced by characters—is first of all a narrative. Plays and novels share the common features of a chrono-logic of events, a set of characters, and a setting. Therefore, at a fundamental level they are all stories. The fact that one kind of story is told (diegesis) and the other shown (mimesis) is secondary. By "secondary" I do not mean that the difference is inconsequential. It is just that it is lower in the hierarchy of text distinctions than the difference between Narrative and the other text-types.

It might be argued that I am simply reversing Aristotle's emphasis: that as he, normatively, favored drama and mimesis, I am favoring narrative (in the narrow sense) and diegesis. But I hope that my purpose does not seem prescriptive. I am not vindicating epic at the expense of drama: I am simply saying that they have something in common—plot and characters—and that it is not so far-fetched to say that these are properties of Narrative, at least in the sense in which I use the term. At the level of greatest abstraction, that sense includes story but removes from discourse any specification of the *kind* of method of transmission.

Of course, to speak of any of these things is to abstract it—artificially, and only for the purposes of discussion—from the totality of the text as we experience it. A "story" cannot occur independently of its "discourse." Nor can the story-discourse composite occur independently of some actualization or embodiment in a medium, whether written words (novels, short stories), spoken words and other physical actions of actors (plays), shadows on the screen and sounds reproduced through a sound track (movies), or whatever.

That plays consist mostly of dialogue is of secondary narratological significance. Dramas written for performance differ from other narratives only in their actualization: that is, theatrical production (or its intention, though "closet dramas" do not have even that intention). In that sense, drama is not a class that competes with narrative; rather it is simply one of the narrative kinds. It is not even true that plays imitate speech alone, since most scripts specify nonverbal events in the form of stage directions. In productions these are actualized by actors' movements. At the level of semiotic abstraction, there is no difference between a sentence in a novel like "John left the room" and the playwright's instruction to an actor to exit, stage left. Both the sentence and the actor's walking off are delegated signifiers of (nonverbal) action.

Theater is a medium available for the presentation of stories; it is one of several ways of bringing a narrative to life. By the same token, the mere fact that a given short story contains only dialogue does not make it a play; it too, is one means of presentation. The same could be said of various interior-monologue novels and stories that represent nothing but a character's thoughts. In these, what the narrator shows is "mental speech" (on the convention that thoughts appear in our minds in verbal form).

Unless we coin another term—and it is not clear that we should— "Narrative" still seems best to cover both diegetic and mimetic forms as these are opposed to other text-types such as Argument and Description. If we adopt an appropriately broad sense of the term, mimetic forms—dramas, films, ballets—are just as much "narrated" as short stories and novels.

Let us turn to problems inherent in such terms as "voice," "knowledge," and similar metaphors. The assumption that stories are only and always narrated by human beings doubtless arose with their bardic origin, and some narratologists (of "contextualist" persuasion) remain convinced that we must start our theories from oral anecdotes. When stories came to be written, narrators retained (though not inevitably) strong personal marks—referring to themselves as "I"; offering judgments, opinions, generalizations; describing their own persons or habitats, and the like. The term "voice" was naturally, if figuratively, tranferred to represent the means by which those activities occurred. It is a metaphor that continues to be widely used but insufficiently examined by narratology, functioning centrally in such otherwise divergent theories as Gérard Genette's and Mikhail Bakhtin's, Wayne Booth's and Franz Stanzel's. Yet no one, to my knowledge, has asked whether it really clarifies what it is supposed to name. How effective is the metaphor of a "voice speaking" when applied to shown or even "impersonally" told narratives? It is ill suited to describe screen or stage actualizations of narratives, and even more awkward when we want to talk about such literary narratives as "The Killers."

As I have argued in previous chapters, a better model views Narrative as an invention, by an implied author, of events and characters and objects (the story) and of a modus (the discourse) by which these are communicated. The narrator is the discoursive agent charged with presenting the words, images, or other signs conveying this invention. He/she/it may do so by presenting—"narrating" in the broad sense—whether that means telling, showing, or some combination of the two. Even though many are uncomfortable with the notion of nonhuman "agency," there is sufficient precedent in the word's etymology to justify such a notion. *Webster's Third New International Dictionary* offers three senses in which a non-human "agent" is allowed for:

1a: Something that produces or is capable of producing a certain effect: an active or efficient cause: a force effecting or facilitating a certain result.

2a: One that acts or exerts power (as by driving, inciting, or setting in motion): a moving force (the distinction between [agent] and patient, between something which acts and some other thing which is acted upon).

4: a means or instrument by which a guiding intelligence achieves a result.

The last sense, in particular, is attractive to narratology, since it enables us to see the narrator as a means or instrument and the implied author as (the record of) a guiding intelligence.

But even our more gifted narratologists find it hard to shake the anthropomorphic bias of "narrator." Some—for example, Roger Fowler—insist on finding in "The Killers," that archetypical (and overdiscussed) "camera-eye" story, a human narrator:

Although . . . the narrator [of "The Killers"] is resolutely silent, non-committal, unobtrusive and unintrusive, *he* [italics added] provides a definite viewing position, like a fixed camera within the lunch-room. The narrow limits of the scene are set by the outside door (which is obviously viewed from within) and the hatch to the kitchen, which is seen from the counter side. Within the room, the eyes focus in turn on a small set of objects: the door and the hatch, the counter and the people positioned at it, the clock. Changes of viewpoint are definite and clear: one very brief glimpse into the kitchen, and the excursion to Ole Andreson's with Nick Adams. In the latter scene the narrator is an invisible man who walks in step with Nick, stands close beside him, sees exactly and only what his eyes see (but not *with* Nick's eyes: there is no penetration of Nick's consciousness). In each part of the story there is severe visual economy, concentration on what is near at hand and relevant.[12]

Notice the subtle but critical shift from the narrator "providing" a definite viewing position to "*his*" *occupying* it. The narrator is said, in effect, to leave "his" post in the discourse and to enter the scene of the story. The narrator is treated as a character, indeed a male character, an "invisible man who walks in step with Nick." This assertion, I take it, is meant not figuratively but literally; the narrator has crossed the line from discourse to story. But what justification is there for assuming that the narrator is a real, if "silent" and "invisible," human male?[13] Why should our operative metaphor be human "eyes" with a direct (not windowed) view? Why should the model suggest a human presence *on* the scene, walking "in step with Nick Adams," instead of a narrative agency out in the discourse, reporting actions and scenes without any explanation or apology about how the information was obtained? I would argue that the narrator, by definition, does not *see* things in the story world; only characters can do that, because only they occupy that world (see the discussion of "filter" in Chapter 9). The narrator's task is not to go strolling with the characters but to narrate what happens to them, whether by telling or showing.

The same problem arises in Lanser's discussion of the state of the narrator's "knowledge":

This narrator knows precisely no more and no less than what a towns-person sitting in Henry's lunchroom would be expected to know. He knows the name of the lunchroom and the fact that it has been made over from a saloon; he knows the first names of George and Nick and Sam; he knows that Ole Andreson had been a heavyweight fighter; he knows the name of the rooming-house where Ole lives. But he does not know the names of the men who enter the lunchroom until those men themselves reveal their names. He describes these two intruders as if seeing them for the first time; he does not describe Nick Adams or George or Sam.[14]

This is a correct account of what the discourse presents, but "knows" is an odd word to apply to a heterodiegetic narrator, who necessarily inhabits the discourse with its built-in vantage on the story. What a *character* knows is a function of his or her situation *in* the story. But a heterodiegetic narrator reports the story: he/she/it doesn't (at the moment of reporting at least) *experience* it. The limitations on such a narrator's capacity to render this or that detail of the story depends not on "knowledge" but on how much the implied author has delegated to him/her/it to present—as opposed to how much has been left to the reader to infer.

The failure to restrict the narrator to the domain of discourse gives rise to all sorts of critical speculation: "Despite the technically heterodiegetic status of the narrator, then, this voice displays the limited privilege of an invisible eyewitness—indeed, an eyewitness who is a member of the local community—who operates like an unnamed *homodiegetic* voice." "Technically heterodiegetic" but really homodiegetic, though unnamed—a narrative voice that is in actuality a character, an invisible male eyewitness who lives nearby. The narrator's sex, Lanser continues, is beyond dispute: "It is especially safe to refer to the narrator of this story as 'he,' not only because of the rules for equivalence between author and narrative voice, but because the story is taken from a collection entitled *Men without Women*."[15] No one, I guess, would argue that the narrator of "The Killers" is a woman; but is that the only alternative? Why can't the narrator be simply a discourse agent without gender, as the narrative agent frequently called "the camera" is without gender?[16]

Lanser's account goes on to contend that the narrator is "one of the gang" (the town gang, not Al's and Max's gang), adducing five sentences as proof:

[Al] was like a photographer arranging for a group picture.

In their tight overcoats and derby hats [Al and Max] looked like a vaudeville team.

[Nick] had never had a towel in his mouth before.

[Nick] was trying to swagger it off.

It sounded silly when [Nick] said it.[17]

But clearly every one of these could be explained more simply and directly as free indirect thought. The third seems just a truncated version of a sentence like "Nick had never known the feeling of a towel in his mouth before." This sentence must represent Nick's inside view: a putative anonymous townsman narrator would hardly know whether Nick had had a towel in his mouth before. Similarly, the fourth sentence could be explained as a short version of "Nick knew he was [or "could feel himself"] trying to swagger it off"; the context suggests not a judgment of the narrator on Nick's bravado but Nick's own self-consciousness about it. And the fifth sentence seems short for "Nick knew or felt that it sounded silly when he said it." As for the first two sentences, they can easily be read as representing the collective viewpoint of George, Sam, and Nick, though once Nick's centrality is established, we might want retrospectively to limit the observation to him.

Though explicit inner views are sparse in this short story, they do seem to afford the limited insight into Nick's consciousness that critics have found in this and other Nick Adams stories. And though the focus on Nick's filter is predominantly one of "interest" rather than perception or conception, it is sustained rather clearly. For example, the story remains "his" when he goes to see Ole Andreson, leaving George and Sam behind. Interpreting these five sentences as Nick's perceptions leads to a simpler and more coherent reading than one which, in its insistence on finding a human being "responsible" for the narration, invents invisible companions marching along next to him. Throughout the Nick Adams stories, Nick is protagonist, though not one given to internal speculation about the things happening around him. The thrust of these stories is the impact on his youthful consciousness of the harshness of the world, even though his absorption of the information is not commented upon. Why devise some ghostly townsperson when so obvious and, indeed, traditional an explanation is at hand?

We need a definition of "narrator" which can allow for non-human as well as human, nongendered as well as gendered agents. We do have many gaps to fill in reading narratives, but it has not been demonstrated that the need to make the presenting agent a *person* is one of them, especially in cases where the text seems to go out of its way to avoid such identifications.

We also need to recognize that the narrator cannot impinge on story space but must stay within the bounds of discourse space. Discourse space may be physically evoked (as, typically, in frame narratives, say the boat on the Thames in Conrad's *Heart of Darkness*), or it may be only an intellectual or conceptual space (the space occupied by Tristram Shandy or the *narrator* Pip as they recall the events of their stories), or it may be no space at all. But whatever form it takes, discourse space must not be confused with the story space that it looks out upon. If we are to preserve the story and discourse distinction, we must recognize in discourse space a separateness analogous to the space on this side of a pane of glass or camera lens.

I do not deny that the narrator has a point of view (or "slant"), but I do deny that the narrator can inhabit both discourse and story at the instant of narration (except, of course, in embedded narration). The act of telling or showing the story should not be confused with the act of experiencing the events, of "seeing" them as a character inhabiting story-time and -space sees them. The narrator does not "see" anything from a perspective within the story: he/she/it can only report what *happens* from a post outside. The difference is crucial.

CHAPTER 8

The Cinematic Narrator

By its nature, cinema resists traditional language-centered notions of the narrator. Clearly, most films do not "tell" their stories in any usual sense of the word. The counter-intuitiveness of a film's "telling" calls into question "enunciation" theories of cinematic narration. In the 1960s Christian Metz and other film theoreticians, attracted by the success of linguistics, applied linguistic principles to the study of the fiction film. Metz quickly realized, however, that film is not a "language" but another kind of semiotic system with "articulations" of its own. Still, neither he nor other enunciation theorists[1] have succeeded in separating out film's more generally semiotic properties from the linguistic formulas. As David Bordwell has shown,[2] Metz could not, for example, illustrate the utility for film narratology of the linguistic distinction between *histoire* and *discours* drawn by Emile Benveniste.[3]

Among the many critical difficulties of enunciation theory, the most obvious is that verbal activity furnishes no easy analogy with visual activity. Benveniste's theory cannot demonstrate (as Metz suggests) that the camera's "look" constitutes a narration or that the *viewer* somehow becomes the "enunciator."[4]

Bordwell's own theory of film narration is so admirably constructed as to deserve widespread acceptance and extended discussion. My only real criticism is that it goes too far in arguing that film has no agency corresponding to the narrator and that film narrative is best considered as a kind of work wholly performed by the spectator.

Bordwell allows for film a "narration" but not a narrator. In a move resembling that of reader-response theorists, he founds his theory squarely on the viewer's activity, seeing in it an act of "construction." From the various cues streaming off the screen and loudspeaker, the audience "constructs" the narrative through intricate hypothesizing, entailing the entire range of mental activity from perception to cognition. Bordwell winnows the literature on visual perception and perspectival systems in art, enriching his findings with sophisticated notions of discourse processing. Bordwell's viewer is not a passive object "positioned" by what happens on the screen but an active participant—indeed, an agent—who virtually creates the film's narration. Utilizing concepts like "schemata" and "templates," Bordwell sketches a persuasive model of what the viewer *does* to turn the flashes and sounds impinging on her attention into a series of perceptible images, which she then interprets as a story.

The theory rests on the Russian Formalist distinction between *fabula, syuzhet,* and *style* (terms whose differences from the narratological "story," "discourse," and "actualization" are important, but not in the present context). The fabula, says Bordwell, "embodies the action as a chronological cause-and-effect chain of events occurring within a given duration and a spatial field." *Syuzhet* is "the actual arrangement and presentation of the fabula in the film."[5] The fabula is a totally implicit—or, from the viewer's perspective, inferred—structure. The syuzhet presents only a small selection of the "total fable."[6] A syuzhet (or "discourse") approach to narrative structure is preferable to a passive "enunciatory" one because it "avoids surface-phenomena distinctions (such as person, tense, metalanguage) and relies upon more supple principles basic to all narrative representation."[7]

" 'Style' [in turn] names the film's systematic use of cinematic devices"; unlike the syuzhet (which is a component of narrative in any medium whatsoever), it is medium-specific. Bordwell treats style and syuzhet as comparable systems (though the latter tends to "dominate" the former): "Syuzhet and style each treat different aspects of the phenomenal process. The syuzhet embodies the film as a 'dramaturgical' process; style embodies it as a 'technical' one."[8] Applying the word "embodies" to both these levels is a bit problematic, however, unless the embodiment is understood to be layered. To my mind, it makes sense to say that the syuzhet "arranges" the fabula into a text, but the style *actualizes* that arrangement; that is, it "embodies" the total narrative. Again, none of these—we must always remember—have any *independent* existence; they are all constructs proposed by theory, the better to explain the workings of film narrative.

Bordwell believes that narration is a dynamic process: "Formal systems both *cue* and *constrain* the viewer's construction of a story." But his emphasis is on what the viewer makes of the visual and auditory data impinging on her consciousness more than on the nature of the data themselves. The very term "construction" suggests that the important work is done by the viewer. In some sense, Bordwell takes the film itself, in its various layered structures, as already given. Thus, he rejects the notion of a cinematic narrator inherent in the film and argues instead for something he calls "narration": "Narration is *the process whereby the film's syuzhet and style interact in the course of cuing and channeling the spectator's construction of the fabula*" (original emphasis).[9]

It is a little unclear how this process occurs, whether it is internal to the viewer—in which case style and syuzhet "interact" only within her perception and cognition—or whether there is some kind of interchange between the screen and the viewer. If the latter, then "narration" at least partly inhabits the film—in which case, we can legitimately ask why it should not be granted some status as an agent. But Bordwell is opposed to the notion of narrative agency because "narrator" connotes "human being" to him. "If no voice or body gets identified as a locus of narration," he asks: "can we still speak of a narrator as being present in a film? In other words, must we go beyond the process of narration to locate an entity which is its source?" His answer is an unqualified no:

> In watching films, we are seldom aware of being told something by an entity resembling a human being. . . . narration is better understood as the organization of a set of cues for the construction of a story. This presupposes a perceiver, but not any sender, of a message. . . . On the principle that we ought not to proliferate theoretical entities without need, there is no point in positing communication as the fundamental process of all narration, only to grant that most films "efface" or "conceal" this process. Far better, I think, to give the narrational process the power to signal under certain circumstances that the spectator should construct a narrator.[10]

What does it mean to say that a film is "organized" but not "sent"? Who or what organizes it—not originally, of course, but right there on the screen during projection? Bordwell does not tell us. He seems concerned only with the agent of perception, not the agent of narration; that is, he equates the agent of perception with the act of narration. But surely the film—already "organized"—somehow gets to the theater and gets projected; *something* gets "sent." If we argue that "narrator" names only the organizational and sending agency and that that agency need not be human, as the dictionary tells us it need not, much of Bordwell's objection seems obviated, and we are spared the uncomfortable consequences of a communication with no communicator—indeed, a creation with no creator. We need *some* theoretical concept to explain the preexistence of what Nick Browne calls the "authority which can be taken to rationalize the presentation of shots."[11]

In my view, it is not that the viewer constructs but that she *reconstructs* the film's narrative (along with other features) from the set of cues encoded in the film.[12] Bordwell admirably describes many of these cues, but he does not explain their mode of existence in the film, only in the viewer. By "mode of existence" I don't mean how some real production team *put* them in the film but how they exist in any projection. The viewer certainly hasn't put them there, so it seems a bit odd to talk about "narration" as if she had.

Bordwell relies on Gérard Genette and Meir Sternberg, but I doubt that either would countenance, for general narratology, a narrative text without a narrator. Though conceding that Sternberg thinks of narrators as "conscious agents," Bordwell believes that film deals only in "processes." He argues that a process can be called, say, "knowledgeable" in the same way that a picture can be called "graceful." There is good reason to agree that a painting or a piece of music or a poem or a film is an "aesthetic object" and that "gracefulness," "cheerfulness," and the like may be said to be among its properties or "aesthetic qualities."[13] But it is one thing to argue that "gracefulness" is a property of an aesthetic object and quite another to make the object, "narration" (rather than the agent, "narrator"), the subject of verbs that *perform* things. Such verbs, by definition, presuppose agency. Objects and processes may have qualities, but only agents can do things. There is something disconcerting about such statements as "A film's narration can be called more or less knowledgeable." To say that an aesthetic object or process is "graceful" means that it strikes some observer as possessing grace. To say that it is "knowledgeable" is to say that it *knows* something, but if it knows something it must be more than an object or a process—it must be an agent (though the agent need not be human: my computer, for example, "knows" a lot). Normally, "process" refers either to a natural happening or to something set in motion by someone or something. But if something can know, present, recognize, communicate, acknowledge, be trustworthy, be aware of things, then surely it is too active a concept to be a mere happening or process. Knowing, presenting, recognizing, and the like are deeds, and deeds logically entail a doer. If "narration" indeed "does" these things, it is by definition an agent, and so requires not the object-nomimalizer "-tion" but the *nomina agentis* "-er."

The status of "narration" in Bordwell's narrative hierarchy is also unclear. On one occasion he seems to treat "narration" as the synonym of "syuzhet": "In most narrative films the narration does rearrange fabula order, principally through verbal recounting and in expository passages. It is more unusual to find the syuzhet *enacting* fabula events out of chronological sequence." But in a footnote explaining the difference between his own use of "syuzhet" and "fabula" and Genette's *récit* and *histoire*, he defines "narration" as syuzhet plus style (what I would call the actualization of the narrative in a medium).[14] Thus it is unclear whether he means to put "narration" at the same level with fabula or at a level higher.

Bordwell argues that "narration" controls the amount and placement of fabula information in the syuzhet through three instruments, which he names "knowledge," "self-consciousness," and "communicativeness."[15] The first and third are nominalized forms of the verbs "know" and "communicate," and the second is a nominalization of an adjective generally applied to human beings. Bordwell uses the terms quite consistently, and they have a certain viability, once you get used to them. But this personification of narration, a mere "process," seems to mystify more than it clarifies. Consider "knowledge": Bordwell asks, "What *range* of knowledge does the narration have at its disposal?" The "range" goes from highly restricted to total knowledge. This corresponds to literary criticism's well-known distinction between "limited" and "omniscient" points of view (or what I shall call "slant"). But whence the knowledge? Since Bordwell rejects the concept of the implied author,[16] he can only mean that "narration" itself decides how much it shall permit itself to know: this much, but not that much. But if, as I have argued above, it is already incongruent to attribute "knowledge" to a literary narrator how much more so to attribute it to a mere "process." Here, if we really must speak of "knowing," we should advert to the overall design of the text, the textual intent, *bref*—the implied author.

"Self-consciousness" entails similar problems. Bordwell does not use this term in its usual literary critical sense: that is, to refer to those (typically Modernist and postmodernist) effects by which the narrator comments on—and thereby demystifies—the process of narration itself.[17] He means by it, rather, the extent to which "the narration displays a recognition that it is addressing an audience," "narration's greater or lesser acknowledgment that a tale is being presented for a perceiver." It is a little hard to understand how "narration" can do this kind of acknowledging. Films do not frequently address the "dear viewer" the way the literary narrator may address the "dear reader." One of Bordwell's examples is Eisenstein's "having characters look at or gesture to the audience," a device also occurring in *Annie Hall*. But why should we understand it to be the "narration" (or even the narrator) who addresses us at such moments, rather than the characters—especially since Bordwell goes on to have it both ways? "Self-consciousness" is marked not only by characters addressing the audience but also by those turning away from it: "Antonioni will stage scenes with characters turned away from us, and the overt suppression of their expressions and reactions becomes in context a token of the narration's awareness of the viewer."[18]

Finally, "communicativeness": "Although a narration has a particular range of knowledge available," writes Bordwell, "the narration may or may not communicate all that information." That is, "the degree of communicativeness can be judged by considering how willingly the narration shares the information to which its degree of knowledge entitles it." "Communicativeness" is independent of "knowledge," he claims; both an omniscient text such as *The Birth of a Nation* and a restricted one such as *Rear Window* may be highly communicative. In the former, the "narration" knows everything; in the latter that narration is "generally communicative in that (on the whole) it tells us all that Jeff knows at any given moment." *Shadow of a Doubt* also restricts itself to the filter of a single character, Charlie.

But in that film, unlike *Rear Window*, at a certain moment "the narration holds back exactly the sort of information to which it has earlier claimed complete access, even though it immediately thereafter resumes his filter."[19]

I go into Bordwell's excellent theory in such detail because, except for our differences on the cinematic narrator, it is so close to my own. We both want to argue that film *does* belong in a general narratology; we both want to argue that films are narrated, and not necessarily by a human voice. We differ chiefly in the kind of agency we propose for the narrative transmission. It comes down, as I say, to the difference between "-tion" and "-er."

But there is one other difference, turning on the word "knowledge." In my theory, the narrator communicates all of and only what the implied author provides. How the narrator came to "know" the provided information seems a nonquestion. Without the implied author, it is pointless to talk about "knowledge," even if we substitute "narrator" for "narration." The question is one not of knowing but of how much and what information the cinematic narrator is programmed by the implied author to *present*. Only the implied author can be said to "know," because the implied author has invented it all. For each reading or viewing the implied author invents the narrative, both discourse and story. The cinematic narrator presents what the cinematic implied author requires. Just as it is the implied author who chooses what the adult Pip tells in *Great Expectations*, it is the implied author of *Rear Window* who decides what the "camera" shows "on its own," what it shows as filtered through Jeff's perception, and what it does not show at all. And just as literature has a place for "career-authorship," so does cinema. Indeed, much of *auteurisme* can be better explained as cinematic career-authorship. Part of what Bordwell calls the "transtext" is implicit in the signatures on films: a "Hitchcock" film is likely to entail suspense; an "Antonioni" film is likely to contain *temps mort* holds on bits of the landscape; a "Fellini" film is likely to merge on-screen and commentative music.

Bordwell too readily rejects the need for the concept of cinematic implied authorship, a concept that I find no less vital to cinematic than to general narrative theory. Films, like novels, present phenomena that cannot otherwise be accounted for, such as the discrepancy between what the cinematic narrator presents and what the film as a whole implies. "Unreliable narration," though not frequent, exists in cinema as well as in literature. As I argued in a previous chapter, unreliable narration presents the clearest but not the only case for the implied author. If the sole source of the ostensible story is a narrator, and if we come to believe that the "facts" are not as the narrator presents them, there can only be some other and overriding source of the story, the source we call the implied author. This possibility exists in the cinema just as much as in literature, though it has not been exercised very often—because, perhaps, the viewing public is not as ready for narrative ironies as is the reading public.

Still there are a few clear-cut examples. The most frequently discussed is Hitchcock's *Stage Fright* (1950).[20] The first half of the film contains a notorious "lying flashback": a false version of a murder is related by Johnny (Richard Todd), an unreliable homodiegetic-narrator. In the first shot we see a frontal view of Johnny and Eve (Jane Wyman) speeding to Eve's father's house. Johnny is saying, "I had to help her [Charlotte Inwood, played by Marlene Dietrich, who has goaded him into murdering her husband]. Anybody would. I was in my kitchen about five o'clock. The door bell rang . . ." Dissolve to what purports to be the "story itself"—Johnny opening the door, then a close-up of Charlotte's bloodstained skirt and Dietrich's voice begging him to help her. Next, Johnny is shown going to Charlotte's home, opening the bedroom door, looking at a poker on the ground near Inwood's corpse, stepping over him, and getting a fresh dress from the closet.

In our first viewing we have no reason to believe that this is not an accurate rendition of events. Only retrospectively, after Johnny admits to Eve his criminal tendency and a previous murder, do we realize that the camera has conspired with Johnny to deceive us, that Johnny's flashback was a lie. Johnny could not have seen Charlotte's husband *already* dead on the floor, because he had killed Inwood himself. Clearly, Johnny *narrates* the first, untrue version of the story, not only in his dialogue with Eve in the car but also *by means of* the ensuing visual sequence. The camera collaborates with, subserves the narrator by misrepresenting, "mis-showing," the facts of the case. Here, seeing is precisely not believing. What we see is literally untrue: it was not the case that Johnny returned for the dress and that he entered the room to see the body already dead. Nor is it the case that "the camera" narrates the false sequence "on its own." Rather, everything that we see and hear follows Johnny's scenario. Thus, even when his voice-over falls silent, he remains the controlling, if unreliable, narrator of the flashback.[21]

So, for this film at least, it does not seem true that "personified narrators are invariably swallowed up in the overall narrational process of the film, which they do *not* produce."[22] At the narrative level, Johnny and Johnny alone "produces" the segment in any narratologically meaningful sense of that word, since every cinematic tool—editing, lighting, commentative music—works to actualize his lie. During these scenes, Johnny prevails over the cinematic narrator. He is "responsible" for the lying images and sounds that we see and hear. Only later does the conventionally reliable cinematic narrator, reappropriating all the cinematic tools, take up the true story. Our judgment that Johnny's version of the story is unreliable depends on our decision that the later version of the story is reliable. And we must acknowledge that this does not happen by chance but is part of a design of communication. Who has invented both the incorrect and the correct versions? Bordwell's theory would have to say "the narration." But which narration, since there are two competing ones? Controlling both narrations there must be a broader textual intent—the implied author. It is the implied author who juxtaposes the two narrations of the story and "allows" us to decide which is true.[23]

In short, in cinema as in literature, the implied author is the agent intrinsic to the story whose responsibility is the overall design—including the decision to communicate it through one or more narrators. Cinematic narrators are transmitting agents of narratives, not their creators. Granted, *Stage Fright* is an unusual movie, but it cannot be ignored in constructing a theory of cinematic narration, for it is precisely the unusual possibility that tests the limits of a theory. A theory of narrative cinema should be able to account not only for the majority of films but also for the narratively odd or problematic ones. Besides, it may well be that unreliable narration will someday become as common in film as it is in the novel.

But the utility to cinematic narration of the concept of the implied author does not rest on a narrator's outright prevarication alone. Other kinds of films also illustrate the need for recognizing a separate principle of invention and intent. In Alain Resnais's *Providence* (1977) the first half of the film represents the fantasies of the protagonist, aging novelist Clive Langham (John Gielgud). Langham's voice-over, we eventually surmise, is somehow constructing the images filling the screen. These are more or less hypothetical rough drafts for scenes in a novel he is struggling to write. During these moments of his fantasy, it is *he*, not some disembodied "narration," who generates what passes before our eyes. Later, as he celebrates his birthday with his sons and daughter-in-law, an impersonal extradiegetic narrator assumes control of the cinematic apparatus. Again, both narrators have been introduced by the overriding intent of the film, the implied author.

In short, for films as for novels, we would do well to distinguish between a *presenter* of the story, the narrator (who is a component of the discourse), and the *inventor* of both the story and the discourse (including the narrator): that is, the implied author—not as the original cause, the original biographical person, but rather as the principle within the text to which we assign the inventional tasks.[24]

For if we deny the existence of the implied author and the cinematic narrator, we imply that film narratives are intrinsically different, with respect to a fundamental component, from those actualized in other media. But that implication contradicts the principle that Bordwell himself correctly endorses: namely, that narration is a "process which is not in its basic aims specific to any medium."[25] The substitution of "narration" for "narrator" does not advance Bordwell's desire to find cinema's actualizations of the "more supple principles basic to all narrative representation" (since, presumably, he accepts the existence of "narrators" in literary narratives). It is awkward to a general theory of narrative to say that some texts include the component "narrator" and others do not. As Sarah Kozloff puts it, simply but incisively, "Because narrative films are narrative, someone must be narrating."[26] Or if not necessarily someone, at least something.

Let me recapitulate my conception of the cinematic narrator. Though film theory tends to limit the word "narrator" to the recorded human voice "over" the visual image track, there is a good case to be made for a more general conception of "cinematic narrator." Films, in my view, are always presented—mostly and often exclusively shown, but sometimes partially told—by a narrator or narrators. The overall agent that does the showing I would call the "cinematic narrator."[27] That narrator is not a human being. The *nomina agentis* here refers to "agent," and agents need not be human. It is the cinematic narrator that shows the film, though it may on rare occasions (as in *Stage Fright*) be replaced by one or more "telling" voices on or off the screen.

The cinematic narrator is not to be identified with the voice-over narrator. A voice-over may be one *component* of the total showing, one of the cinematic narrator's devices,[28] but a voice-over narrator's contribution is almost always transitory; rarely does he or she dominate a film the way a literary narrator dominates a novel—that is, by informing every single unit of semiotic representation.[29] The normal state of affairs, and not only in the Hollywood tradition, is for voice-over narrators to speak at the beginning, less frequently at the end, and intermittently (if at all) during the film. Some films do use the technique more extensively. In a few cases the voice-over narrator seems to control the visuals: in *Stage Fright*, *Providence*, and Robert Bresson's *Diary of a Country Priest* (1950), the human narrator's voice dominates, at least in part of the film.[30] In *All About Eve*, Addison De Witt's narration controls the whole introductory set of flashbacks that present the history of Eve's rise in the theater. In the freeze-frame description discussed in Chapter 3, it can reasonably be argued that it is Addison who has frozen the frame, just as he previously tuned out the voice of the old actor presenting the award. In the film's coda, however, after Eve receives the award and goes home, only to find her own little stagestruck groupie waiting to follow in her footsteps, the general cinematic narrator assumes control.[31] At first, then, the image track seems to be the character's construction; that is, the images are at the service of—are an alternative means of communicating—what he says. Later, the general cinematic narrator takes control. But both narrators are the instruments of the implied author.

The cinematic narrator is the composite of a large and complex variety of communicating devices. Some of them are partially shown in this diagram, which makes no pretense to completeness; my purpose is rather to demonstrate something of the multiplexity of the cinematic narrator:

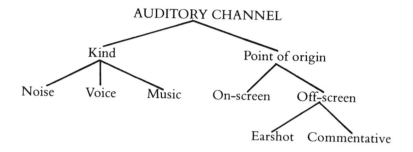

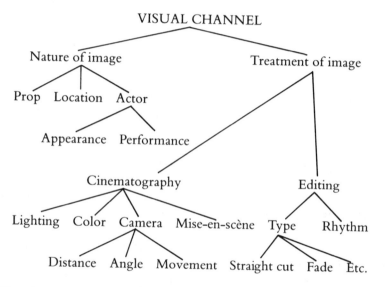

The cinematic narrator is the composite of all these plus other variables. Their synthesis *as* the narrator, of course, is achieved by the semiotic processing performed by the viewer, the details of which are admirably described by Bordwell. That processing goes beyond the merely perceptual; for example, the clutching of two right hands is perceivable by all viewers but is interpretable as a "handshake" or "arm-wrestling" only by those who know the rules of a language and culture that include such signifieds.

The different components of the cinematic narrator as diagrammed usually work in consort, but sometimes the implied author creates an ironic tension between two of them. It is not uncommon, even in

Coming to Terms

Hollywood films, for the visual track to undercut the story told by a character-narrator's voice-over. In Terence Malick's *Badlands* (1973), for example, the voice of the heroine, Holly, tells a romanticized account of her escapade with the murderer Kit which is totally belied by the sordid action as we see it with our own eyes.[32]

This kind of partial unreliability is unique to two-track media such as the cinema. The disparity is not between what the cinematic narrator says and what the implied author implies but between what is told by one component of the cinematic narrator and shown by another. Whereas in totally unreliable narratives such as *Stage Fright* the conflict must arise through disparities between all the representations of the narrator and what the viewer must infer from the film as a whole, the partially unreliable narration of *Badlands* arises explicitly from a conflict between two mutually contradictory components of the cinematic narrator. Normally, as in *Badlands*, the visual representation is the acceptable one, on the convention that seeing is believing. In theory, at least, the opposite could happen as well—that is, the sound track could be accurate and the visual track unreliable— but in practice, that effect seems very rare; Sarah Kozloff found only one example, in *An American in Paris* (1951).[33] The reason for this imbalance seems fairly obvious. The errant homodiegetic voice-over can easily be understood to have some motive for skewing the events. In *Badlands*, Holly is a naive adolescent, and so we hypothesize that she romanticizes the escapade. After all, she lives in a society so boring that any notoriety, even that of criminals, overrides questions of mere morality. But when the camera is aberrant and the voice-over "straightens it out," the effect is odd and self-conscious. In *An American in Paris*, as each of the three protagonists introduces himself, the camera focuses on the wrong person; the voice-over redirects it. A more usual if weaker case of visual unreliability occurs when the visual track presents a shallow picture of events, which are interpreted with greater profundity by the voice-over narrator; this is the strategy of Bresson's *Journal of a Country Priest* and Stanley Kubrick's *Barry Lyndon* (1975).[34]

There remains a final question about unreliability: does it make any sense to call narrators "unreliable" who are without personality or, as I have called them, "covert"? (This class includes virtually all cinematic narrators and many heterodiegetic narrators of novels and short stories.) It is hard to think of any reason for doing so. Unre-

136

liability depends on some clearly discernible discrepancy between the narrator's account and the larger implied meaning of the narrative as a whole. But that discrepancy would seem to depend pretty much on personality: there has to be some *reason* for us to distrust the narrator's account, and the only possible reason would be something in his character. Where there is no character—and hence no motive for giving a questionable account of the story—how can we even recognize that the account is unreliable?

We must remember, finally, that the cinematic apparatus is not always committed to the iconic; sometimes it too employs arbitrary conventions. Obviously, the natural language used in dialogue track, voice-over, or captions is entirely arbitrary. Sometimes a single caption can undercut the hypothesis suggested by all the rest of the film: in Dusan Makaveyev's *Montenegro*, we learn in a caption over the final images that the heroine has just poisoned her whole family. But even the visual track may be noniconic. Say, for example, that the narrator wants to convey the idea that a train trip took a long time. Especially in films of the 1930s, the camera might very well show a montage of overlapping shots of spinning locomotive wheels. From the montage the viewer could infer that the trip took longer than its discourse representation.

The argument for an impersonal agent as cinematic narrator finds interesting support in the narrative theories of Ann Banfield. Banfield argues (in *Unspeakable Sentences* and elsewhere) that certain linguistic features such as special tenses (the *passé simple* in French) and the unusual collocation of preterits with present time and place deixis (as in "He *saw now* that he *was* mistaken") distinguish literary narratives from ordinary communicative uses of language. Its sentences are literally "unspeakable": they cannot occur in normal conversation. Precisely because it is unlike normal discourse—which always posits a speaker and an audience and thus subjectivity—the space of literary narrative, Banfield believes, is empty and timeless. In her view, the narrator-subject as conventionally conceived must be absent from a text that includes such sentences as "This was now here."

I do not agree totally with this theory, since it goes on to deny the very existence of the narrator. Many first person narratives, for example, clearly entail the time and place marks of ordinary discourse. But for certain kinds of "third person" effects, and thus for much of cinematic narration, the theory affords an interesting way of grasping the notion of nonhuman narrative agency. The technology of film, Banfield contends, like that of the telescope and the microscope, "allow[s] the viewing subject to see, to witness, places where he is not, indeed, where no subject is present." It also reveals "the appearance of things *when* no one was present," as, for example, a stellar explosion that took place millions of years before man evolved.[35] Clearly, this kind of model helps us understand how we so readily conceive of a non-human narrator; how, for example, we can speak of "the camera" as such an agent, how, in *Rear Window*, a nonhuman cinematic narrator can roll up the blinds and take us on a visual tour of the courtyard. For that is the predictable response of ordinary moviegoers: confronted with the beginning sequence of *Rear Window*, they will interpret the scanning views of the interior of a courtyard as a tour of the courtyard by the camera "on its own." When the shades roll up, we know that what we see is being presented by a "subjectivity reduced to nothing else but what the instrument can record"; this is quite different from later viewings that are filtered through the perception of Jeffries. At such moments, the visible details of the courtyard correspond to what Banfield, following Bertrand Russell, calls *sensibilia*: "those objects which have the same metaphysical and physical status as sense-data, without necessarily being data to any mind." That is, to any mind *inside* the fiction: they are, of course, data to the real audience in the movie theater, though data perceived at second hand. They are not seen or heard but rather overseen and overheard, as the "impressions" of an impersonal narrative agency. These images (Banfield might contend) would still exist even if no one had bought a ticket and the projectionist had gone out for a smoke: "Each gathering of sensibilia, as on the ground glass of the telescope, represents . . . a perspective definable independent of whether or not it is given to any observer."[36]

Banfield's concern is literary, but she finds in the work of Gilles Deleuze a similar attitude concerning film. Deleuze reminds us that Dziga Vertov's "kino-eye" is not limited as a human eye is; it is ubiquitous, the product as much of montage as of cinematography. And its powers are, to use Banfield's terms, "private and subjective," yet "impersonal." Deleuze would argue that it is precisely the objectivity of the cinematic narrator that requires us to "construct," rather than just to "see," since what the kino-eye presents us with is a construction of views that no human eye *could* see.[37]

CHAPTER 9

A New Point of View
on "Point of View"

RECENT NARRATOLOGISTS have pretty much abandoned the term "point of view" as loose and imprecise. Various terms such as "focalization" have been proposed to replace it, but like "point of view," these do not face the main problem. That problem, as I see it, is the need to recognize *different* terms for the two different narrative agents, narrator and character. To explain why, we need to examine briefly the various senses of "point of view" in the language at large.

My desk dictionary lists two senses: "a point from which things are viewed," and "a mental position or viewpoint." (The *Oxford English Dictionary* and *Webster's Third* list additional senses, including the narratological one.) The basic distinction is between a physical place from which something is seen (a "vista" or "lookout"), and a viewer's mental attitude or posture. The second sense is clearly a metaphoric transfer from the first. We literally stand at some point (say, the top of a skyscraper) to see something (say, the rest of the city). All three components of the situation—the thing seen, the place from which it is seen, and the act of seeing—are literal. But when the place "from which" becomes, figuratively, the human mind, the meanings proliferate. We "see" not only physical objects but memories, abstract ideas, relationships, and so on: hence the complexity and vagueness of the term "point of view."

The mind, including its perceptual equipment, can be understood either as the organ of figurative "seeing" or as the equivalent of the literal post from which the seeing takes place. "From my point of

view the Transamerica Building is an architectural travesty" is meaningful even if I say it at a cocktail party in Barcelona. The Transamerica Building remains a visible object, but the act of "seeing"
entails a figurative use of the term "point of view." The "seeing" can
refer to acts of memory, judgment, opinion, or whatever.

Further, since "see" can mean more than merely "optically perceive," "point of view" can have as its object nonvisible things.
"From my point of view, the president's stand on flag burning is
indefensible." The president's stand, the thing "seen," is an abstraction, conceived figuratively as occupying a kind of space; it is part of
the same figure that articulates my "perceiving" from my own mental "place"—my ideological "stance," to vary the metaphor. The
metaphoric transfers thus add to literal perception such mental activity as cognition, conceptualization, memory, fantasy, and the like.
Thus,

ORGAN OR FACULTY	PLACE OF SEEING	THING SEEN
(1) Literal: eyes	Literal: skyscraper	Literal: city
(2) Figurative: visual recall	Figurative: "post" in mind	Literal: Transamerica Building
(3) Figurative: judgment	Figurative: "post" in mind	Figurative: president's stand

But "point of view" permits even more extensive metaphoric
transfer. Take the sentence "From the point of view of the fetus, the
abortion was unfortunate." A fetus neither perceives nor conceptual-
izes, but it is not unusual in English to assign it a "point of view."
What is entailed is a component of "interest": beings and even inani-
mate objects can be understood to have a stake in actions or events
that relate to them. So it is possible to make such statements as "From
the dog's point of view, the water hose spelled trouble"; "From the
redwood forest's point of view, the sound of chain saws was apoc-
alyptic"; "From the point of view of law enforcement, automatic
weapons are a disaster"; "From the point of view of the bond market,
the increase of unemployment is a godsend."

Further, "point of view" is also subsumed under ideology in the broadest sense. One can cite the ideological point of view of someone who is not alive: "From Franklin Roosevelt's point of view, Reagan's self-characterization as his successor was ludicrous." Doubtless, further extensions could be made, but these are sufficient to suggest that "point of view" in ordinary usage covers far more than mere perception or even cognition.

All these senses and implications of "point of view" have been transported from the language at large into narratology. But we may ask whether the narratological properties that we wish to identify are well captured by this term—or indeed by *any* single term—or whether its complexities render it imprecise and confusing. The question is not whether the functions of perception, cognition, empathy, and so on, need to be named. Obviously they do. The question is whether the *same* name (whether "point of view" or "perspective" or "vision" or "focalization") should cover the mental acts of different narrative agents. I believe that it should not, that the separate mental behaviors, stances, attitudes, and interests of narrators and characters require separate terms.

Let us consider a rather straightforward literary example. *Dombey and Son* begins as follows:

Dombey sat in the corner of the darkened room in the great arm-chair by the bedside, and son lay tucked up warm in a little basket bedstead, carefully disposed on a low settee immediately in front of the fire and close to it, as if his constitution were analogous to that of a muffin, and it was essential to toast him brown while he was very new.[1]

No reader, I take it, believes that the maker of the analogy between the baby and a toasted muffin is Mr. Dombey, a man far too complacent about his first male offspring to entertain such a thought. So these are clearly the narrator's words (or, to be scrupulous, they are words assigned to the narrator by the implied author). It is traditional to say that the analogy represents the narrator's "point of view," which is here, as often in Dickens's novels, whimsical and gently ironic. But I would argue that the narrator is not to be imagined as literally *contemplating* the new baby and deciding, in that contemplation, that he resembles a muffin.

The convention has it, rather, that the narrator is performing his usual task of *reporting* this scene, and he introduces the muffin analogy the better to convey its unique flavor. The narrator, in this case omniscient and unidentified, is a reporter, not an "observer" of the story world in the sense of literally witnessing it. It makes no sense to say that a story is told "through" the narrator's perception since he/she/it is precisely *narrating*, which is not an act of perception but of presentation or representation, of transmitting story events and existents through words or images. It is naive, I think, to argue that this omniscient narrator "got" this information by witnessing it. He is a component of the discourse: that is, of the mechanism by which the story world is rendered. No one wonders whether the narrator ever inhabited the story world of *Dombey and Son*. Though fictional, he is a different *kind* of fiction from Dombey or Dombey, Jr. He resides in an order of time and place different from that occupied by the characters; his is a different "here-and-now." And that's true for every narrator, no matter how minimal his/her/its distance from the "here-and-now" of the story (as, for example, in the epistolary novel).

The narrator may have his own "view of things," of course. But we must lock "view" with stern quotation marks to indicate the exact nature of the metaphor. Since it makes so little sense to say that the narrator literally sees Mr. Dombey sitting there admiring his son, we might ask whether "view" is not positively misleading as a term to describe the narrator's situation. It seems better to distinguish between narrator's and character's mental experiences in the story world as different *kinds* of experiences, but that is hard to do if we refer to both by the same term, whether "point of view," "perspective," or "focalization."

I am not asserting, of course, that only narrators have attitudes. Characters also have them (along with a whole range of other mental experiences), and they may differ sharply from those of the narrator. A particularly clear example occurs right after our introduction to Mr. Dombey. Though others understand that Mrs. Dombey was a "lady with no heart to give him," Mr. Dombey

would have reasoned: That a matrimonial alliance with himself *must*, in the nature of things, be gratifying and honourable to any woman of common sense. That the hope of giving birth to a new partner in such a house, could not fail to awaken a glorious and stirring ambition in the breast of the least ambitious of her sex. That Mrs. Dombey had entered on that social contract of matrimony: almost necessarily part of a genteel and wealthy station, even without reference to the perpetuation of family firms: with her eyes fully open to these advangages. That Mrs. Dombey had had daily practical knowledge of his position in society. That Mrs. Dombey had always sat at the head of his table, and done the honours of his house in a remarkable lady-like and becoming manner. That Mrs. Dombey must have been happy. That she couldn't help it.[2]

Since it is the narrator who has just reported that there is reason to believe Mrs. Dombey a "lady with no heart to give," he cannot lay claim to these sentiments or the language that expresses them. They are entirely Mr. Dombey's attitude, his "view" of things.

It is high time that we introduce a terminological distinction between these two loci of "point of view": that of the narrator, and that of the character. I propose *slant* to name the narrator's attitudes and other mental nuances appropriate to the report function of discourse, and *filter* to name the much wider range of mental activity experienced by characters in the story world—perceptions, cognitions, attitudes, emotions, memories, fantasies, and the like.

"Slant" well captures, I think, the psychological, sociological, and ideological ramifications of the narrator's attitudes, which may range from neutral to highly charged. (I use the term in a totally nonpejorative sense. "Angle" would work just as well.) The slant may be expressed implicitly or explicitly. When the narrator's slant is explicit—that is, put into so many words—we call it "commentary," particularly "judgmental commentary." Such commentary should not be confused with the characters' comments, anchored as they are to an observational post *within* the story world. Attitudes, of course, are rooted in ideology, and the narrator is as much a locus of ideology as anyone else, inside or outside the fiction. The ideology may or may not match that of any of the characters. And it may or may not match that of the implied or real author. It might be argued that in a sufficiently broad definition, attitudes are *all* that "narrator's point of view" feasibly refers to.

Further, though it seems infelicitous to say that a narrator "looks" at events and existents in the story world, that does not mean that he cannot look at events and existents in the *discourse* world that he occupies, to the extent that that world is fleshed out. The unnamed narrator of *Heart of Darkness* perceives sights and sounds, including Marlowe's voice, in that boat on the Thames. Mr. Lockwood perceives, conceives, imagines, meditates about life at Wuthering Heights before Mrs. Dean begins her story. But, I contend, it is in the nature of the case that neither can pierce the discourse membrane to experience the story world directly; they can experience it only vicariously, through the words of others. They *re-report* what others tell them. Marlowe and Mrs. Dean did, of course, experience the original events, but they did so in their capacity as characters, not as narrators. "Slant" delimits the mental activity on *this* side of the discourse-story barrier.

"Filter," on the other hand, seems a good term for capturing something of the mediating function of a character's consciousness—perception, cognition, emotion, reverie—as events are experienced from a space within the story world. The effect has been well understood since Henry James. The story is narrated *as if* the narrator sat somewhere inside or just this side of a character's consciousness and strained all events through that character's sense of them. The very word "inside" implies, logically, the discourse-story barrier discussed above. And the barrier, structurally, remains, whether the narrator continues to speak in his own voice or falls silent for long stretches or for the entire text. What I like about the term "filter" is that it catches the nuance of the *choice* made by the implied author about which among the character's imaginable experiences would best enhance the narration—which areas of the story world the implied author wants to illuminate and which to keep obscure. This is a nuance missed by "point of view," "focalization," and other metaphors.

Further, the terms "slant" and "filter" correspond to the vital distinction, originally made by Gérard Genette, between who "tells" and who "sees" the story. In my view, the latter could only mean that character, that *occupant* of the story world, who has perceived the events that transpire. The narrator can only report events: he does not literally "see" them at the moment of speaking them. The heterodiegetic narrator *never* saw the events because he/she/it never occupied the story world. The homodiegetic or first-person narrator *did* see the events and objects at an earlier moment in the story, but his recountal is after the fact and thus a matter of memory, not of perception. He tells or shows what he remembers *having seen.* In other words, narrative discourse recognizes two different narrative beings moving under the same name: one, the heterodiegetic narrator, inhabits only discourse time and space; another, the homodiegetic or character narrator, also speaks from discourse time and space but previously inhabited story time and space. Only Pip-the-character saw those things out on the marsh, "back then." It is Pip-the-narrator, a different order of narrative being, who "now" recounts those events in an unspecified but distinctly posterior discourse time and space. In this later moment and other place, what the narrator conveys can only be memories of perceptions and conceptions internal to the story, not the perceptions and conceptions themselves. This is no less true in narrations that occur only minutes after the story events, as in epistolary novels. If we are to preserve the vital distinction between discourse and story, we cannot lump together the separate behaviors of narrator and character under a single term, whether "point of view," "focalization," or any other.

Continental narratology, however, has insisted that *somebody* always "sees" or "focalizes" the story, that if no one inside the story is given the special privilege of such "sight," then the narrator must be assumed to have it. "The only focalization logically implied by the 'first-person' narrator," writes Genette, "is focalization through the narrator."[3] But surely speaking of the narrator as "focalizer" blurs the distinction that Genette himself introduced to clear up traditional confusion between voice and point of view—between "who speaks" and "who sees." The narrator's comments are not of the same order as a character's perceptions, even if he is reporting what he saw or felt "back then" when he *was* a character. The use of "focalization," or any other single term, to refer to the quite different mental process of characters and narrators violates the distinction between story and discourse.[4] Even for so-called "camera-eye" narration it is always and only *as if* the narrator were seeing the events transpire before his very eyes at the moment of narration. If we do not understand this, we cannot clarify but must fall victim to the very illusion that it is our task to analyze. As Genette puts it, fictional discourse simulates a reproduction: that is, an *invented* production. It does not see; it produces. That production is offered sometimes as a memory (a reproduction), sometimes as the sheerest fantasy. (Lawrence Sterne and others rub our noses in the artifice.) Even when the narrator takes pains to make it seem as if he were "right there," witnessing the things as they "really" happened, all fictional narratives remain artifice, convention, produced illusion.

Only characters reside in the constructed story world, so only they can be said to "see," that is, to have a diegetic consciousness that literally perceives and thinks about things from a position within that world. Only their "perspective" is immanent to that world. Only they can be filters. The narrator cannot perceive or conceive things *in* that world: he can only tell or show what happened there, since for him the story world is already "past" and "elsewhere." He can report them, comment upon them, and even—figuratively in literature, literally in cinema—visualize them, but always and only from outside, from a post out in the discourse. The logic of narrative prevents him from inhabiting the story world at the moment that he narrates it.

Of course, this convention, like any convention, can be undermined—but when it is, the anomaly is clear. In *The French Lieutenant's Woman* the narrator, clearly a twentieth-century type who talks about Freud and World War II, disguises himself late in the book as a Victorian gentleman and transports himself back to 1867, to the railroad carriage occupied by the protagonist Charles Smithson (much to the latter's annoyance). But the joke works only to the extent that we understand the infraction, the narrative scandal entailed. And we continue to believe that it is the modern narrator who recounts the appearance and actions of the "character" he has thus created, by the suspension of some principle of verisimilitude.

Some theorists might argue, however, that the distinction between being "inside" and being "outside" the story gets blurred in certain kinds of narrative, in those, for instance, utilizing free indirect thought. But let us ask whether that is so. Consider the first two paragraphs of Virginia Woolf's *Jacob's Room*:

> "So of course," wrote Betty Flanders, pressing her heels rather deeper in the sand, "there was nothing for it but to leave."
> Slowly welling from the point of her gold nib, pale blue ink dissolved the full stop; for there her pen stuck; her eyes fixed, and tears slowly filled them. The entire bay quivered; the lighthouse wobbled; and she had the illusion that the mast of Mr. Connor's

little yacht was bending like a wax candle in the sun. She winked quickly. Accidents were awful things. She winked again. The mast was straight; the waves were regular; the lighthouse was upright; but the blot had spread.[5]

The narrator, from a post outside in the discourse, is rendering Betty Flanders's continuing grief over the death of her husband, Seabrook, two years before. Betty is writing a letter about having had to leave her native town after her husband's death. The narrator tells us that her pen sticks and the ink wells, and that her eyes follow suit, welling with tears. Then we enter her mind, though the filtration is "psycho-narrated"—rendered in the narrator's own words. The mental content is not conceptual but perceptual. That is, the entire bay does not quiver for the *narrator*, nor does the lighthouse wobble. It is Betty who sees, through tears, these visual aberrations. But the next sentence *does* contain the very words that pass through Betty's consciousness: it is free indirect thought. The sentence is the equivalent of "Betty felt once again that accidents were awful things." That might or might not be a sentiment that the narrator shares and indeed utters here; it is precisely the nature (and charm) of indirect free discourse to make it hard to know. But even if both the feeling and the language might be *shared* by character and narrator, that does not seem reason for arguing that the demarcation between the story world and the discourse world is blurred.

The same logic, I think, applies to interior monologue. In the "Penelope" section of *Ulysses*, for example, the ruminations are totally those of Molly Bloom, in her own words (or sounds). She is not functioning as narrator, not telling anyone a story after the fact, but simply carrying on normal thinking processes in the present story moment. The thought stream is simply quoted by a totally effaced narrator. The convention is exactly the same as quoted dialogue: hence the appropriateness of calling it "free direct thought." There is no particular reason to argue that the narrator, though silent, has left the discourse world.

"Point of view" ("vision," "perspective," "focalization") has named still a third narrative function: that is, the presentation of a story in such a way that a certain character is of paramount importance. But this is quite different from filtration, since we may or may not be given access to that central character's consciousness. This function, I think, should be called *center*. Thus, Milly Theale, Gatsby, and Stavrogin are centers but not main filter characters in *The Wings of the Dove*, *The Great Gatsby*, and *The Possessed*. In one sense, each is the most important character in the novel, but we have less direct access to their consciousness than to that of other characters. Centering without filtration is a useful technique for depicting enigmatic characters.

A final narrative function traditionally named by "point of view" is what I call *interest*. Consider this remark on the very first page of *Oliver Twist*:

> In this workhouse was born—on a day and date which I need not trouble myself to repeat, inasmuch as it can be of no possible consequence to the reader, in this stage of the business at all events— the item of mortality whose name is prefixed to the head of this chapter.[6]

The narrator's slant is again one of Dickensian irony, as if it were hardly worth his while, or the reader's, to care much about this "item of mortality." But the item in question is Oliver Twist, whose name appears on the title page and who proves to be the central character of the novel. We immediately infer that for the newborn babe—that is, from his "interest point of view"—it *is* a matter of concern that he was born in a certain workhouse on such and such a date. Since he is too small to see or to understand or to have an attitude about such matters, he cannot be a filter. We need another name to describe this narrative effect, and I propose *interest-focus*. (The term is not redundant with "center," since even a minor character can be interest-focused.) "Interest" point of view is of particular importance in narrative media like film. Quite often we do not see things from some character's optical point of view or know what she is thinking, but we identify with her, interpret events as they affect her, wish her good luck or good comeuppance.

Even if "slant," "filter," "center," and "interest-focus" do not meet general approval, I would argue the need for terms reflecting these distinctions. The external-internal tangle that "focalization" gets into would be resolved because, by definition, a term such as "filter" would be recognized as internal to the story world and "slant," by contrast, as external to it. Separate terms would enable us to characterize texts more accurately than would any single term. Slant, we could say, may or may not work in conjunction with filter. If it does, we can distinguish limited filtration from multiple filtration. Either term may or may not imply the transmission of information belonging to the narrator alone and presented in the form of commentary. Camera-eye narration, then, is simply slant without filtration and without narrator's commentary. Any of these can be conjoined with or without centering and/or interest-focusing on a certain character.

The Fallible Filter

The distinction between filter and slant is important for a proper understanding of "reliability." In particular, it helps clarify a certain confusion about the *locus* of reliability. We must distinguish between two kinds of "untrustworthiness." In the first, the *narrator's* account of the events (including what any character says or thinks) seems at odds with what the text implies to be the facts. That is what is generally meant by "unreliable narration." In the second, a *character's* perceptions and conceptions of the story events, the traits of the other characters, and so on, seem at odds with what the narrator is telling or showing. I propose that we call the latter effect *fallible filtration*.

The narrators of Ring Lardner's "Haircut," Albert Camus's *La chute* and Mark Twain's *Huckleberry Finn* are unreliable, whether from mendacity, naiveté, or *inconscience*. The protagonists of Jane Austen's *Emma* and Henry James's "The Liar," on the other hand, are fallible filters. Different terms are needed for these different kinds of distortion of story information. The term "unreliable" seems suitable only where the narration itself is problematic, since the word presupposes that there somewhere exists a "reliable" account. Though this "reliable" account goes unstated, like any irony, it is quite distinctly *there*. Indeed, as Booth points out, we are often far more certain of ironic meanings than of straight ones.[7] Readers might reach a greater degree of consensus about what "really" happened in an unreliably than in a reliably narrated story.

But what is "unreliable" in fallible filtration is not the narrator's account of story events but only the thoughts or speeches of the filter character. This fallibility may be implicit, or it may be stated directly by the narrator. The effect of a character's misguided thoughts needs another name than "unreliability" for the same reason that narration and filtration themselves should be distinguished and not blurred under a single rubric like "point of view" or "focalization." "Fallible" seems a good term for a filter character's inaccurate, misled, or self-serving perception of events, situations, and other characters, for it attributes less culpability to the character than does "unreliable." After all, the character has not *asked* that her mind be entered or her conversation overheard by a narrator and reported to a narratee. She communicates only intradiegetically, with other characters in the story. She is normally not aware of *being* in a story monitored by a discourse. As long as she is a character in and not the narrator of the main story or of a story-within-a-story, she does not purport to be giving an account of that story. She cannot misrepresent it, because she is not attempting to represent it; rather, she is *living* it. So she can hardly be responsible to the narrative in the way that a narrator is. She may be lying or acting unreliably in other ways, with diegetic consequences to herself and other characters; within her own mind she may be fooling herself; but as a character she has no direct access to the discourse, to the transmission of the story, and therefore cannot be accused of unreliable narration. The milder characterization "fallible"—"liable to mistake or to error"—seems preferable to the stronger term "unreliable," since it does not connote a knowledge of textual intention or the intent to deceive some narratee.[8]

Confusion about this distinction began with the very first example that Booth picked to illustrate unreliable narration: namely, "The Liar."[9] Though much of Booth's account of Henry James's novella is accurate and sensitive, it does not recognize an essential fact: that the protagonist, Oliver Lyon, cannot be an unreliable narrator for the simple reason that he is not a narrator at all. He is, rather, a fallible filter. Of course, the story transpires very much in Lyon's head. Though Booth may have somewhat overstated the case for Lyon's "viciousness," one can hardly disagree that Lyon rationalizes some rather deplorable behavior on his own part. Still, he does so in the privacy of his own mind, not as a representation to a narratee. Indeed, as a character he has no consciousness of the existence of a narratee. It is one thing to ask, "Is Lyon really villainous and vicious?" Booth finds him so, and his reading certainly seems preferable to those of critics who swallow Lyon's interpretation of events whole. But it is another—and more narratologically relevant—thing to ask, "How do we know that Lyon's views are flawed?" We know not by listening to him *tell* the story but by listening to a covert narrator represent his thoughts and intentions.

In unreliable narration, the implied author constructs a narration that the implied reader must call into question.

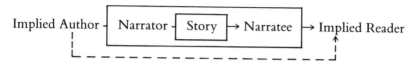

(The broken line indicates the secret ironic message about the narrator's unreliability.)

In fallibility, on the other hand, the narrator asks the narratee, his or her interlocutor in the discourse, to enjoy an irony at the expense of a filter character.

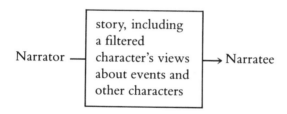

The message about the character's fallibility goes from narrator to narratee and is not countermanded by the implied author. The narrator reports the character's thought or speech but in addition implies or asserts a certain unacceptability of that thought or speech.

Explicit fallibility, that announced by the narrator, is simply a special case of narrative commentary—in particular, the kind of commentary that I have called "interpretation." On the first page of *Emma*, the narrator states unequivocally that Emma has rather too much her own way and a disposition to think a little too well of herself. In "A Painful Case," Joyce's narrator describes Mr. Duffy's habitual reference to himself in the third person as an "odd auto-biographical habit." That sort of judgment clearly helps to ironize Duffy's intense distance from life.

But there is also implicit fallibility, which can only be inferred by the narratee. At a critical moment in Joyce's "Clay," we read that

Maria "felt a soft wet substance and was surprised nobody spoke or took off her bandage." Maria, the fallible filter, does not know—or, better, does not allow herself to guess—that the substance is clay, a traditional symbol of death. The substance she touches is nowhere named in the story except in the title. The irony, pathetic as it is, is between the narrator and the narratee at Maria's expense; it is part of the larger irony that Maria goes around cheerfully concealing from herself the sad figure that she cuts in Dublin. Similarly, in "A Little Cloud," when Little Chandler acknowledges that he will never be a popular poet but that English critics may some day recognize him as a minor member of the Celtic School, there is reason to infer that he will continue to delude himself, that he is never going to publish anything.

There is no unreliable narration in Joyce's *Dubliners*. No deep reader, I think, has proposed that events or characters were other than as the narrator represents them. Where there is irony, it clearly turns on the narratee's sharing of the narrator's attitude toward the character's misguided attitudes. So it would not be precise to speak of the characters as unreliable; rather, they are fallible—Maria in her pathetic way, Chandler in his dreamy way, Duffy in his isolated way. Both fallible filtration and unreliable narration are forms of irony, but the ironized targets differ. In fallible filtration the irony inheres in a secret message between the narrator and the narratee at the expense of a character. In unreliable narration the irony inheres in a secret message between the implied author and the implied reader at the expense of the narrator.

In many traditional texts, such as *Tom Jones* and *Emma*, the implied author's message does not differ essentially from the narrator's; we do not search for differences between what the implied author intends and what the narrator tells or shows. We cannot find a reason for believing that the implied author does not stand behind the narrator's irony at the expense of fallible characters like Tom and Emma. But in "Haircut" or the section of *The Sound and the Fury* narrated by Jason Compson, there is good reason to doubt that the implied author endorses the barber's account of Jim Kendall's decency or Jason's racial and religious attitudes. The drift of the narrative works against such presumptions. For example, Jim clearly is not a good fellow at all but a bastard, a sadist who perpetrates practical "jokes" out of sheer nastiness; thus, Whitey the barber is an unreliable narrator because his account of the story is flawed. We recognize the flaw even though he is our only source for the story itself. The value structure and understanding of the world presupposed by the implied author prevents us from endorsing Whitey's interpretation of those events. To succeed, the story obviously must persuade us that Whitey's admiration for Jim and his gullible acceptance of the "official" story of the "accidental" shooting are misguided.

Though a character can be shown by the narrator to be fallible either explicitly or implicitly, a narrator can be unreliable only implicitly, since the narrator is the unique source of the story. The implied reader can only infer the real purport of an unreliably narrated story. In fallible filtration, on the other hand, there is always the possibility of an explication. The reliable narrator is free to explain and comment on the characters' misapprehensions, though in many cases she ("covertly") elects to let them reveal themselves.

Unreliable narration entails a special kind of irony. In ordinary, nonfictional irony we usually understand the speaker to be in on the joke. On one occasion, for example, the *New Yorker*'s "On the Town" reporter damns with faint praise or in other ways ironizes the many publicity parties that she is invited to. The repetition of the word "great," so frequently bandied about at a party thrown in honor of the "personality" Merv Griffin, calls his "greatness" into question. We can be pretty sure that the reporter wants us not only to understand that she doesn't mean what she says but that she is *consciously* practicing irony. Reporter and reportee are in on the joke about the persons and events reported. Those persons and events, not the reporter, constitute the butt. In a reading of this kind of irony—which we might call "speaker-conscious irony"—two conditions seem to operate: the reader or hearer understands (1) that the speech entails two conflicting messages, an ostensible one and an implicit one that is different from the ostensible and may even contradict it; and (2) that the speaker is conscious of that underlying message, intends it, and thus wants us to privilege it over the ostensible message.

But unreliable narration shares only the first condition, not the second. It is "speaker-unconscious": that is, the narrator is the butt, not the objects and events narrated. The unreliable narrator cannot know the disparity between the two messages presented by his discourse. He delivers what he understands to be a single, straight-forward message, but the implied reader must infer that the ostensible message is being canceled or at least called into question by an underlying message that the narrator does not understand. The narrator is being ironized in the *act* of narrating. Much of the effect rests on the implied reader's understanding that the narrator is unconscious or at least ambivalent about the duplicity, distortion, or naiveté of his account. The implied reader understands the implied author's ironization of the narrator, though the dramatized narratee may or may not understand it.

Slant and Filter in the Cinema

Like literary narrators, cinematic narrators have their slant. Ideological slant tends to be implicit, though in some films it is spelled out in so many words by a voice-over or captions. A growing critical literature documents the capitalist or bourgeois slant of the classical Hollywood film (not to speak of its sexist and racist slants as well).[10] Slant has been found not only at the more abstract levels of narrative but also at that of actualization or "style."[11] Hollywood films are usually characterized by a "seamless" style in which the actualization hides all marks of artifice, accounts for all projected story space and time, and motivates all shot transitions in a totally unobtrusive or "transparent" way. The seamless style presents events and characters under the aspect of the totally "natural"—a "natural" which, of course, heavily supports the status quo. Hollywood films disguise under the mask of "ordinary realism" what is in fact a highly ideological view of the world. Soviet filmmakers of the 1920s, more conscious of their ideology, proceeded from a quite different stylistic supposition. They developed techniques, such as Eisenstein's montage of conflict, designed to galvanize the audience into an attitude receptive to the idea of revolution. At the level of individual style we find idiosyncratic ideological or psychological slants: the typically pessimistic slant of Alfred Hitchcock's narrators, the buoyant slant of Federico Fellini's, the puritanic and "standing tall" slant of John Ford's, the "sexual buddy" slant of Howard Hawks's, the musing, environment-sensitive slant of Michelangelo Antonioni's, the heroic nationalist slant of Leni Riefenstahl's, and so on.

Much is known about the ideological and stylistic aspects of narrator's slant. The difference between cinematic slant and cinematic filter, however, especially the marking of characters' perceptions and cognitions, is less clearly understood. Unlike literature, cinema literally shows spaces, mediated or not by a character's gaze. The unmediated camera view may be called "perceptual slant." But the logic of the story-discourse distinction argues that perceptual slant is a different narrative phenomenon from perceptual filter. If we are to sustain this cardinal distinction, if we are to recognize that film is simply one among several media that actualize narrative, we must avoid the metaphor that the camera "sees" the events and existents in the story world at such and such a distance, from such and such an angle. Rather it *presents* them at those distances and angles. In other words, perceptual slant (not filter) frames the cinematic narrator's transmission of visual and auditory imagery. Metaphorically, the fictive world is presented to the real audience "under glass," even though audiences are strongly induced to ignore that fact. The intensely realistic illusions created by cinematic technology—both photographic and acoustic—are so seductive that even sophisticated film theorists sometimes forget the theoretical partition separating the story world from its discourse and actualization.

That partition is more clearly apparent in paintings, especially narrative paintings. Paintings are so clearly surface objects that no one would think of speaking of *their* representations as "seeings." There *is* no camera to confuse the issue. Viewers do not get so engrossed in story content as to forget the surface quality of the impression: the fact that figures represented on the canvas, no matter how lifelike, are "really" daubs of pigment a few millimeters thick. Perhaps because of the absence of temporal constraints (we may take only a second to view a painting, or we may contemplate it until the museum closes), we cannot forget the painting's two-dimensionality even as we read the story out of the brush-strokes. Consider, for example, Tintoretto's *Christ at the Sea of Gallilee*: the scene represents the moment (in John 21:7) when Peter, upon seeing Christ on the shore, "did cast himself into the sea."[12] In the near left foreground Christ is represented in quarter profile, facing out to sea, his right index finger extended diagonally into deep story space; Peter's halo-encircled head is depicted at an appropriate counterangle. We interpret his gaze as locked on Christ's, and we see that he has already put one leg into the water. The interchange of looks is set at about a forty-five degree angle from the picture plane. (This is a typical cinematic technique for framing dialogue interchanges between characters.) Clearly the painterly narrator does not "see" this scene but rather presents it for *us* to see, as a registration upon a two-dimensional surface. It is the convention of classical narrative paintings that our perception necessarily occurs *on this side* of the picture plane; we are separated from the events by the transparent membrane of discourse. No viewer doubts that the story event is taking place "on the other side," in a projected story world.

The cinema frame, too, presents events and characters from a post this side of the story world; there is never any question about what is included and what excluded from our perception. (This will presumably change when cinema goes holographic.) In literature, however, framing (insofar as it exists in the reader's consciousness at all) is figurative and elastic. In even the most descriptive or "cinematic" novel, insofar as we "see" anything, it is only a sketch of what is necessary to accommodate the action. The scene (if it is imaged at all) is very fuzzy around the edges. But when we watch a film, we are rigorously limited to a "this-much," a totally discrete selection of story space represented in a rectangular frame of a certain dimension. Of course, we tend to "forget" the frame's existence as we get into the story, so powerful are the diegetic intimations of off-screen space. If we recall scenes in well-loved films, chances are we will not remember them as framed by a rectangle. Remembered films are more like remembered novels: we remember plots and characters more readily than the actual framing of scenes.

The convention is that the particular rectangle of visible material constitutes a "favored view," a selection by the implied author which the cinematic narrator is delegated to present. That selection entails a certain distance and angle, certain lighting conditions, and so on—those that maximize the story's impact. The same is true of the juxtaposition of shots. In Hitchcock's *Sabotage* (1936), for example, the opening shots juxtapose familiar views of London—Oxford Street, Big Ben and Parliament, Picadilly Circus, and so on—with a bare light bulb. After the light bulb flickers and goes off, so do the lights of the public buildings. The interpolation of the light bulb (presumably any old light bulb in London) among the shots of the buildings is to convey the notion that electric power *in general* has failed; if only the lights of the buildings went out, we might merely assume that it was closing time. Not only are the views "favored," but so are their combinations.

Functioning as an additional constraint on this convention is the further convention that the images may filter through some character's perceptual consciousness. The many ways by which perceptual filter can be effected—especially through eyeline match, shot-countershot, the 180-degree rule, voice-off or voice-over, plot logic—are well known. Through these devices, films deftly lock the audience into a character's perception. But it is important to recognize—and not often enough urged—that character's gaze and narrator's representation operate on different sides of the story-discourse partition. The character's perceptual filtration of objects and events is always additional to the camera's representations; that is, the filter occupies a space between the "naked occurrence" of the images and the audience's perception of them. The camera's slant remains in place, even when it is temporarily mediated by the character's perceptual filter.

Sometimes the cinematic narrator, through camera movement of angle or other means, seems to be communicating the story directly or unmediately, as for example in the establishing moments of a film before any character appears. The view of the Manhattan skyline in Woody Allen's *Manhattan* (1979) and the Ruritanian village in Hitchcock's *The Lady Vanishes* (1938) are shown directly, through the narrator's slant. At other times the representation of the story world is filtered through a character's perception and interest-focus; or it is filtered through one character's perceptual filter and another character's interest-focus; or it is presented from no one's angle of perception but from a character's interest-focus. These possibilities are well analyzed by Nick Browne with respect to a sequence in *Stagecoach* (1939). In the scene at the dining table at the Dry Fork coach station, one series of shots filters through the perception and interest of Lucy, a model of propriety, the pregnant wife going to Lordsburg to join her husband, a cavalry officer. But another series is not "associated with or justified spatially as the depiction of anyone's glance."[13] This *non*-glance-motivated series is no less common a phenomenon than the filtered kind (hence the inadequacy of the suture theory of film construction). As Browne points out, the specific mental dispositions of the three characters involved—Lucy, Dallas the prostitute, and

Ringo the escaped prisoner—cannot be easily keyed to the camera placements. Rather, they invoke a general *social* situation:

> The permanent and underlying fact about the mise-en-scène which justifies the fixity of camera placement is its status as a social drama of alliance and antagonism between two social roles—Lucy, an insider, a married woman and defender of custom; and Dallas, an outsider and prostitute who violates the code of the table. . . . The shots [that] might be called "objective," or perhaps "nobody's" shots, in fact refer to or are a representation of Lucy's social dominance and formal privilege. [They] show a field of vision that closely matches Lucy's *conception* of her own place in that social world: its framing corresponds to her alliance with the group and to her intention to exclude the outsiders, to deny their claim to recognition. It is in other words not exactly a description of Lucy's subjectivity but an objectification of her social self-conception. Though Lucy is visible in the frame, [the sequence] might be said, metaphorically, to embody her point of view.[14]

That "metaphorical embodiment" is what I call "interest-focus"; in fact, Browne has anticipated my use of the word: "These shots might perhaps be read as statements of the 'interests' of characters." And, as Browne is quick to suggest, interest focus, unlike strict perceptual filter, can attach to more than one character at a time. For not only is Lucy involved in and conscious of the social situation described by Browne, but so is Dallas; at stake for her is "exclusion and humiliation," which we are moved to repudiate as "unjust." Interest-focus also attaches to the Ringo Kid, who clearly feels the tension in the air. Cinema enables "us as spectators to be two places at once, where the camera is and 'with' the depicted person." In the sequence from *Stagecoach*, the viewer is several "places" at once—"with" the fictional viewer, "with" the viewed (Dallas), and even "with" onlookers (the Ringo Kid).[15]

So we see that "perceptual filter" technically codes the viewer's reconstruction of story space. "Interest-focus," on the other hand, depends on contextual signals presented by the story. The latter is often but not exclusively "social" (in Browne's sense). There is, for example, a conventional code of the camera's "following" a character, keeping him on the screen: hence Hitchcock's success in getting us to root for villains like Bruno in *Strangers on a Train* (1951). There is also the star effect: we know even before the film begins that we will spend most of our time in the interest-focus of any character played by, say, Cary Grant or Katherine Hepburn.

Conventional wisdom has it that cinema cannot convey a character's conceptual thinking with the kind of precision that it conveys perceptual filter and interest-focus. In an early book on the subject, George Bluestone wrote:

> The rendition of mental states—memory, dream, imagination—cannot be as adequately represented by film as by language. If the film has difficulty presenting streams of consciousness, it has even more difficulty presenting states of mind which are defined precisely by the absence in them of the visible world. Conceptual imaging, by definition, has no existence in space. [Thus] the film, by arranging external signs for our visual perception, or by presenting us with dialogue, can lead us to *infer* thought. But it cannot show us thought directly. It can show us characters thinking, feeling, and speaking, but it cannot show us their thoughts and feelings.[16]

In literature, simple verbs such as "think" and "remember," with the use of quotation marks and the like, can introduce thoughts as easily and exactly as "say," "tell," and "reply" introduce dialogue. In film, dialogue is not a problem (especially since the advent of sound), but the expression of thought is. There has always been considerable resistance to the use of voice-over to convey mental activity. Many filmmakers—even those who do use voice-over freely as a component of the cinematic narrator—disdain as artificial its application to characters' thoughts, considering it an overly easy solution to the problem. The same disdain does not apply to the *visualization* of conceptual thought in "mindscreen" effects. Of course, the very artificiality of the voice-over representation of characterial thought can suit certain "campy" or comic projects: Woody Allen's *Annie Hall* (1977) is a case in point.

But like all artistic limitations, the problem of conveying thought can turn into a virtue. It challenges the artist to rise above mere technical constraints. One solution is to write screenplays that maximize the power of context to imply, more or less specifically, what a character is thinking. This can make the mental content all the richer to us, since there is more for *us* to reconstruct. Another solution is to people screenplays with characters whose thoughts are *intentionally* obscure.

Here we touch upon the secret of such an artist as Antonioni. Consider the scenes in *L'Avventura* (1959) that turn on the protagonist Sandro's frustration about his career as an architect. Few words are spoken, and those in no way express this frustration, but the action is so devised and photographed that a reasonably sensitive viewer can guess what is going on in Sandro's mind. As he shows Claudia the architectural splendors of Noto from the roof of a church, Sandro explains that he has given up the active practice of architecture for the more profitable job of cost estimating. He says this with relative equanimity. But later, he becomes preoccupied and moody. Resisting Claudia's charming flirtatiousness, he takes a walk in the town piazza. He purposely ruins an architecture student's drawing of a detail of a building, denies doing so when challenged, and boasts about the number of brawls he was involved in when he was the student's age. Back at the hotel he intercepts Claudia, who has dressed and is coming to meet him, and leads her back into their room. He goes out on the balcony, restlessly puffs on a cigarette, and then throws it into the street. At this inappropriate moment he tries to force the bewildered Claudia to make love. She refuses, despite his insistence. Then they talk desultorily about the search for Anna.

Clearly, what is really bothering Sandro is neither Anna's disappearance nor Claudia's response to his erratic amatory demands. Rather, it is his sense of impotence about not working at his profession, not practicing the art which he loves and which fulfills him. He is a victim of what Antonioni called *una malattia dei sentimenti*, "a malaise of the feelings." He attempts to escape his professional frustration by using sex as an anodyne. Along with escape goes distraction, which, in Antonioni's films, is a mental gesture of escape.[17] Antonioni excels in conveying the indirections of visible behavior and imbuing them with a sense of suppressed anguish. For him, cinema's technical difficulty in depicting characters' thoughts is not a burden but the motivation to explore a uniquely human dimension of experience, an exploration that few other filmmakers have attempted.

CHAPTER 10

A New Kind of Film Adaptation:
The French Lieutenant's Woman

FILM ADAPTATIONS often face a familiar charge: that they fill in too many gaps. Here is Wolfgang Iser's view:

> Without the elements of indeterminacy, the gaps in the texts, we should not be able to use our imagination.
>
> The truth of this observation is borne out by the experience many people have on seeing, for instance, the film of a novel. While reading *Tom Jones*, they may never have had a clear conception of what the hero actually looks like, but on seeing the film, some may say, "That's not how I imagined him." The point here is that the reader of *Tom Jones* is able to visualize the hero virtually for himself, and so his imagination senses the vast number of possibilities; the moment these possibilities are narrowed down to one complete and immutable picture, the imagination is put out of action, and we feel we have somehow been cheated. This may perhaps be an over-simplification of the process, but it does illustrate plainly the vital richness of potential that arises out of the fact that the hero in the novel must be pictured and cannot be seen. With the novel the reader must use his imagination to synthesize the information given him, and so his perception is simultaneously richer and more private; with the film he is confined merely to physical perception, and so whatever he remembers of the world he had pictured is brutally cancelled out.[1]

Iser's critique of film adaptation (and, by implication, the rest of cinema as well) seems a little unreasonable. Need "imagination" be so exclusively identified with pictorial imagining or "picturing?" Are narrative gaps solely ones of picturing—in other words, are films "gapless" because visually explicit? Obviously not; as Bordwell points out, gaps occur in films not only at the general narrative level—in story ellipses—but also at the stylistic or "surface" level. Filmmakers like Antonioni purposely avoid the kind of communication that comes naturally to literary narrative—verbal clues about what characters are thinking, either directly or as refracted by dialogue. However specified his films may be at the gross visual level, they are extremely "gapped" at a more profound level, since most of his characters will not or cannot say what is really on their minds.

Iser seems to be blurring the distinction between the right to an absence of visual closure (readers "may never have had a clear conception of what the hero actually looks like") and the right to refuse to form a mental image. The sentence "the reader of *Tom Jones* is able to visualize the hero virtually for himself, and so his imagination senses the vast number of possibilities" constitutes something of a non sequitur: visualizing from words does not necessarily lead to a large number of possible visualizations. It is just as easy to interpret "That's not how I imagine him" as meaning that a given reader is so attached to a *certain* image of Tom that he or she refuses any other ("he can't possibly look like Albert Finney").

Though the visual imagination may be less stimulated by a film than by a novel, the conceptual imagination may be very much stimulated by, say, a face filled with emotion that goes unexplained by dialogue or diegetic context. In a way, the challenge is greater, and our capacity to interpret faces is not innately up to our capacity to image from words. Film has just as much room for artistic gapping—though it is an artistry of its own. In some cases, the film is better suited to a subject than the novel that inspired it.[2]

Still, good film adaptations of good novels are not a plentiful commodity, for reasons that are of narratological interest. The central problem for film adapters is to transform narrative features that come easily to language but hard to a medium that operates in "real time" and whose natural focus is the surface appearance of things—hence film's traditional difficulties with temporal and spatial summaries, abstract narratorial commentary, representations of the thinking and feeling of characters, and so on.[3] Though such aspects of narration in cinema can be introduced through a certain artifice—

for example, through the voice-over convention—historically, the best filmmakers have preferred purely visual solutions. Even films that use voice-over narration generally do so in an intermittent rather than a sustained way. Films prefer to rely on the audience's ability to infer things that a literary narrator might put explicitly into words. But like most general truisms, this one is simplistic. It does not take into account the attempts to "cross over": for example, the self-imposed camera-eye restrictions of a Hemingway on the one hand, or the "novelistic" *bricolage* of Jean-Luc Godard on the other. What a medium can "do" narratively depends very much on what its creator wants it to do, on the genre that he works in, on the kinds of conventions she can persuade her audience to accept, and so on. Any insistence that the visual is king can be sustained only by excluding from the canon some of cinema's most brilliant works.

A lot of ink has been spilled in recent years on the film adaptations of novels.[4] But too much of the discussion has centered on questions of story content, with particular respect to "fidelity," as if the source novel were some sacrosanct object whose letter as well as spirit the film had to follow. This approach often leads to an unproductive prescriptivism that finds the film inadequate because it does not "read" like the novel. (It has also given rise to "faithful" but empty adaptations, such as the Jack Clayton–Francis Ford Coppola version of *The Great Gatsby* in 1974.) The theoretical nature of adaptation is rarely addressed. Critics generally fail to distinguish between inadequacies deriving from the medium as such and those deriving from the artistic infelicities of specific filmmakers. Obviously, film cannot reproduce many of the pleasures of reading novels, but it can produce other experiences of parallel value. More sophisticated critics treat novel and film as separate, if analogous, narrative experiences, just as they do the histories of Plutarch and the plays of Shakespeare.

This chapter, in any case, is concerned not with fidelity but with the different solutions that novels and films prefer for common narrative problems—problems of "service" among text-types, narrative discourse, filter and slant, and the like. There are many ways for a filmmaker to adapt a novel, and it is useful to study them all. But I limit my discussion to only one question, though in many ways the most challenging one. How do intelligent film adaptations grapple with the overtly prominent narrator, the expositor, describer, investigator of characters' states of mind, commentator, philosophizer? It is easier to base a film on a novel that is already covertly narrated, totally or predominantly "shown" by a camera eye. The greater challenge is presented by novels with talkative, expatiating narrators; by the same token, these offer opportunities for more creative cinema. By examining even a single imaginative adaptation, we can learn something useful about the expressive possibilities of the two media, at least at the present moment in film history.

To preserve the "sound" of a prominent narrator's "voice," film's most obvious option is to replicate it, to make it literally audible. Excellent adaptations have been made using voice-over narration— some memorable ones are *Tom Jones* (1963), *Lolita* (1962), *A Clockwork Orange* (1971), *The Diary of a Country Priest* (1950), *Rashomon* 1950), *Apocalypse Now* (1979), *Sophie's Choice* (1982), *Kiss of the Spider Woman* (1985). In a pioneering article on the subject, Martin Battestin shows in detail how the film version of *Tom Jones* combines an "authorial" voice-over with "old-fashioned" movie devices (editorial wipes in various geometric forms, accelerated motion, and the like) to create an effect analogous to that of the novel's "old-fashioned" narration. Battestin argues that "analogy is the key" to good adaptation, and his is certainly a more enlightened view than that held by the fidelity mongers.[5]

The question of analogy is of considerable interest to a narratology concerned with the similarities and differences of narrative media. Since voice-over has been studied in considerable detail—most recently and efficaciously by Sarah Kozloff[6]—I will say nothing more about it here. Nor shall I take up purely visual ways of conveying the mental experiences of characters. These, too, have been well-studied, in the effect dubbed "mindscreen" by Bruce Kawin—a technique featured in *8 1/2* (1963), *Wild Strawberries* (1957), *Annie Hall* (1977), and other films.[7] I turn, rather, to an innovative solution to the problem of communicating the overt narration of a novel, the solution used in the film version of *The French Lieutenant's Woman* (1981), written by Harold Pinter and directed by Karel Reisz.[8] My discussion of this film does not argue the superiority of its particular technique of adaptation to those used by other films, nor do I propose it as a model. I discuss it simply as one particularly clever way among others through which the medium can accommodate problems of narrative transference. Some of the acclaim showered on the film was prompted by its formal sophistication. It is the kind of film that has a serious practical impact on film history, since it has educated the audience to new possibilities of narrative innovation.

First, let us consider what the film had to deal with. The narrative structure of the novel by John Fowles is at once highly traditional and provocatively postmodernist or "self-conscious."[9] Like the Victorian forebears it parodies, it is a wondrously "loose and baggy monster." Its narrator is flamboyantly voluble, richly endowed with powers to summarize, enter characters' minds, describe people and places, interpret, judge, generalize (often quite gratuitously), draw abstract conclusions, discuss what might have happened but didn't, meditate upon the nature of novels in a "self-conscious" way—and so on. This kind of narration is obviously more difficult for a film to emulate than that of such homodiegetic novels as Stefan Zweig's *Letter from an Unknown Woman* (1932).

The film version makes no attempt, through voice-over or other means, to replicate heterodiegetic narration. It goes an entirely different route, relying on a special kind of implication. But like the novel, it "self-consciously" addresses the question of its own narrative processes. It proposes a not unfamiliar analogy: just as the self-conscious literary narrator may comment on his own narrative techniques, the self-conscious cinematic narrator may show not only the movie being made but the process of making that movie. The novel's self-consciousness climaxes in the double ending, an ending—the narrator argues—made inevitable by the Darwinian world of chance mutation.[10] The film's self-consciousness, on the other hand, rests on the fact that the medium permits a given signifier—an actor—to signify more than one character. Obviously, that cannot happen in literature, which is made of words, not actors; although Borges's narrator can *assert* that there were two Don Quixotes, identical in every respect, that has to be demonstrated verbally, its oddness literally spelled out. But the use of a real British actor, Jeremy Irons, to represent ("stand for, signify") a fictional British actor named Mike, who in turn plays the Victorian gentleman Charles, is literally possible in cinema (and theater). This power enables the film to deal self-consciously with the actor's dilemma: falling in love not with the actress but with the character the actress is playing.

Because of temporal and other constraints, of course, film versions often alter some of the intent and overall meaning of the novels they are based on. Let me briefly describe the differences between the two versions of *The French Lieutenant's Woman*. Actually, these have not been sufficiently attended to by critics and reviewers. Some of the correspondences they have attributed to the adaptation are simplistic and even inaccurate; for example, it is not true,—as Jay Boyum asserts—that "the book is essentially a novel within a novel" and therefore readily translated to the screen as a movie within a movie.[11] The novel is a narrative framed by the commentary of the narrator, a commentary that is itself not narrative but descriptive and expository-argumentative.[12]

The novel concerns the struggles of a young English gentleman, Charles Smithson, to surmount the smugness and insularity of the Victorian Age. He is led to do so through the love of Sarah Woodruff, a woman who, the narrator profusely assures us, lives far ahead of her time. But whether Charles can lift himself by his bootstraps sufficiently to meet her demands is so problematic that the novel offers two endings, and in only one does he manage to do so.

A large part of the novel's commentary is devoted to the historical meaning and implications of Charles's effort to modernize his thinking. The focus is on Victorian history; our own era is brought in only to shed more light on the nineteenth century. The film, on the other hand, problematizes *both* eras, at least with respect to amatory attitudes. Instead of a voluble narrator, the film offers a counterpart story of modern love, the romance of the two actors who play the novel's protagonists in a projected screen version of *The French Lieutenant's Woman*.

The novel is unimaginable without the wide-ranging narrator's commentary. Since Charles himself is largely unconscious of his historical situation, the narrator must be there to explain it to us in the fullest possible detail. The narrator is endowed not only with total knowledge of the mid-Victorian scene but also with the "foresight" afforded by his temporal vantage in the year 1967, exactly one hundred years after the date of the story.

Charles is totally and bewilderingly absorbed by his love for Sarah Woodruff. Sarah is the "French lieutenant's woman," notorious in Lyme Regis for her reputed seduction and abandonment by a French naval officer. Actually, the seduction never occurred; she uses the story as a way of asserting her difference from the rest of her community and, indeed, her era. Though Sarah's is the one consciousness that the novel does not generally enter—the narrator proclaiming his own uncertainty of her psyche and motives—she is portrayed as a kind of evolutionary mutant, a woman far ahead of her time who escapes the stereotypes of Victorian morality by asserting her rights to physical love, profession, and equality with men. She is a mystery to Charles, but despite the narrator's protestations of his own inability to explain her, she is rendered as a relatively lucid object. He analyzes her, this way and that, through the explanatory microscope of a hundred years of intellectual history. For example, to explain her "uncanny . . . ability to classify other people's worth," he says that it was "as if, jumping a century, she was born with a computer in her heart." But to Charles she is a sphinx, and the price he pays for her is, by his standards, enormous. In dropping his conventionally submissive fiancée, Ernestina, he faces the worst punishment imaginable to a Victorian upper-class male: to "forfeit . . . the right to be considered a gentleman."[13] It is one thing to be a gentleman scientist; it is quite another to have the important half of that appellation ripped away by public scandal.

To make things worse, Sarah disappears, and Charles does not see her again for two years. She turns up at the house of Dante Gabriel Rossetti, as model, protegée of the Pre-Raphaelite group, and mother to boot. The novel offers two possible endings between which the narrator refuses to choose. In the first, Charles learns that the child is his own; he accepts both mother and daughter, and they live happily ever after. In the second, Charles is so furious that he does not notice the child and rejects Sarah's invitation to remain a Platonic friend. Though in despair, he will not kill himself, the narrator assures us, because experience is beginning to provide him with the first "atom of faith" in himself. Charles has experienced a kind of existentialist salvation, which is speeding up his own evolution.

The novel parades these events in a leisurely way, ornamenting them with extensive and vigorously intrusive commentary on the Victorian age and its differences from our own. The narrator is obsessed with history; even the date, 1867, was chosen because it was the year of the publication of the first volume of Marx's *Kapital*, of the Second Reform Bill, and of John Stuart Mill's campaign for the emancipation of women.[14] The narrator comments endlessly on the political, economic, scientific, social, linguistic, and even sartorial aspects of Victorian life. Each chapter begins with an epigraph from a contemporary account, not only from famous writers—Thomas Hardy, Alfred Tennyson, Jane Austen, Matthew Arnold, Lewis Carroll, John Henry Newman, A. H. Clough, Leslie Stephens, G. M. Young, Charles Darwin, and Karl Marx—but also from such pedestrian documents as the *Report from the Mining Districts*, the *City Medical Report*, the report of the Children's Employment Commission, even an ordinary citizen's letter to the *Times*. These quotations and attendant commentary provide a panoramic contrast between the Victorian way of looking at life and our own; love is an important but by no means the only sector of the panorama.

It almost seems at times that the story is only a pretext for the commentary, that the narrative has come to subserve the argument. The narrator acknowledges as much. Among other self-consciousnesses is that of the possible subversion of one text-type by another:

> Perhaps I am trying to pass off a concealed book of essays on you. Instead of chapter headings, perhaps I should have written "On the Horizontality of Existence," "The Illusions of Progress," "The History of the Novel Form," "The Aetiology of Freedom," "Some Forgotten Aspects of the Victorian Age" . . . what you will.[15]

The narrator is very much concerned with the "evolutionary leap," which is the central clue to the nature of Sarah's "mystery." As a twentieth-century Darwinian, he understands that Sarah's "difference" is a product not of hysteria but of biological development—hence the quotation from the biologist Martin Gardner which begins the last chapter: "Evolution is simply the process by which chance (the random mutations in the nucleic acid helix caused by natural radiation) cooperates with natural law to create living forms better and better adapted to survive." Just so, we are led to infer, it was chance chromosomal distribution that made Sarah rebel against straitlaced Victorian notions of woman's place, urged her to strike out on her own, and cast her up on the wave of the future. Presumably, the same chromosomal randomness selects men who can cope with this new female sense of independence and separate purpose, for only such men will be attractive as mates to such women. The narrator argues: "There is no intervening god . . . only life, as we have, within our hazard-given abilities, made it ourselves, life as Marx defined it—*the actions of men* (and of women) *in pursuit of their ends.*"[16] The narrator does not identify sentimentally with Charles's unhappy fate in the second ending but expresses a more general optimism about the development of love relationships. If Charles is not yet sufficiently evolved to understand and accept a Sarah breathtakingly ahead of her times, some more advanced fellow can.

In contrast, the film offers merely anecdotal visual citations of Victorian history: miserable working conditions (shots of women laborers flooding out of hideous factories); the prevalence of prostitution (the scene in Haymarket); Victorian medical practice (Dr. Grogan, Lyme's general practitioner, delivering a baby in an asylum). Basically, the film's only real theme is love—Victorian versus modern. And even that undergoes a sea change. The novel's narrator examines Victorian love clinically, as one among other aspects of the history of the era. The elaboration is expository and comparative; he explains erotic states of mind that moderns might find incomprehensible. The film, on the other hand, immerses the viewer in the experience of Victorian love in a way calculated to seem familiar, for all its Gothic trappings[17]—empathy is always the cinema's long suit.

The need to fix as clearly as possible its contrast with modern Eros drives the Victorian half of the film to something of an extreme. Not only is the novel's ambiguous double ending given up, but the film's final vignette of Sarah and Charles rowing off into a peaceful and soul-satisfying future on a quiet lake is far more romantic—one is tempted to say more willfully clichéd—than even the "happy" ending of the novel. The filmmaker was obviously seeking maximal dramatic contrast with the modern lover's plight, trapped by the rock music, the screeching acceleration of Anna's car, and his fantasies of Sarah-in-Anna's-body. The film ends implying that the hero cannot hope to recapture the solid security of Victorian love—clearly a simplification of the complexities of the novel's erotic theme.

The film projects an implied reader whose tie is more fundamentally with the "human" Victorian characters than with the modern actors—"human" in quotation marks because what is involved, of course, is simply the *convention* of romantic love as metonymy for "humanity." It is this convention that gives meaning to the first exchange of gazes between Charles and Sarah on the Cobb. Nothing more need be said. The novel, however, insists on saying more, on explaining these stares in a way that goes far beyond the sentimental convention of "love at first sight":

She turned to look at him—or as it seemed to Charles, through him. It was not so much what was positively in that face which remained with him after that first meeting, but all that was not as he had expected; for theirs was an age when the favored feminine look was the demure, the obedient, the shy. Charles felt immediately as if he had trespassed; as if the Cobb belonged to that face, and not to the Ancient Borough of Lyme. It was not a pretty face, like Ernestina's. It was certainly not a beautiful face, by any period's standard or taste. But it was an unforgettable face, and a tragic face. Its sorrow welled out of it as purely, naturally and unstoppably as water out of a woodland spring. There was no artifice there, no hypocrisy, no hysteria, no mask; and above all, no sign of madness. The madness was in the empty sea, the empty horizon, the lack of reason for such sorrow; as if the spring was natural in itself, but unnatural in welling from a desert.[18]

Obviously, this extended entry into a character's mind cannot be accommodated by simple eyeline matches. Meryl Streep and Jeremy Irons are excellent players, and they get a great deal of purport into their gazes. But there is no way that they or any other actors could guarantee, by facial expression alone, the nuances of such a passage. The filmmaker has the dilemma of choosing between a mute scene, which provokes a stereotypic response, and some unduly artificial device such as voice-over. In this case, he chooses the former. Only later, and by other means, does he convey mental entries, interpretations, and commentary.

Whereas the novel's implied author undertakes to recover the reality behind our clichéd attitudes of the "Victorian," showing us how exotic a time it was, the film, relying on what we share (or think we share) with the Victorians, represents modern life as the less comprehensible. These diverging intentions result in important changes in plot and theme and, above all, character. For example, unlike the novel, in which it is Sarah who is enigmatic, the film problematizes the modern actress, Anna. Consider the crucial event of both versions, the disappearance of Sarah. In the novel she vanishes and is rediscovered only by chance. She makes no attempt to reestablish her relationship with Charles; she is quite content to remain unmarried. Though she acknowledges that she threw herself at Charles in Lyme and Exeter and that there had been "a madness" in her at that time, she stoutly avers that she was "right to destroy what had begun between us."[19] In the film, however, it is she who notifies Charles's detectives, once she feels that she has recovered from her "illness." She is contrite and begs Charles's forgiveness. The film Sarah is simpler, more predictable, more sentimentally conceived. We are asked to believe that she simply went off for a long time to make herself a better mate for Charles. She is made "purer," the better to establish a pointed contrast with Anna, her modern counterpart.[20]

There are other important differences between the two works, but let us turn to what they have in common to illustrate the film's unique solutions to the novel's discursive challenges. Of course, what was already straightforwardly scenic in the novel could easily be transferred to film: for example, the lovers' fourth meeting (Chapters 20–21) at which Charles hears Sarah's account of her affair with the French lieutenant. As in most of the film, there are few changes in the dialogue; Sarah narrates her adventure very much in the terms she uses in the novel. But the inner views require different treatment. In the novel, the narrator is constantly into and out of Charles's mind, interpreting and explaining feelings that Charles could hardly articulate, let alone confess to, and presenting the complexity of his motives to a degree that the film wisely makes no effort to match. Charles's conscious intention is to be sympathetic and helpful (as his position as an English gentleman requires) but also distant, "a little regal with this strange supplicant at his feet." He fancies himself Dr. Grogan's surrogate, offering a "talking cure" to the poor woman's hysteria. Of course, even as Charles assures himself about his intentions, the narrator keeps us aware of the extent to which he falls under her allure.

Though it primarily tells the event through Charles's filter, the novel also informs us of what Charles does *not* think. When Sarah observes that once begun, the path she had descended with Varguennes was "difficult to reascend," the narrator notes: "That might have been a warning to Charles; but he was too absorbed in her story to think of his own." The climax of the scene is reached when Sarah claims that her "fall" has given her a freedom unknown to the middle-class housewife. The narrator conveys Charles's confused response—he feels touched, then disturbed, experiencing a glimpse of "the dark shadows where he might have enjoyed it himself."[21]

The film makes no attempt to interpret Charles's intricate state of mind, offers nothing to correspond, for example, to the novel's whimsical metaphor of the "little spray of milkwort from the bank beside [Sarah], blue flowers like microscopic cherubs' genitals."[22] Meryl Streep could, of course, have plucked a spray of milkwort, but its colorful symbolism would have been lost on anyone who hadn't read the novel. A quick cut to figurative cherubs' genitals would have been a nice metaphoric touch, à la Eisenstein, but few in the audience would have gotten the point. It is hard to imagine any straightforward dramatic playing of the scene that could capture the narrator's many ludic, godlike observations.

The interchange between Charles' thoughts and the narrator's commentary is extremely fluid. The narrator is at Charles's elbow to explain, with the certainty of historical generalization, how he can entertain what strike us as mutually contradictory feelings:

Such a sudden shift of sexual key is impossible today. A man and a woman are no sooner in any but the most casual contact than they consider the possibility of a physical relationship. We consider such frankness about the real drives of human behavior healthy, but in Charles's time private minds did not admit the desires banned by the public mind; and when the consciousness was sprung on by these lurking tigers it was ludicrously unprepared.[23]

The narrator readily generalizes outward from the fiction to the real Victorian and later eras; he takes deep pleasure in what, to a narrow Lubbockian view, would seem diegetic indulgence.[24] For better or worse, he is not satisfied with explaining Charles' behavior under a single general topic. Without missing a beat, he proceeds to another short generalizing essay, this time on the Victorian fondness for small closed spaces. Ruminations on claustrophilic architecture lead in turn to speculations on painting.[25]

The film version of this scene makes no effort to comment on the times. It finds no acceptable way to expatiate on Victorian painting or architecture, or on the Victorian refusal to entertain—even in the privacy of one's own mind—what society has declared unspeakable. But it does convey a great deal about the personal, human elements of the situation—mostly by implication—through details of acting, composition, camera movements, editing, and music. What it shows is simpler and less determinate (which is not to say less precise) than what the novel tells us. Charles's apprehension is conveyed mostly by the actor's facial expression and posture, the set, and a distinctive camera movement. In the novel, Sarah introduces Charles to her hideaway and offers him her usual perch, a "great flat-topped block of flint . . . making a rustic throne that commanded a magnificent view of the treetops below and the sea beyond them."[26] In the film, however, there is no royal seat and nothing regal about his posture: he sits uncomfortably cross-legged on the ground at some distance behind Sarah, a most reluctant confessor. To highlight his sense of growing emotional entrapment, the film sets the scene among trees with long lateral boughs. Their slender lines intersect the couple's bodies, suggesting the threads of a spider's web. The camera conspires to heighten the effect: it tracks slowly around in a circle, making the boughs seem to form ties between the couple. Though neither Sarah nor Charles moves, the camera reduces the distance between them by lining them up, Charles directly behind Sarah. The visual effect is to imply something like "Charles felt himself increasingly entangled in Sarah's affairs." "Entanglement" may be a less intricate feeling than those so elaborately conveyed by the novel—a witch's brew of superiority, protectiveness, envy, and "unconscious" lust—but it *is* a feeling, one crucial to the plot, and one effected totally by strictly cinematic means.

The central problem facing this adaptation was not how to render the novel's plot details. Its dialogue is largely copied, and the actors do roughly what the characters in the novel do. Rather, the challenge was to capture the narrator's commentary, commentary that is not only elaborate but modern in its slant. Though not averse to the idea of self-conscious metanarrative, the film does not turn the twentieth-century narrator into a character—as the novel briefly does, bizarrely, through the mysterious man with the "massively bearded face" who makes his appearance in Charles's railroad carriage (chapter 55). Rather, the film introduces a modern framing story that Fowles himself found a "brilliant metaphor" for the original.[27] The modern story concerns the behind-the-scenes affair between the actors, Mike and Anna, who play the roles of Charles and Sarah. But since each story comments on the other, in the thematic sense, at least, it is difficult to know which is framing which. It is wrong, I think, to equate the modern story with the second ending of the novel, as Susanna Barber and Richard Messer do, conjecturing that "like Charles, Mike feels the pain of a kind of rebirth."[28] And the relation between the stories needs to be more precisely stated than by referring vaguely, as Boyum does, to some kind of "double vision."[29]

There is more contrast than similarity between the film's two stories. In the final chapters of the novel, the issues are drawn clearly: Sarah loves her work with the Pre-Raphaelite Brotherhood; she is "not to be understood," even by herself; and her intellectual and spiritual development has led her to conclude that she cannot love Charles, or anyone else, as a wife should."[30] But in the film, Anna's motives seem to be kept totally obscure. Despite muttering David's name in her sleep (to Mike's discomfiture), her relationship with her French lover seems quite passionless. She says she envies Sonia, Mike's wife, but when asked why, she mumbles something banal about Sonia's gardening ability. And her final "escape" from Mike is wrapped in mystery. For his part, Mike is no Charles: he does not throw away his present life, reject his family, and run after Anna.

No, the modern story is not a replay of the Victorian. Rather, it attempts to dramatize the novel's *commentary*, though not by simply assigning the narrator's lines to one of the characters. That would have been the Jamesian solution, utilizing the modern actors as *ficelles*. (On only one occasion does a character, Anna, comment on the Victorian situation, and her observation is immediately undercut by Mike's crude jest about the "two point four fucks a week" enjoyed by the Victorian gentleman.)[31] The commentary, rather, is implicit: it inheres in the juxtaposition of the two stories, the acted-out contrasts between Victorian and modern attitudes toward Eros. These differences are left to the audience to infer. The inferences we draw may be less specified than what we learn from the explicit pronouncements of the novel, but they are certainly viable enough. The film makes us believe that Victorian love has as much to tell us about modern love as vice versa.

To put the matter in more text-theoretical terms: where the novel's commentary explicitly conveys exposition and argument at the service of the narrative, the film implies commentary through the very invention of the juxtaposed modern story. The basic implementing technique here is "crosscutting" (Christian Metz's "alternate syntagm" or "alternate montage"),[32] a venerable editing technique already perfected by D. W. Griffith. A more elaborate name is "imbricated montage," the separate but interspersed assemblage of shots back and forth between two different strands of a story which ultimately get tied together.[33]

What makes the intercutting in *The French Lieutenant's Woman* unusual is that the modern story is not just one component or strand of a total story. The interrelations between the two are much more complex. At one level, the modern story serves as a surrogate discourse of the Victorian story, a dramatized alternative to more directly vocal narration. At another level, the modern story is autonomous; it goes beyond framing and even commenting on the Victorian story to present, in its own right and with seemingly "irrelevant" details, a certain modern state of affairs. This autonomy is hard to recognize in the early part of the film, where the focus remains persistently on the Victorian tale, and the modern sequences are brief and elliptical, each usually consisting of a single shot. It takes us a while to understand why we should be concerned about the actors playing the Victorian characters. Only toward the end of the film does their drama begin to approximate and even outweigh that of the Victorians, the outcome of which becomes fairly predictable once Charles learns Sarah's whereabouts. The last three sequences of the modern story, on the other hand, are particularly complex, incorporating a large number of diverse shots.

Since the modern story unfolds in so fragmentary and unexpected a manner, it is useful to consider in detail how it intersects, point for point, thematically and formally, with the Victorian story, which it ultimately displaces as the focus of dramatic attention. As we perform this recuperation, we will note seven additional sequences proposed by the screenplay but not used in the film (I shall put the deletions in brackets).

1. The modern story opens in Anna's hotel room; she and Mike have spent the night together, and he answers her makeup call. They joke about how the whole company will now know they are lovers and how that makes her a "whore." [Deleted: Anna sighs with relief as her dresser helps her out of a Victorian corset.]

2. In Mike's bedroom, Anna reads about the number of prostitutes in London; Mike jokingly calculates the Victorian gentleman's average visits; Anna laughs at his statistics. [Deleted: Mike gets into a helicopter that flies over the Undercliff; aerial shots of the Undercliff,

the wild coastal area near Lyme Regis where Charles and Sarah hold their trysts.[34] [Delayed to sequence 11: Anna takes off her wig and stares at herself in the mirror.] [Deleted: In an illuminating—perhaps too illuminating—sequence in Anna's dressing trailer, the couple joke about the scene they have just played: Charles's accidental meeting with Sarah on the Undercliff and his request to stroll with her, a request she refuses in a manner at once mysterious and coquettish. Mike says he enjoyed it and asks Anna whether she found him "sympathetic." She answers "Mmn. Definitely." Mike responds, "I don't mean me. I mean him . . . you swished your skirt—very provocative. Did you mean it?" Anna says, "Well, it worked. Didn't it?" This scene would have constituted the first evidence that Mike is falling seriously for *Sarah*—not Anna, but the character she plays— making Anna's "Well, it worked. Didn't it?" a double entendre that perhaps even she is unaware of.]

3. In a kind of garden shed (perhaps to parody the conservatory in which Charles proposes to Ernestina), Mike and Anna, in modern clothes, rehearse the scene that corresponds to the novel's second meeting of Charles and Sarah on the Undercliff (chapter 16). Sarah is supposed to slip and Charles to catch her; Anna does it poorly at first, making Mike visibly edgy. The second time she finds the right note, and in one of the film's most striking moments Mike stares at her as if she suddenly has *become* Sarah, right before his eyes. His look is so intense that it seems to register his own astonishment as much as Charles's participation in the fictional scene. To emphasize Anna's transformation and Mike's response, the cinematic narrator cuts, in midshot, to the "real" Victorian scene: it is Anna who begins the fall, but Sarah, in red wig and Victorian clothes, who ends it, slipping not to the floor of the garden shed but to the ground of the Undercliff. This shot floats the seed, in a purely visual way, of what the screenplay tried to convey verbally in the preceding deleted sequence— "Did you mean it?"

4. As Mike stands moodily smoking at the window of his hotel room, we suddenly hear for the first time in the *modern* story Sarah's haunting musical theme (scored for string quartet, especially cello), which has been associated with her from the very opening shot.[35] This musical "bleedover" is the first of several that suggest, commentatively, Mike's infatuation with a woman of the previous century. In the diegetic space of the modern story, the theme tells us with

relative precision that Mike is more in love with the character than with the actress who plays her, that the character is *replacing* the actress. When he sees Anna's bare foot sticking out of the dark blanket and white sheet—resembling Sarah's ankle under her black dress and white petticoat—he tenderly tucks it back under the cover. In the context of what we have seen of both men, tenderness is an emotion more characteristic of Charles than of Mike. In her sleep, Anna murmurs the name of David, her French lover. Mike says, "It's not David. It's Mike." Both his anachronistic love and its ultimate disappointment are now clearly foreshadowed.

5. Mike and Anna lie on the beach. Mike asks Anna why she is sad. She denies that she is. [This is all that the film preserves of a three-shot sequence in the screenplay: in the first, Anna walks up to Mike, who has been lying on the beach, and tells him she has had a wonderful walk; in the third, Mike watches Anna, who lies with her eyes closed. In both the actual and the proposed version, Anna's silence about her feelings is the first clear sign of her opacity as a character and of the film's intention to make her, rather than Sarah, the figure of mystery. She could be sad for any number of reasons: because she empathizes with Charles's ostensible rejection of Sarah, because she is facing a hard choice about Mike, because her personal life is a mess—or what?]

6. Anna is through shooting; in modern clothes, she is leaving for London. Mike, still in Victorian dress, is morose; he asks to see her in London. She tells him that that would be difficult. When he insists, she reluctantly agrees. [Deleted: Slightly later in a London bar, Mike tells Anna he has been dying for her. She says that the world in London "isn't real." When he asks her if David "isn't real," she avoids answering, saying she can't wait to be in Exeter. Mike smilingly promises to "have her" in Exeter. Perhaps this scene was dropped because it takes us too much into Anna's mind. In the final version, her motives and decisions are kept largely obscure; we are lodged almost totally in Mike's interest-focus.]

7. Mike sees Anna off at the train station and says, laughingly, "I'm losing you." He asks her to stay, telling her she's a free woman. She responds, "Yes. I am." He says he's going mad. She says, "No you're not." He says he's dying for her. She answers that he just had her, in Exeter.

8. David and Anna sit in their hotel room. He calls and hangs up

when David answers. It is clear that David is suspicious. Cut to Mike's house: Sonia, his wife, asks him if he's all right. Mike suggests inviting some of the cast for a party. He calls the hotel again and asks David if they both will come to the party. David says, drily, "I give you Anna" [!] and hands the phone to her. She accepts the invitation as Mike whispers that he loves her. She responds diffidently so that David cannot infer what is being said. [Deleted: David asks Anna what has been decided about the film's ending; Anna answers that *she* has decided she wants "to play it exactly as it's written." David wonders if that won't lead to a fight. Anna responds grimly, "I hope not." The implication is that she has decided to end her affair with Mike. The shot was doubtless cut for the reason discussed above, that her explicit act of "choosing" undermines some of the ambiguity of her final disappearance.]

9. This sequence occurs in three brief parts: Anna enters a costumer's shop in a London mews; she poses in front of a mirror with the white dress designed for the Windermere sequence, saying "I'm going to like her in this"; she then gets back into the studio car and drives off.

10. A long sequence depicting the party at Mike's house cuts between the intrigue of Mike and Anna's affair and vignettes of the various supporting actors, now out of character and wearing modern clothes. The actress playing Mrs. Poulteney, a mild, pleasant woman, admires Mike's child; when David asks Mike if the film concludes with the happy or unhappy ending, Mike says "We're going for the first ending—I mean the second ending"; Anna expresses her envy for Sonia's garden; "Sam" plays Bach on the piano; and so on. Throughout the sequence Mike tries to get Anna alone; he complains ("This is pure bloody hell") and tells her they must talk "properly" in Windermere. Anna asks what there is to say, but agrees.

11. The film ends with a cast party on the Windermere set. The sound track is dominated by rock music, and the scene is visually chaotic. The camera whirls around as members of the cast dance—"Dr. Grogan" (rather drunkenly), "Mrs. Poulteney," "Sam," "Mrs. Fairley," "Montague," and others. Mike signals to Anna to meet him in the house. As she passes through her dressing room, she stares at herself in the mirror. Sarah's red wig sits next to her on a block. Mike bumps into "Ernestina" on his way to meet Anna; he kisses her perfunctorily, but she clings to him; he gives her an affectionate but

hurried pat and rushes off; she walks sadly away. Reaching Anna's dressing room, Mike fondles the red wig for a moment, then goes into the room in which the last scene of the Victorian film was played. It is empty. Sarah's theme music suddenly replaces the rock band on the sound track. Mike hears a car pulling away. He rushes to the window. The rock music returns. He shouts out "Sarah!" in the definitive corroboration of his obsession.

These eleven sequences constitute a complete account of the film's modern story except for one detail that occurs "self-consciously" as the jewel in its crown (though it apparently was not planned in the screenplay). It entails a crucial "violation" of the integrity of the Victorian story, a slippage from the embedded into the embedding story. It occurs in the Windermere scene, at the moment when Charles accuses Sarah of having ruined his life and of taking pleasure in doing so (here the film's dialogue replicates the novel's). She reaches out in apology. Charles is supposed to reject her, to push her away. He does so with far more energy than necessary.[36] In fact, he knocks her down—so hard that she bumps her head resoundingly on the floor. As she struggles groggily to get up, Charles does a strange thing: his face softens with concern and he seems to ask her with his eyes whether she is all right; she smiles, wanly, that she is—an exchange clearly inconsonant with the (Victorian) action that is supposed to be taking place. Then the scene resumes as "written."

How do we interpret his unwonted violence, his mute checking to see if she is all right, and her equally out-of-character reassuring smile? It can only be, I think, that the tensions of the modern story, for the first and only time, have bled through into the *visuals* of the film-within-the-film. Elsewhere, the modern and Victorian stories are kept scrupulously separate at the visual level (though at the auditory level both "real" and commentative sounds frequently overlap the two stories: in anticipation of the crosscuts, telephones ring, helicopters buzz, trains roar to tell us we are about to resume the modern story). This is the unique visual transgression: although dressed and performing as Charles, Mike's frustration about Anna's "failure" to be Sarah is so great that his anger gets the better of him, and he falls out of character. His passion for Sarah—and his anger with Anna for not *being* Sarah—makes him overdo the scene. Then, realizing that Anna might be seriously hurt, he expresses his apprehension, which is relieved only when she nods and smiles.

Mike wants to play the twentieth-century game by nineteenth-century rules. By falling in love with a nineteenth-century fictional character, he has experienced a charge of nineteenth-century passion. The passion hardly seems to mark an evolutionary leap forward. The film is less sanguine than the novel about the progress of evolution in the emotional sphere.

There are numerous films whose subject is the making of a film: *8 1/2* (1963), *Day for Night* (1973), and *Singin' in the Rain* (1952) come immediately to mind. But *The French Lieutenant's Woman* differs from these in that its concern is not the problem of creativity or the labor of the director but the impact of the "framed" film on the actors. Nor is the film a *mise-en-abyme*: the modern story is not a miniature replica of the Victorian story.[37] On the contrary, its subject is the difference between the two worlds as seen from the *modern* perspective. Only a concern with modern Eros would explain the film's extended preoccupation with Mike's anguish. Mike has fallen anachronistically in love with a fictional Victorian character. Like Pygmalion, he tries to bring his beloved to life, in Anna, but for her own good reasons— though reasons we shall never know—Anna chooses not to play Galatea. This impossible search for a fictional woman out of a bygone era is not a subject proposed by the novel, which handles the modern repercussions of Victorian thought only in the expository-argumentative mode. The film's theme is the plight of the modern actor (perhaps as synecdoche for the modern artist or thoughtful person in general) who gets a taste, if only vicariously, of a better, older way of loving and, hence, of living. Unfortunately for him, the world that made that kind of loving possible no longer exists. The character and the actor thus provide reverse images: just as Charles longs for a woman of the future, Mike longs for a woman of the past. It is in this way that the film reflects something of the novel's commentary on Victorian mores but also commentary on our own.

The cinematography, *mise-en-scène*, editing, and other aspects of the production cleverly underline Mike's dilemma by contrasting the visual qualities of Victorian and modern life. For example, the visuals of the modern story, *Mike's* visuals, especially at the end, seem at once frenzied and banal. Unlike the elegant compositions and lighting of the Victorian portion[38]—the greenhouse proposal, the Undercliff, the bucolic tryst in the ruined barn, the love chamber in Exeter—the modern sequences look flat, mundane, fortuitous.[39] The *mise-en-scènes* showing Anna getting into and out of cars in London, the garden party at Mike's, Anna's hotel room, the cast party at Windermere—all look scattered and slapdash. Unlike the characters they play, the modern actors are randomly strewn about, their movements aimless. Something precious, the film implies, has been lost in our modern haste and casualness. In both editing and movement within the frame, the slow pace of Victorian life is captured and contrasted with the hectic scurrying about, the tensions and uncertainties and ambivalences of modern London.

The effect is achieved with particular brilliance in the editing back and forth between the two stories. Each modern intrusion comes at a moment in the Victorian story with which it has a peculiar and often ironic connection. Charles's absurdly chaste proposal to Ernestina is "interrupted" by the raucous telephone call that awakens the illicit modern lovers. Anna's sadness on the beach seems provoked by the scene she has just played, in which Charles, shocked at his own feeling of lust at the sight of Sam and Mary sporting in the woods, tells Sarah that they must never meet again. As we leave Exeter and the deflowered Sarah thanking Charles for the strength to live that he has given her, we cut to Mike running for the train to London, cheese and onion sandwich in hand; he jokingly protests that he is losing Anna. Charles is about to lose Sarah for two years, but Mike will lose Anna (presumably) forever. Just after Charles desperately experiences the loss of Sarah as he stands in the empty hotel room in Exeter, Mike telephones Anna's hotel room only to hear David's French-accented voice. (As things build up to a climax for Mike, sound bleedovers occur more regularly. For instance, the telephone starts ringing during the previous, Victorian shot of Charles looking wildly about the room in Exeter.)

The more closely we look at the film's editing, the more we realize how cleverly each story intertwines with the other. If the Victorian story does not explain our modern erotic dilemmas, it at least casts them in high relief. Where the novel assumes the task of explaining the less familiar age,[40] the film makes *ours* the less coherent one. Victorian mores, for all their quaintness, are somehow more comprehensible because more "human." The incoherence of our own attitudes is handled mostly by making Anna—not Sarah—the mysterious woman.[41] She says little that helps to characterize her; we don't know whether she abandons Mike so precipitously out of frivolity, fear of deep emotion, confusion, recognition of *Mike's* confusion, or some combination of these.[42] But whatever her motives, they are very modern.

Thus, the film takes from the novel only the erotic theme—in particular, the suggestion that Victorian mores may have been superior to our own. The novel's narrator argues that their very self-restriction may actually have given the Victorians a sexual drive keener than ours, that indeed they may in some unconscious way have *set* such elaborate inhibitions for the purpose of intensifying sexual pleasure, as a person may intentionally fast a whole day the better to enjoy a gourmet dinner in the evening. He speculates that our easy access to sex, our permissiveness and promiscuity, cannot but trivialize the experience for us. He makes the comparison in a vivid metaphor: "If you can only enjoy one apple a day, there's a great deal to be said against living in an orchard of the wretched things; you might even find apples sweeter if you were allowed only one a week."[43] The novel by no means argues the advantages of the present. As critic Charles Scruggs puts it, Fowles is "capable of admiring Victorian culture, and in precisely moral terms. He appreciates its strong sense of purpose, its determination to make life meaningful, because he is so acutely aware that his own age lacks a sense of purpose and meaning."[44] For all its differences and abridgments, the film communicates a similar attitude—indeed, communicates it even more single-mindedly.[45]

The use of one narrative at the service of another is, of course, common in both literature and film. Its usual form is that of the *Arabian Nights* or the *Canterbury Tales*: the served narrative is the frame story, and the serving narrative is a story that performs some explicit function in the frame—diverting, illustrating, or whatever. Or vice versa: the frame story is a mere pretext to get to the meat of the narrative, which lies in the framed story (*Wuthering Heights, The Turn of the Screw*). In either case, the intentions are usually clear. But in the film version of *The French Lieutenant's Woman*, both the "direction" of the service and its exact force are kept uncertain, implicit, highly subject to interpretation. The tactic is very much in keeping with—indeed, is the counterpart of—the "self-consciousness" of the novel. John Fowles said in an interview that " 'this whole fiction-as-illusion thing' only interested him as a way of sharpening the illusion—'not dispensing with it but learning to live with it.' "[46] The film version uses the same means to "sharpen the illusion" of both the Victorian and the modern story, particularly the latter, which in my view is one of the better accounts of modern love that the cinema has given us.

CHAPTER 11

The "Rhetoric"
"of" "Fiction"

One need only consider oft-neglected rhetoric . . .
                                          —Mikhail Bakhtin

WAYNE BOOTH's famous book is a spirited defense against the imposition of general rules on fiction. His recruitment of "rhetoric" for this defense raises an interesting and important narratological question, especially at a time when critics of a totally different persuasion, such as Terry Eagleton, also want to recuperate the term.[1] How do the words "rhetoric," "of," and "fiction" interact in such a phrase?

The question "What does 'rhetoric of fiction' mean?" really asks "What shall we *allow* it to mean?" Let us assume that "fiction" means "narrative fiction": that is, narratives that make no claim to factuality. Thus, we can expand the discussion to fictions in all media. "Rhetoric" is not so easily defined, but some of its definitional problems are more easily solved than others. Many (including Eagleton) have pointed out that it can refer either to a practice or to a discipline: for example, either "the use of verbal means to suade" or "the formal *study* of such means." An easy solution would be to refer to practitioners as "rhetors" and to students of the subject as "rhetoricians." But that does not resolve the ambiguity of the name of the discipline itself. As Christine Brooke-Rose notes, the ambiguity is shared with other disciplines: the term "history" refers both to the events that have transpired and to discourse about those events.[2] The same thing is true of such terms as "linguistic" (*linguistique*) and "poetic" (*poétique*). Paolo Valesio resolves the ambiguity by using the plural form for the discipline, on the precedent of "linguistics" and "poetics."[3] But "rhetorics" has not caught on, in English at least.

Rehabilitators of rhetoric in the twentieth century have set themselves two goals: to achieve a total rhetoric, and to make it descriptive rather than prescriptive. A total rhetoric would address all aspects of textual construction, global as well as local. One of the reasons for the long decline of rhetoric between Aristotle and George Campbell was the narrowing of focus. Rhetoricians became more and more obsessed with niceties of style at the expense of structure and global design. Only among modern thinkers such as Chaim Perelman do we find a renewed interest in questions of the overall construction and logic of texts, their strategies as well as their local tactics.[4]

The second goal of a modern rhetoric is to describe rather than prescribe and proscribe: that is, to study what rhetors do rather than to dispense rules about what they *should* have done. I. A. Richards and Kenneth Burke have helped us understand that the modern rhetorician's task is the construction of theory and the observation of actual practice, not a set of recommendations about how to write and speak. Booth's book, too, is a reaction against the prescriptivism of critics who, following Percy Lubbock, argue that the only correct approach to the novel is the dramatic.

Then there is the word "of." What do we mean when we speak of the rhetoric *of* something? Oddly enough, "rhetoric" does not become more stable in such an expression as the "rhetoric of fiction." For one thing, we have the ambiguity between the practice and the discipline just mentioned: do we mean "the rhetoric that fiction utilizes to promote its ends?" or "that rhetoric as studied by the rhetorician?" This ambiguity is not very troubling, because theoreticians are obviously concerned with practice as explained by a discipline, a theory. But more problematic ambiguities hide in the wings. Booth acknowledges as much in his afterword to the second edition of *The Rhetoric of Fiction*: "A distinction between two notions of rhetoric run throughout the [first edition of the] book, but it is not always maintained consistently."[5] I address this matter of consistency later, but first I want to consider a problem that Booth does not raise. This is the question of the *end* of rhetoric—obviously a vital matter that entails the whole distinction between the rhetoric of fiction and the principal goal of narratology: that is, a description of the structure of this one text-type.

To address the question of fictional rhetoric's end we must turn to the senses of "rhetoric" in general. I mention only three, though I know there are others worth discussing. The first can be dismissed in short order: it is that in which "rhetoric" means the second-level study of something, the elementary study being its "grammar." Thus, a rhetoric of yoga or computer programming would include instruction in stretches or programs too advanced for the beginner. This sense is obviously irrelevant to narratology.

A second sense equates rhetoric with verbal (or, more generally, semiotic) communication *tout court*. This contrasts with a third, more restricted sense in which the term is ordinarily understood: namely, the use of communicative means to suade. I say "suade" and not "*per*suade" to emphasize, as Aristotle does, that rhetoric concerns the urgings of the text, the "available means," rather than its ultimate success or failure with real audiences. Rhetoric, in this sense, has nothing to do with public opinion polls. The practical effect of texts on public attitudes is more properly a subject for the social sciences.

On the face of it, the second or broad sense might seem most suited to what we want to talk about. But if rhetoric is equated with nothing less than the whole of verbal (or other semiotic) communication, there is no reason for separating it from the purely descriptive study of language, particularly those branches that concern units larger than the sentence and travel under the names "discourse analysis," "pragmatics," and the like. In the other direction, the definition suggests a concern with the means in and of themselves, without respect to the larger purposes of the text. Such a rhetoric would be simply a taxonomy. But the term "narratology" or "grammar of narrative" suffices to represent the purely taxonomic interest. To be of any use at all, "rhetoric of fiction" should mean something else.

If we emulate Kenneth Burke (and who would provide a more distinguished model?), we can assign to the phrase "grammar of fiction" the "grounding in formal considerations"—that is, the "purely internal relations" among narrative fictional terms—and reserve "rhetoric of fiction" for the study of how the terms were put to specific ends, measured as effects on implied audiences. But this is very close to the third sense of "rhetoric"—the traditional one that ties rhetoric to suasion. The rhetoric of fiction, then, must treat the issues of textual analysis in ways different from those of its academic neighbors. What is it that the reader of fiction is suaded to do? What is the end of a rhetoric (that is, practice) of fiction?

Booth says in his original preface that by "rhetoric of fiction" he means the "techniques of non-didactic fiction, viewed as the art of communicating with readers—the rhetorical resources available to the writer of epic, novel, or short story as he tries, consciously or unconsciously, to impose his fictional world upon the reader."[6] Many have discussed that definition, but I want to look at it once more for my own purposes. Applying "rhetoric" to fictional texts obviously stretches the term a bit. Fictions are traditionally said to make no claims to factuality. How can such a text "suade" somebody to do something or to adopt or to stick to some attitude? If there is no such world as Oz and no such girl as Dorothy, what is it that the reader is suaded to do or believe?

Booth's definition works easily if we adapt it to nonfictional texts, especially arguments. Consider a deliberative text, one presented to a legislative body. A characterization of the rhetoric of deliberation as the "technique of texts of legislative persuasion, viewed as the art of communicating with legislators—the resources available to the legislator as he tries to impose his view or proposal upon his colleagues" is comprehensible and easily acceptable. So is a characterization of the rhetoric of forensic appeal as "the technique of legal briefs, viewed as the art of communicating with a judge or jury—the resources available to the lawyer as he tries to impose his interpretation of the facts of the case and consequently the applicability or inapplicability of the appropriate laws." But how do we apply this kind of frame to texts whose principal end is not to prove something but to involve us in their fictional worlds?

Does "impose" or "communicate with the intent to impose" (or any of various synonyms—"control," "manipulate," "guide," "order" and so on) equal "suade"? That seems to depend on how we interpret "imposition" and on what we take to be fiction's end. The legislator and the lawyer desire to impose their views to some practical end beyond the design of the text itself, namely the institution or repeal of a law, or the acquittal or conviction of a defendant. They hope that the audience will take some stance toward the issue raised by the text. They would hardly be satisfied with the knowledge that their audience simply enjoyed the text. Though it speaks of other sorts of values, particularly moral ones, much of Booth's book and the tradition from which it derives concern *aesthetic* ends, the suitability of fit, so to speak, between technique and the audience's sense of fulfillment or closure.

But even textual enjoyment and fulfillment are not simple matters. Ancient rhetoric accounted for them by means of a subclass described as "epideictic," from the Greek word for exhibition, display, showing off in public speaking. Though the original subject of epideictic texts was praise or blame of the institution or person that was subject of the speech, another assumption arose even in the ancient era: namely, that the praise or blame could apply to the text's own form and style. Clearly, the ancient rhetor's solicitation of approval of the form of his speech, quite apart from its content, prefigures the novelist's solicitation of the reader's acceptance of the validity of the *way* the novel is put together, regardless of what the novel is about. The author of a nondidactic fiction asks that you approve not of what his characters do but rather of the way in which those doings are presented and the strength and quality of the illusion they build in your mind. It is not implausible to refer to this solicitation as a kind of suasion and hence of rhetoric, though it seems crucial to remember that the end it seeks is significantly different from that which ordinary rhetoric seeks. The expression "rhetoric of fiction," I believe, best refers to a fiction's suasion that its unfolding *form* be accepted.

In Booth's view, the end desired by this form-directed rhetoric is a maximal heightening of the fiction's effect. As part of his argument against the dogmatic followers of Henry James, Booth tellingly invokes the master's own denial that the scenic art alone should prevail in fiction. He recalls James's belief that the purpose of any technique is to heighten the *intensity* of the fictive illusion, and therefore that on occasion direct commentary by the narrator is justifiable. Though the viability of this position hardly needs more support, Booth's "intensity" is very much what the early Burke calls "saliency," for him the chief and only real semantic constant of form. Formal techniques, he wrote in "Lexicon Rhetoricae," "impart emphasis regardless of their subject. Whatever the theme may be they add saliency to this theme, the same design serving to make dismalness more dismal or gladness gladder."[7]

In attaching "rhetoric" to form, however, we must not imply that the rhetoric of fiction deals with different materials than its grammar does; the materials are the same. Rather, rhetoric looks at those materials from a different perspective. It is concerned less with defining or taxonomizing definitions of techniques, such as narrative voice or analepsis ("flashback"), than with showing how they apply to the text's end—the set of explicit and implicit suasions of the implied reader. The question that rhetoric poses about, say, analepsis is whether it engages the implied reader more powerfully than does normal discourse order. Let us refer to this kind of rhetoric as "rhetoric to aesthetic ends," or "aesthetic rhetoric."

The other kind we can call "rhetoric to ideological ends," or "ideological rhetoric." Booth's decision to exclude from his purview didactic fictions or fables shows his desire to focus on the aesthetic function of fictional rhetoric.[8] Fables use fictional narrative to advance explicit propositions about the real world, propositions that could quite as readily be advanced through other types of discourse: Exposition, Description, Argument. For them, aesthetic rhetoric is only at the service of ideological rhetoric. Nondidactic fictions, on the contrary, may or may not imply propositions, or even those attenuated propositions traditionally called "themes." Some texts— the clearest examples are dadaistic or surrealistic—go far to avoid propositions. But to ensure their own self-consistency, even they use an aesthetic rhetoric, albeit a rhetoric often designed to attack the notion of any conventional ideological rhetoric.

Let me expand a bit on the nature of rhetoric to aesthetic ends, that is, suasion to accept the form of the narrative as most appropriate to its content. I believe that Booth is right in using the term "rhetoric" to refer to this function. Other terms, of course, are possible. One advanced recently, under the influence of French thought, is "seduction." "Seduction" privileges the emotions over the intellect, and it is true that ancient rhetoric acknowledged *pathos* along with *logos*. Clearly, both the heart and the mind are induced to follow a narrative through to its conclusion. Each has its own pleasure, but it seems unnecessary to separate them. Rhetoric has never insisted on a cut-and-dried distinction between the two faculties.[9]

Many theorists believe that a central purpose of fictions is to create their own believable worlds, imaginary spaces containing plausible (or at least self-consistent) characters and actions. In this view, the end of aesthetic rhetoric is verisimilitude, the creation and maintenance and, as James and Booth insist, the intensification of the illusion itself. What is at issue in this kind of rhetoric is not a "message," or even any reference to the real world at all, but an imaginary situation that is sui generis, homogeneous, conceivable, and hence "acceptable" (in some relatively vague but recognizable sense of the word). Booth says that through rhetoric the reader learns to know where, in the world of possible values, he stands—that is, to know "where the author *wants* him to stand." But, we must add, these are *possible* values, including some that readers in the real world might not endorse (as, say, in an "anti-anthropic" science fiction novel or, to cite a notorious case, in Lewis-Ferdinand Céline's *Journey to the End of Night*). Of course, the reader will agree to "stand" in that place only for the nonce, for the occasion of the reading itself. You might or might not start working for a Marxist revolution after reading Maxim Gorky's *Mother*, but the decision could hardly be called an important *literary* consequence of Gorky's suasion. Obviously, no viable aesthetic rhetoric of fiction could demand practical or real-life consequences of a novel's suasions.

David Lodge, himself a novelist and astute narratologist, remarked that " 'Rhetoric' is Professor Booth's term for the means by which the writer makes known his vision to the reader and persuades him of its validity."[10] Booth's "communicate to impose" becomes Lodge's more specifically rhetorical "persuade," and Booth's "fictional world" becomes Lodge's "vision." Lodge's terms in some ways legitimate, better than do Booth's own, the use of the term "rhetoric" in its traditional sense. If all we mean by "rhetoric" is the art of *communicating* with readers, we are not totally justified in using the term. The world is filled with nonsuasory communication, communication that does not try to impose opinions upon its audience. For example, brokers routinely purchase newspaper ads to announce issues of stocks and bonds that have already sold out. Their intention is neither to urge the public to buy nor even to boast of their success as underwriters but merely to follow correct procedure. It is not accidental that many critics since the eighteenth century have located literature's texts at the opposite pole from direct urgings. If rhetoric is simply equated with communication, then both terms get muddled, and an important distinction is lost.

But what does "validity" mean? Dictionaries say: " 'Valid,' from Latin 'validus,' meaning strong, as in 'valorous': sound, just, well-founded, cogent, authoritative, effective, having force." The novel's narrative technique becomes rhetorical when it functions to suade us of the text's right to be considered *as* fictional narrative, of its existence as a nonarbitrary and noncontingent utterance, one that has its own force and autonomy, its own right to be taken seriously as a legitimate member of the class of texts we call narrative fictions.

Since much in fiction is, by definition, unencumbered by claims to factuality, it cannot be that "valid" refers to truth in any ordinary sense. Both the rhetoric of fiction and the rhetoric of history use narration, but only the latter also suades us to believe that its stories are factually true. Obviously, Mark Twain's novel does not argue the actual existence of a boy named Huck Finn who did such and such. Validity must mean rather that Huck's (or any character's) fictional existence has some other kind of force: for example, that it is plausible, acceptable, feasible; the fictional world that he occupies is coherent, believable, verisimilar in itself. Validity, we might say, is the *internal* thrust of *Huckleberry Finn*'s aesthetic rhetoric. *Externally,* insofar as it is a relatively realistic fiction, the novel's aesthetic rhetoric purports to suade us that the way the story is told corresponds to life in rural midwestern America in the mid-nineteenth century. It suades us to accept the proposition that if there had been such a boy at such a place and such a time, he would elect to tell his story himself and in that way.

What, then, would bad aesthetic rhetoric be? Presumably, it would make the wrong choice of techniques to effect a narrative's ends. But this is not so easy to demonstrate. Consider an issue that arises in fiction conveying the experience of uneducated characters. D. H. Lawrence's "Love among the Haystacks," for example, is a story about the love affairs of two sons of a Midland farmer. To represent the banter between the two brothers and talk with their father and a third brother, the narrator carefully "quotes" the local dialect. But that dialogue is mixed with his own typically Laurentian diction, which is filled with more elegance and eloquence than such farmers could muster. For example, just after one brother, Maurice, says "Tha sees . . . tha thowt as tha'd done me one, didna ter?" the narrator adds, "He smiled as he spoke, then fell again into his pleasant torment of musing." The character would not, indeed, could not *say* "pleasant torment of musing"; more important, the elaborately paradoxical feeling would never *occur* to him, even in cruder verbiage. Nor does it help the story very much if we read the statement as the narrator's own observation: clearly, the implied author's intent is to characterize Maurice's mood in ways sympathetic to Maurice. But can we say that the contrast in diction is rhetorically infelicitous? Is it infelicitous that Maurice speaks dialect with Paula but that Geoffrey shifts to standard English when speaking with Lydia? (No dramatic reason is given for either move.) It all depends on how much one likes Lawrence. His admirers will be untroubled, taking the refined diction as evidence of the nobility of the simple soul. Anti-Laurentians will find in the dictional disparity between characters and narrator the dilemma of much of Lawrence's fiction: for all its desire to record accurately the speech of the simple but passionate and therefore noble folk whose attitudes it wishes to celebrate, it unwittingly patronizes them. Unlike, say, the narrator of the first three stories of James Joyce's *Dubliners*, whose literary diction can be rationalized by assuming that he later emerges from his meager childhood milieu to *become* a writer, the well-spoken Laurentian narrator seems to condescend to the characters from some lofty vantage of knowledge, intelligence, and artistry. That runs counter to the apparent intention of the fictions as a whole. For anti-Laurentians, Lawrence's verisimilitude founders on the implied author's inability to strike a harmonious balance between the narrator's voice and the voices of the characters.[11]

What sorts of tools are utilized by the aesthetic rhetoric of fiction? Presumably, anything that can find its way into a text. Consider, for instance, features of language and style. Henry James's style argues, among other things, the leisure to weave an elaborate meditative web. Hemingway's, on the other hand, argues the need for grace under pressure. Another rhetorical tool is the manipulation of cultural codes, as Roland Barthes demonstrated in *S/Z*. In point of fact, however, what rhetoricians of fiction usually talk about is that set of devices specially favored by narrative texts which are the ongoing concern of narratologists: filter and slant, narrative voice, chronological relations between story and discourse, and so on. Aesthetic rhetoric addresses such questions as "Why does the choice of first-person narrative voice make Huck's story plausible, viable, esthetically whole?" No one, I think, would argue that the implied author of *Huckleberry Finn* makes the wrong choice, that some other kind of narrator would render a more plausible account of the events and characters and settings of that novel. The assignment of the role of narrator to Huck himself permits access to a consciousness, in the discourse as well as in the story, which is peculiarly suited to the aesthetic design of the novel. Booth's book is filled with examples of how such choices function toward aesthetic ends, and his best demonstrations show that alternative technical choices would not have served the text's ends as well.

Let us turn now to Booth's inconsistencies (some of them acknowledged), not so much to criticize them as to learn from them. Again what seems involved are two senses of the word "rhetoric." In the afterword to the revised edition, Booth characterizes the first sense as "the rhetoric *in* fiction, as overt and recognizable appeal (the most extreme form being authorial commentary)." The second is "fiction *as* rhetoric in the larger sense, an *aspect* of the whole work viewed as a total act of communication."[12]

But these are not logical opposites, as we might expect of a dichotomy proposed to exhaust the universe of possibilities. The opposite of "in" is not "as" but "out" or "outside of." The opposite of "overt" is "covert," and the opposite of "recognizable" is "unrecognizable." Further, though it is clear what "overt" or "recognizable" appeal means, it is not clear that such appeal is best described as being "in" the fiction (as we might say that Lovelace's seductive rhetoric is "in" *Clarissa*).[13]

Booth puts his finger on one source of this difficult problem, but I believe that the inconsistency derives from still another ambiguity of "rhetoric": namely, between rhetoric as a *kind* of text and rhetoric as a *function* of texts of any kind. Thus, what Booth calls "overt rhetoric" (also "direct rhetoric," "direct-address rhetoric," "direct guidance," "recognizable appeal," "separable rhetoric," "obvious rhetoric," "extraneous rhetoric," "extrinsic rhetoric," "consciously direct rhetoric," "authoritative rhetoric," "authorial rhetoric," and "rhetoric in the narrow sense") is *text* that is rhetorical in its content as well as in its function. Such text advertises itself as rhetoric, for example, by using value-laden words that work expressly to shape the audience's attitudes toward events, behaviors, characters, and settings. Booth's examples illustrate the point very well: the assertion by the biblical narrator that Job "was perfect and upright"; the assertion by the Homeric narrator that the Greeks were "heroes" with "strong souls"; the assertion by Fiammetta, the narrator of the ninth story of the fifth day of Boccaccio's *Decameron*, that Monna, the heroine, was "no less virtuous than fair."

"Covert rhetoric," on the other hand, works only implicitly as rhetoric; it pretends to be quite another kind of text. For instance, a dramatized scene seems not to urge but simply to *be*. Still, Booth would say, it functions in a deeply rhetorical way. (Other names by which he refers to "covert rhetoric" are "disguised rhetoric," "ostensibly dramatic move[s]," "objective" and "impersonal" text, text "pure" of rhetoric, "intrinsic rhetoric," and "acceptable rhetoric"— acceptable, presumably, to Lubbockian purists.) Booth argues that "anything that heightens," anything "that can be made public"— indeed, everything in the narrative text—is rhetorical. Rhetoric is implicit even in the original given, James's *donné*, or what Burke calls the "author's original symbol" (as opposed to the technical and formal complications of its presentation to an audience). For Booth, even "at the instant when James exclaims to himself, 'Here is my subject!' a rhetorical aspect is contained within the conception: the subject is thought of as *something that can be made public*, something that can be made into a communicated work." What is needed, and what Booth finds in James's project, is a "general rhetoric in the service of realism, rather than a particular rhetoric for the most intense experience of distinctive effects."[14]

But I wonder whether the agglomerated elements that work rhetorically in a fiction can be homogenized under the term "general rhetoric." For all its utility, direct characterization by narrator-authorized adjectives, say, remains only a technical device, one narratological choice among others available to the implied author. And it becomes rhetorical only when its end is clear: that is, when we can explain how it achieves an effect of audience control. Some kinds of aesthetic ends discussed by Booth are speed, economy, verification, and reinforcement. For example, in the Boccaccio story, the heroine's mind is entered briefly to substantiate the narrator's independent praise of her virtue; in *Emma*, Mr. Knightley's dialogue is used to reinforce the narrator's occasional, relatively muted comments on Emma's shortcomings. And so on. These examples are perfectly straightforward and clear. But a problem arises for me when the word "rhetoric" is attached not only to the whole two-part complex

(1) technical choice + (2) end

but also to technical choice alone. For example, in discussing Joyce's endorsement of reader's guides and skeleton keys to *Ulysses* and *Finnegans Wake*, Booth writes, "The reader's problems are handled, if they are to be handled at all, by rhetoric provided outside the work." The problem here, and in similar passages, is the metonymic or synecdochic slide from a total complex to only the first part or means of that complex. (This kind of slippage resembles one faulted by I. A. Richards: the use of the term "metaphor" to refer not only to the whole complex, "vehicle-plus-tenor," but also to "vehicle" alone.) Aside from the confusing redundancy with "grammar," which we have already discussed, the danger of equating rhetoric with technique alone, rather than technique-plus-end, is that it is thereby transferrable to a class of texts, a kind of genre. But the rhetorical is only one of several functions of technical choice in a narrative text (another, for example, is the mimetic function).

Further, what troubles me about saying that everything in a narrative text is rhetorical is that rhetoric thereby ceases to be a *distinctive* function of the text. This is well illustrated by Booth's expression "rhetoric of dissimulation." Precisely because a technique *can* dissimulate, it should be called not a kind of rhetoric but rather a narrative feature that functions rhetorically, a surrogate for express urgings. For example, "telling," direct assertion by the narrator on his or her own authority, is often replaced in the Jamesian project by materials that are in themselves not rhetorical but dramatic, embedded "naturally" in the story itself. The *ficelle*—the minor character invented "only" to function as expository sounding board—is not a rhetorical device as such but simply one more part of the rendered story. Information that could have been presented by "direct" rhetoric (the authorial narrator's own statement) gets presented through a surrogate, a mouthpiece—a Maria Gostrey (in *The Ambassadors*), a Henrietta Stackpole (in *The Portrait of a Lady*)—who has some degree of diegetic respectability and who fits, in some not improbable way, into the story. The implied author introduces such characters to avoid inflicting on the implied reader a narrator endowed with "unnatural wisdom." Like a master illusionist explaining his bag of tricks, James unmasks the device in the very coinage *ficelle* (a metaphor based on the French word for a puppet's strings), but we rhetoricians should not confuse the surrogate with what it surrogates for: bare pronouncements by an authoritative narrator. For the trick actually works: the majority of James's readers (poor folk unblessed by narratological training!) do not bracket off Maria Gostrey or Harriet Stackpole as mere rhetorical devices.

In other words, *ficelles*—like inner views, chronological rearrangements, and the like—are not themselves "pieces" of rhetoric; they are not urgings, either direct or indirect, overt or covert. They are narrative techniques, options in the narrative grammar available for the author's use. From the narrative-grammatical point of view, *ficelles* are characters like any others. However, as Booth says, they perform rhetorical *functions*. This, I think, is the important point. Textual rhetoric is immediately recognizable as such even if extracted from the context; appeal inheres in the very words and grammar. But the *ficelle* and other narrative devices become rhetorically functional only in context, even as they continue to operate in normal diegetic ways. Maria Gostrey may be a *ficelle*, but she doesn't cease being a character for all that, a character whose existence, personality, and actions are perfectly verisimilar in the world constructed by the novel. In other words, when we are calling a *text* "rhetoric" (rather than using the word in some other sense, such as the study of the behavior of rhetors), we are really speaking of what might more precisely be called "text-whose-rhetorical-intention-is-transparent," or even "text-that-*expresses*-its-rhetoric." But most narrative techniques do not express their rhetoric. Only professionals (authors, critics, and theorists), would think of calling them "rhetorical." There is no point in referring to direct interpretations by the narrator as explicit rhetoric if we recognize no implicit rhetoric. And the use of "dramatic" techniques to solve problems of controlling audience attitudes, I suggest, is not so much "implicit rhetoric" as it is a selection among narrative techniques to perform rhetorical functions.

I am not really arguing anything very different from what Booth says himself when he observes, for instance, that "the rhetorical dimension in literature is inescapable." His "dimension" is pretty much what I mean by "function." Both terms allow for *other* fictional dimensions alternative to the rhetorical. It is just that I want to *underline* the distinction between "rhetoric-as-text" and "rhetoric-as-textual-function" and to suggest that the former is so fraught with potential misunderstanding that it may be prudent not to use "rhetoric" in that sense.

Booth's book may seem to deny a distinction between aesthetic and ideological rhetoric or to affirm, rather, that there is only one rhetoric and that it works to endorse "values." Remember how convincingly he pulls the rug from under Chekhov, who "begins bravely enough in defense of neutrality, but . . . cannot write three sentences without committing himself." Chekhov, like all artists who aspire to the condition of God paring His or Her fingernails, commits an "elementary and understandable confusion between neutrality toward *some* values and neutrality toward *all*."[15] No one can deny the untenability of Chekhov's position. Even a total nihilism would obviously presuppose the value of something—namely, nothing. Booth's book often adverts to moral values, and it would be foolish to deny their importance to narrative fiction. But after studying the book for many years, I have concluded that in practice it really emphasizes aesthetic rather than ethical values. It generally considers ethical values in the context of how they work for the particular fiction in which they arise, not how they relate to behavior in the real world. In one or two places, Booth makes the point rather explicitly; for example, in a discussion of the historical relativity of artists' commitment "to causes of their time," he notes that "the test is whether the particular ends of the artist enable him to do something with his commitment, not whether he has it or not." And what is that "something" if not "something artistic," "something beautiful?" Whatever the political, moral, social, economic, or other values the author entertains, the artist "can seldom afford to pour his untransformed biases into his work."[16]

For all its discussion of morality, then, the primary orientation of *The Rhetoric of Fiction* is aesthetic—which is fine for formalism but not for more recent trends in textual theory. Even Burke, who is so often relevant to contemporary discussion, fails us here; the notion of art as "equipment for living," for example, treats the ideological aspect of fiction a bit like a plaything, a hypothetical model to be learned from, rather than the repository of ideas that are in their own right important and maybe even implementable.

Rhetoric working to aesthetic ends suades us of something interior to the text, particularly the appropriateness of the chosen means to evoke a response appropriate to the work's intention. Rhetoric working to ideological ends suades us of something outside the text, something about the world at large. The latter need not be a proposition; even nondidactic fiction radiates ideology.

It is not always easy to separate the ends of the two kinds of rhetoric, but let me take a stab. Consider the rhetoric of an infrequently discussed classic by Virginia Woolf, *Jacob's Room*. I have argued that rhetoric directed toward either aesthetic or ideological ends rests securely on the grammar of fiction, the set of narrative tools available to the author. Thus, a given narrative technique may work in one way to support the aesthetic end and, at the same time, in another way, to urge some proposition or to resonate thematically with the real world. A narrative device fundamental to *Jacob's Room*, as it is to *Mrs Dalloway*, is what I have called "shifting limited mental access," or an abrupt entry into the mind of one character after another but *without* the suggestion of omniscience. "Shifting limited access," I explained in *Story and Discourse*, moves to the next character's mind without hinting that an all-knowing narrator is manipulating the movement for tidy plot reasons: "In such passages, the narrator does not ransack mind after mind . . . for answers to hermeneutic questions. The mental entries seem matters of chance, reflecting the randomness of ordinary life."[17]

Jacob's Room was the first of Woolf's novels to use the device with any frequency. Sometimes the shift in consciousness seems to derive from the physical proximity of strangers: in the first chapter we shift abruptly from the mind of Betty Flanders, mourning her husband's death, to that of a total stranger named Charles Steele, whose sole interest in Betty is as a dab of color on the canvas he is painting. Elsewhere in the novel, however, physical proximity is of no significance; simultaneity is the only basis for the conjunction of thoughts. Jacob, in Greece, puts down the *Daily Mail* in disgust; at the same moment, his friend Bonamy, back in London, laments to himself: "[Jacob] will fall in love."[18]

But what about the rhetoric? What is the aesthetic-rhetorical and what the ideological-rhetorical force of the technique of shifting limited mental access in *Jacob's Room*? The device helps suade us aesthetically to accept the Woolfian fictive universe, one in which, says David Daiches, "experience is flux, and the lives of different [people] shade imperceptibly into each other."[19] Whether the real world is actually like that, of course, is not at issue. But when we *do* consider the text from the perspective of real-world concerns—that is, consider it ideologically—we may note that the suddenness of the transfer from consciousness to consciousness dovetails with, and so supports, a picture of modern life filled with empty busyness, distraction, and lack of commitment. This impression is confirmed by the contents of the novel: the meaningless roar of motor traffic outside Jacob's room in London, the idleness of interminable party conversation, the breeziness of Sandra's infidelity and her husband's calm acceptance of it. Rapid shifts of consciousness echo a heightened sense of the speed of modern means of communication: the radio, the telephone—all those lightning channels and nothing much to say. Ideologically, shifting limited access prompts a meditation about human communication—that it does not seem to improve in quality as it becomes enormously faster and easier.

Another end supported by shifting limited access in *Jacob's Room* is spatial. The implication is that in such a fictive universe, distance is nothing: there is no longer a faraway, because people can communicate instantaneously over vast distances. Still another implication is sociopolitical: despite elaborate class differences, everybody is pretty much in the same boat when it comes to feelings—of insecurity, of elation, of calm, and so on (this is corroborated by Woolf's unprecedented decision to give proper names to even the veriest bystanders).

Shifting limited access used toward aesthetic and ideological ends is, like any technique, context-sensitive. A hypothetical example will help demonstrate that point. Imagine such access in a novel set in medieval times, say a successor to Umberto Eco's *Name of the Rose*. For the Middle Ages, too, the technique could help invoke a fictive universe in which "experience is flux, and the lives of different [people] shade imperceptibly into each other." But the rapid shifts of consciousness would not have the same ideological resonances as those we feel in *Jacob's Room*, simply because the world was such a different place back then. We would have to look to other possible historical correlations for ideological reference.

Shifting limited access is very widespread in *Mrs Dalloway*, too, but works to different ends, not only aesthetically but ideologically. In *Jacob's Room*, we travel through various consciousnesses feeling the impossibility of knowing what anyone else is like, let alone what a half-formed Cantabridgian like Jacob, who perishes in a ghastly war, might have become. The irony, of course, is that for all the easy fluidity of mental access with which the narrator is "empowered," she is not permitted, any more than the simplest bystander, to make head or tail of this young English gentleman. In *Mrs Dalloway*, at least in that part of it filtered through the consciousnesses of Clarissa and Peter Walsh, another kind of irony seems to be at work, something like this: "Though we may understand a loved one very well indeed, so well that her consciousness seems the virtual mirror-image of our own, she may be the last person we can stand to be with, even for two hours, let alone for a lifetime."

I am not claiming that these sentences capture the theme of the novel but merely that they provide a reasonable description of ideological (as opposed to aesthetic) ends that shifting limited consciousness seems to promote. To the extent that its use enhances, makes salient, intensifies the illusion of the novel, we can say that the technique is functioning in good aesthetic-rhetorical fashion. At the ideological level, on the other hand, we would want to ask how the choice of shifting limited access confirms or undermines projections of the real world beyond the fiction. For example, the shifts between Clarissa's and Septimus's consciousness argue how comparable are the fates of the powerless, whether they are powerless for reasons of gender or of "mental illness" (quotation marks of irony here), in a society where power resides in the hands of such insensitive and authoritarian males as the psychiatrist Bradshaw. Similarly, in *Jacob's Room*, the odd perspective chosen by the unnamed but clearly female narrator is strongly ideological. For instance, there is a wonderful description of a heated argument inside Jacob's room at Cambridge by a narrator who can only *be* outside, prowling in the courtyard, straining but unable to hear what is being said, drawing only rough inferences from the gesticulations of this or that young man as he passes the window.[20] Why is she outside in the cold if not because she is a woman? The whole effect argues the cultural isolation of intellectual women in early twentieth-century England, excluded from the centers of learning, made to feel like interlopers (at one point, Jacob mutters to himself that women, like pet dogs, should not be allowed into King's College Chapel).[21] The theme of exclusion, of course, is one that Virginia Woolf expresses through nonfictional rhetoric in *A Room of One's Own* and elsewhere.

Let us turn to a cinematic example: Michelangelo Antonioni's film *The Passenger* (1975) is a meditation on the mysteries of identity and on the impossibility of escaping one's fate.[22] It is a study in what Otto Rank calls *doppelgängerism*, the idea "that a person's past inescapably clings to him and that it becomes his fate as soon as he tries to get rid of it."[23] David Locke (Jack Nicholson), a reporter covering a rebellion in Chad, strikes up an acquaintance with a mysterious and gentle man named Robertson who bears a striking resemblance to himself. That very day Robertson dies of a heart attack. Discovering his body, Locke impulsively switches passports and takes on Robertson's identity. He discovers that Robertson was a gunrunner supplying arms to the rebels and that his own life is in danger. In Barcelona, he meets and falls in love with a young French architecture student, but she cannot help him escape the assassination planned for Robertson.

The task of *The Passenger's* aesthetic rhetoric is to suade us of the plausibility of Locke's fate. We must be led to believe that the only other white man in a remote Chadian hotel is a dead ringer for Locke, that he would die precipitously of natural causes, and that only Locke would know of his death. The resemblance is achieved, superficially, by casting in the role of Robertson a look-alike for Jack Nicholson. But a more profound rhetorical move is to wrap the event in mysterious and even mystical circumstances. When Locke first discovers Robertson's corpse and his passport under the body, the plaintive sound of an African flute is heard on the soundtrack. Locke goes to the window and opens the shutters. The camera pans across the desert. We hear the same flute music a few moments later in a mysterious flashback to the living voice of Robertson conversing with Locke.

We are not at all prepared for the flashback; indeed, it occurs in a rather deceptive way. As Locke is comparing Robertson's passport photo with his own, there is a knock at the door. He looks up. But then we hear *his* voice saying, "Come in," and Robertson's responding, "Sorry to barge in like this." What we hear is not Robertson's real voice, but a recording of it made by Locke during their meeting the day before. As the voices continue, Locke carefully removes Robertson's photo from his passport with a razor blade. The source of the voices appears briefly in a shot of Locke's tape recorder. Suddenly, Locke looks up, thoughtfully. Following the direction of his gaze, the camera pans across the wall to the open window. Robertson appears on the balcony followed by Locke. In other words, over the real sounds made by the tape recorder, the image track presents a flashback of Robertson and Locke in conversation a few hours earlier. It is a flashback *visible* to Locke, a "mindscreen" memory effect done as a straightforward point-of-view shot. Turning to the same desert view that Locke contemplated after Robertson's death, Robertson comments on how beautiful and still and "waiting" the landscape is. Locke responds that he prefers men to landscapes.

The mixture of visual flashback and contemporary sound is strange, and its strangeness matches and, in a sense, motivates the strangeness of the men's resemblance and the opportunity that Robertson's death affords Locke to change identity. Especially the remark about "waiting" ties their fates together. The desert awaits Robertson's death, which is imminent, and Locke's as well; he will wait peacefully for his—that is, Robertson's—assassin in another small hotel in an equally desolate landscape, in Spain.

Though politics is the ostensible motor running the film's narrative machinery, the ideological point suggested by this scene is metaphysical, not political. The film really turns on the personal fate of a single man facing some ultimate existential questions: Who am I? Shall I try to be someone else? Will I feel any different if I do? Should I run from it or accept my death peacefully? What is it that I am running from? What is it that I am dying of? The unusual framing of this scene, in which a person has an unprecedented opportunity to drop his own identity and take up someone else's, is a good example of innovative cinematic rhetoric working to sophisticated ideological ends. Everything about the sequence suggests a slant of philosophical quietism, one that accepts death as part of life, an ideology that is comforting but unsentimental. The point is supported and confirmed by another unique technical effect at the end of the film, an extremely long tracking shot in which the camera exits through the bars of Locke/Robertson's window, makes an extended tour of the street outside, and then returns. At the very moment of Locke's death, the camera is more preoccupied with the living environment in front of the Hotel de la Gloria than with the assassination taking place inside the room and the disposition of the corpse. Both these sequences provide a rhetoric to confirm an ideology much in the spirit of the existentialism of Alan Watts: "Death is the goal of life. Nonbeing fulfills being; it does not negate being, just as space does not negate what is solid. Each is the condition for the reality of the other."[24]

The study of rhetoric can help narrative theory if its limits are clearly recognized. The more closely they are defined, the better.

Rhetoric should not be used as one more synonym for "communication" in the loose sense but should refer rather specifically to end-oriented discourse, where "end" is conceived as the suasion of the audience. In my view, there are two narrative rhetorics, one concerned to suade me to accept the form of the work; another, to suade me of a certain view of how things are in the real world. The investigation of these two rhetorics and their interaction strikes me as a crucial project for students of literature and of film.

Notes

Notes to Introduction

1. America alone has produced significant works by Robert Alter, Ann Banfield, David Bordwell, Wayne Booth, Edward Branigan, Peter Brooks, Nick Browne, Ross Chambers, Dorrit Cohn, Jonathan Culler, Lubomir Doležel, Fredric Jameson, Brian Henderson, Benjamin Harshaw, Linda Hutcheon, Bruce Kawin, Jeffrey Kittay, Susan Sniader Lanser, Steven Mailloux, David Miller, J. Hillis Miller, Bruce Morrissette, Toma Pavel, James Phelan, Mary Louise Pratt, Gerald Prince, Peter Rabinowitz, Ralph Rader, David Richter, Paul Ricoeur, Robert Scholes, Barbara Herrnstein Smith, Susan Suleiman, Hayden White, and others. Abroad, narrative questions have been illuminated by scholars like Mieke Bal, Roland Barthes, Claude Bremond, Christine Brooke-Rose, Gérard Genette, A.-G. Greimas, Lucien Dällenbach, Umberto Eco, Roger Fowler, Michael Halliday, Philippe Hamon, Stephen Heath, Wolfgang Iser, David Lodge, Frank Kermode, Brian McHale, Christian Metz, Shlomith Rimmon-Kenan, Franz Stanzel, Meir Sternberg, and Tzvetan Todorov. And, of course, the treasures of Russian thought continue to be revealed: Eikhenbaum, Tomashevski, Tynjanov, Propp, Shklovski, Bakhtin. Wallace Martin (*Recent Theories of Narrative* [Ithaca: Cornell University Press, 1986]) has recently put much of this work in historical perspective, and there has even appeared a useful *Dictionary of Narratology*, by Gerald Prince (Lincoln: University of Nebraska Press, 1987). My debt to these authors goes without saying.

2. Seymour Chatman, *Story and Discourse: Narrative Structure in Fiction and Film* (Ithaca: Cornell University Press, 1978).

Notes

Notes to Chapter 1

1. So Gérard Genette puts it in "Frontiers of Narrative," in *Figures of Literary Discourse*, ed. Marie-Rose Logan, trans. Alan Sheridan (New York: Columbia University Press, 1982), p. 128. (This essay originally appeared as "Frontières du récit," *Communications* 11 [1966], 152–63.) Roland Barthes also argued the need for a theory of text-types in "An Introduction to the Structural Analysis of Narrative," in *Image Music Text*, trans. Stephen Heath (New York: Hill & Wang, 1977), pp. 79–124: "One of the tasks of such a linguistics would be precisely that of establishing a typology of forms of discourse. Three broad types can be recognized provisionally: metonymic (narrative), metaphoric (lyric poetry, sapiential discourse), enthymematic (intellectual discourse)" (p. 84).

2. The "forms" or "modes of discourse" have been distinguished for centuries but keep cropping up in recent narratological discussion. E.g., they seem to be what Ross Chambers calls "register" in his interesting essay "Describing Description," in *Meaning and Meaningfulness: Studies in the Analysis and Interpretation of Texts*, French Forum Monographs 15 (Lexington, Ky.: French Forum, 1979), pp. 90–101. Chambers recognizes three such registers: narrative, description, and commentary. His formulation, however, like Genette's, explains text-types by privileging narrative. In contrast, I seek to explain the relations among text-types from a point of view that does not privilege any type or medium.

3. This sense of Exposition, of course, is unrelated to the special sense it has in narratology, namely the representation of plot events before the narrative proper begins. See Meir Sternberg, *Expositional Modes and Temporal Ordering in Fiction* (Baltimore: Johns Hopkins University Press, 1978).

4. Gotthold Ephraim Lessing, *Laocoön, Nathan the Wise, and Minna Von Barnhelm*, trans. William A. Steel (London: Dent, 1930).

5. The scholarship is conveniently summarized in Marianna Torgovnick, *The Visual Arts, Pictorialism, and the Novel* (Princeton: Princeton University Press, 1985), p. 31.

6. In Rudolf Arnheim, *Visual Thinking* (Berkeley: University of California Press, 1969), p. 35, as quoted in Torgovnick, *Visual Arts*, pp. 32–33.

7. Thus, I would disagree with Torgovnick's contention that "it makes little more sense to exclude temporality from the nature of the visual arts than to maintain that we perceive literature spatially when we regard an unopened book and feel its dimensions" (*Visual Arts*, p. 33).

8. These terms are not, strictly speaking, equivalent, but there is sufficient family resemblance to permit equating them in this rough way.

9. Michel Beaujour, "Some Paradoxes of Description," *Yale French Studies* 61 (1981), 27.

10. Expositions, on the other hand, are basically explanations (*exponere* = "to put forth, explain"; *explanare* = "to make level or clear"). Thus, they share with descriptions the task of rendering properties, but they do so by a more recognizably discursive logic—analysis, definition, contrast, comparison.

11. The best modern study of argumentation is Chaim Perelman and L. Olbrechts-Tyteca, *The New Rhetoric: A Treatise on Argumentation*, trans. John Wilkinson and Purcell Weaver (Notre Dame, Ind.: University of Notre Dame Press, 1969).

12. The difference between Argument and Exposition seems to be that the arguer presumes the audience already to have a certain attitude, which she tries to alter (or sometimes to reinforce). Generally, Argument presupposes difference of opinion; Exposition presupposes an absence or confusion of opinion. Of course, the clarification itself implies an argument about the preferability of that clarification, so the line between these two text-types is hazy. But the distinction remains useful to the extent that we can distinguish the explicit suasion of an argument from the implicit suasion of an exposition.

13. The example of *The River* is analyzed in David Bordwell and Kristen Thompson, *Film Art: An Introduction*, 2d ed. (New York: Knopf, 1986), pp. 57–62; this is one of the few books that attempt to categorize non-narrative films. Bordwell and Thompson use the term "rhetorical" (p. 81) for the text-type that I call Argument, and they conflate expository and descriptive text-types under the term "categorical."

14. Susan Suleiman, *Authoritarian Fictions* (New York: Columbia University Press, 1983), p. 26. Suleiman's discussion of "exemplum" shows how service is built into the word's very etymology: "The term *exemplum* (Greek *paradeigma*) designated persuasion by induction, or argument by analogy (in contrast to the *enthymeme*, or persuasion by deduction). . . . Aristotle . . . already divided *exempla* into 'real' and 'fictional' ones—the former being drawn from history or mythology, the latter being the invention of the orator himself. In the category of fictional *exempla*, Aristotle distinguished parables, or brief comparisons, from fables, which constitute a series of actions, in other words, a story" (p. 27).

15. Susan Sniader Lanser, in *The Narrative Act* (Princeton: Princeton University Press, 1981), goes too far in equating all fictions with the fable or parabolic genres: "The novel's basic illocutionary activity," she writes, "is ideological instruction; its basic plea: hear my word, believe and understand" (p. 293). Suleiman's *Authoritarian Fictions* takes great care to separate authoritarian—that is, thesis-dominated and hence "argued"—fictions from the rest of the universe of novels and short stories.

16. Jean La Fontaine, *Fables of La Fontaine*, trans. Elizur Wright (New York: Derby & Jackson, 1860).

Notes

17. Henry Fielding, *The History of the Adventures of Joseph Andrews & His Friend Mr Abraham Adams* (1742; Harmondsworth: Penguin Books, 1954), p. 27.

18. Ibid., pp. 156–57. I owe this example, along with general edification about the role of argumentation in fiction, to Glen McClish, "Rhetoric and the Rise of the English Novel" (Ph.D. diss., University of California, Berkeley, 1986), pp. 232–33.

19. Marie-Henri Beyle (Stendhal), *The Red and the Black* (1830), trans. C. K. Scott Moncrieff (New York: Modern Library, 1926), p. 236.

20. Leo Tolstoy, *Anna Karenina* (1877), trans. Joel Carmichael (New York: Bantam Books, 1981), pp. 601–2.

21. Wayne Booth, *The Rhetoric of Fiction*, 2d ed. (Chicago: University of Chicago Press, 1961, 1983), chap. 1.

22. Charles Dickens, *Little Dorrit* (1857; New York: New American Library, 1980), p. 1.

23. Gérard Genette, *Narrative Discourse*, trans. Jane Lewin (Ithaca: Cornell University Press, 1980), p. 101.

24. Genette, "Frontiers," p. 136.

25. Fyodor Dostoevsky, *Crime and Punishment* (1866), trans. Constance Garnett (New York: Macmillan, 1951), p. 2.

26. I take this example from Cleanth Brooks and Robert Penn Warren, *Understanding Fiction*, 2d ed. (New York: Appleton-Century-Crofts, 1959), p. 9, which says that though it is "moving" toward a narrative, and though "one can easily imagine Lady Blessington's becoming a character in a historical novel," this is still a "character sketch"—hence a description.

27. Genette, "Frontiers," p. 134.

28. *The Miscellaneous Works in Prose and Verse of Sir Thomas Overbury, Knt.*, ed. Edward F. Rimbault (London: Reeves & Turner, 1890), p. 69.

29. Quoted in Mieke Bal, "On Meanings and Descriptions," trans. by Robert Corum, *Studies in 20th-Century Literature* 6, nos. 1 and 2 (1982), p. 126.

30. Wallace Martin, personal communication.

31. Bordwell and Thompson, *Film Art*, p. 49.

32. Alain Robbe-Grillet, *Two Novels by Robbe-Grillet*, trans. Richard Howard (New York: Grove Press, 1965), p. 96. As Bruce Morrissette points out in *Novel and Film: Essays in Two Genres* (Chicago: University of Chicago Press, 1985), p. 24, what we get in *La jalousie* is "the phenomenological transcription of the jealous husband's perceptions and sensations." That these are the husband's perceptions and not those of some objective narrator must be inferred, because there are no first person markers indicating him as the speaker. Once we make that inference, Morrissette continues, we must conclude that these perceptions and sensations are really "objective correla-

tives of the subject's thoughts and passions." But in an age of psychological fiction, "thoughts" and "passions" certainly qualify as narrative events, indeed, the critical or even the only events of many fictions. The events of *La jalousie* must be understood to occupy the space in the text between the descriptive statements.

33. Genette, "Frontiers," p. 135.

34. I am indebted to Wallace Martin (personal communication) for this language.

Notes to Chapter 2

1. Gérard Genette, "Frontiers of Narrative," in *Figures of Literary Discourse*, ed. Marie-Rose Logan, trans. Alan Sheridan (New York: Columbia University Press, 1982), p. 137.

2. Gérard Genette, *Narrative Discourse*, trans. Jane Lewin (Ithaca: Cornell University Press, 1980), p. 94 n.12.

3. See Philippe Hamon, "Rhetorical Status of the Descriptive," *Yale French Studies* 61 (1981), 1–26, trans. Patricia Baudoin of Philippe Hamon, *Introduction à l'analyse du déscriptif* (Paris: Hachette, 1981), chap. 1.

4. Ibid., p. 7.

5. See Jean-François Marmontel, "Grammaire et littérature," in *Encyclopédie méthodique* (Paris: Panckoucke, 1782); Hamon, "Rhetorical Status," p. 32 n.2; Paul Valéry, "Degas, danse, déssin," in *Oeuvres*, vol. 2 (Pléiade ed.), pp. 1219–20 (quoted in Hamon, "Rhetorical Status," p. 10).

6. Hamon, "Rhetorical Status," p. 11.

7. Ibid., p. 13.

8. Philippe Hamon, "Qu'est-ce qu'une description?" *Poétique* 12 (1972), 475 (my translation).

9. Meir Sternberg, "Ordering the Unordered: Time, Space, and Descriptive Coherence," *Yale French Studies* 61 (1981), 60–88.

10. James Joyce, *A Portrait of the Artist as a Young Man* (1914–15), ed. Chester G. Anderson (New York: Viking Press, 1973), p. 184.

11. Roland Barthes, "L'effet de réel," *Communications* 11 (1968), 84–89, rpt. as "The Reality Effect," trans. R. Carter, in *French Literary Theory Today: A Reader*, ed. Tzvetan Todorov (Cambridge: Cambridge University Press, 1982).

12. Fyodor Dostoevsky, *The Devils* (1871), trans. David Magarshack (Harmondsworth: Penguin Books, 1953), pp. 188–89.

13. Georg Lukács, "Narrate or Describe? A Preliminary Discussion of Naturalism and Formalism," in *Writer and Critic and Other Essays*, ed. and trans. Arthur D. Kahn (New York: Grosset & Dunlap, 1970), pp. 111–12.

The ideological implications of this distinction between observer and participant are examined by Fredric Jameson in *Marxism and Form: Twentieth-Century Dialectical Theories of Literature* (Princeton: Princeton University Press, 1974), pp. 200–202.

14. Lukács, "Narrate or Describe?" p. 114.

15. Ibid., p. 116.

16. Wallace Martin, *Recent Theories of Narrative* (Ithaca: Cornell University Press, 1986), p. 122.

17. Alexander Gelley, "The Represented World: Toward a Phenomenological Theory of Description in the Novel," *Journal of Aesthetics and Art Criticism* 37 (1979), 187.

18. The point is made clear by Christian Metz in *Film Language: A Semiotics of the Cinema*, trans. Michael Taylor (New York: Oxford University Press, 1974), p. 128: "This in no way implies that the descriptive syntagma can only be applied to *motionless* objects or persons. A descriptive syntagma may very well cover an action, provided that it is an action whose only intelligible internal relationship is one of spatial parallelism at any given moment in time—that is to say, an action the viewer cannot mentally string together in [diegetic] time. Example: a flock of sheep being herded (views of the sheep, the shepherd, the sheepdog, etc.)."

19. Jeffrey Kittay, "Descriptive Limits," *Yale French Studies* 61 (1981), 225–43.

20. Ibid., p. 232.

21. Ibid., p. 239.

22. Gotthold Ephraim Lessing, *Laocoön, Nathan the Wise, and Minna Von Barnhelm*, trans. William A. Steel (London: Dent, 1930), p. 59.

23. Hamon, "Rhetorical Status," p. 17. The passage occurs in Lessing, *Laocoön*, p. 57.

24. Even Kittay seems uncertain about how to analyze the passage: "A reading shows the actions of Hephaistos as a necessary structural component of sorts, as each 'vignette' on the shield originates in the repetitions: 'Then he made . . . ,' 'Then he pictured . . .' Is this passage one of action or of description? Or is this a place where no one should care?" ("Descriptive Limits," p. 241). If we are seriously concerned about the nature of narrative and its delimitation from other text-types, I think we should care. I am trying to show that the antinomy of deep versus surface structure makes it relatively easy for us to do so. Indeed, the only disappointment in Kittay's otherwise brilliant article is its skeptical conclusion: "To read a passage as the representation of the act of making, as *poesis* is, is to find no final difference between description and action" (p. 242). What a shame—after he has seemed to establish the difference in so precise a way.

210

25. Homer, *The Iliad*, trans. W. H. D. Rouse (New York: Mentor Books, 1950), p. 225.
26. Alain Robbe-Gillet, *Snapshots*, trans. Bruce Morrissette (New York: Grove Press, 1968).
27. Cleanth Brooks and Robert Penn Warren, *Understanding Fiction*, 2d ed. (New York: Appleton-Century-Croft, 1959), p. 257.
28. I intentionally say "skewed chrono-logic" and not "flashback" or "anachrony" in Genette's sense. What is happening is not the later discourse representation of an earlier story event. It is rather the reversal of *both* story and discourse order.
29. Hamon, "Rhetorical Status," p. 26.

Notes to Chapter 3

1. The "cinematic narrator," discussed at length in Chapter 8, is the transmitting agency, immanent to the film, which presents the images we see and the sounds we hear. It is not the filmmaker or production team but bears the same relation to those real people as does the narrator to the real author of a novel. Neither is it a voice-over that introduces the action, though that voice-over may be one of its devices.
2. In that sense, narratology would disagree with Aristotle's deprecation of spectacle as "not hav[ing] much to do with poetic art and really be-long[ing] to the business of producing the play" (*Aristotle's Poetics: A Translation and Commentary for Students of Literature*, trans. Leon Golden [Englewood Cliffs, N.J.: Prentice-Hall, 1968], 14.8–10). It is doubtless true that one simply *hearing* the plot of *Oedipus* would experience some degree of fear and pity, but surely an excellent stage or screen performance will intensify the effect a thousandfold.
3. Claude Ollier, "Réponse," *Premier Plan*, no. 18 (n.d.), 26, quoted in Bruce Morrissette, *Novel and Film: Essays in Two Genres* (Chicago: University of Chicago Press, 1985), p. 22.
4. John Fowles, *The French Lieutenant's Woman* (1969; New York: New American Library, 1969), p. 10.
5. I have discussed these matters under the rubric of "determinacy" in Seymour Chatman, *Story and Discourse: Narrative Structure in Fiction and Film* (Ithaca: Cornell University Press, 1978), p. 30.
6. Christian Metz, *Film Language: A Semiotics of the Cinema*, trans. Michael Taylor (New York: Oxford University Press, 1974), pp. 127–28.
7. *L'Avventura: A Film by Michelangelo Antonioni*, ed. David Denby, trans. Jon Swan (New York: Grove Press, 1969), p. 11.

8. Orson Welles, *Touch of Evil*, ed. Terry Comito (New Brunswick, N.J.: Rutgers University Press, 1985), p. 56.

9. Ernest Callenbach (letter to the author).

10. "Camera," here and throughout, is synecdochic for the whole cinematic apparatus.

11. Honoré de Balzac, *Old Goriot*, trans. Marion Ayton Crawford (Harmondsworth: Penguin Books, 1959), p. 29.

12. Rudyard Kipling, "The Man Who Would Be King," in Cleanth Brooks and Robert Penn Warren, *Understanding Fiction*, 3d ed. (Englewood Cliffs, N.J.: Prentice-Hall, 1979), p. 85.

13. Gustave Flaubert, *Madame Bovary*, trans. Francis Steegmuller (New York: Random House, 1957), pp. 273–74.

14. As quoted by Philippe Hamon, "Rhetorical Status of the Descriptive," *Yale French Studies* 61 (1981), 3.

15. Videocassette is available on MCA Video.

16. Metz, *Film Language*, p. 167. Metz's distinction between "achronological" syntagmas (such as "parallel" and "bracket") and "chronological" syntagmas (such as "descriptive") is not clearly drawn. What seems to be at issue is the difference between descriptions that happen *during* story time— that is, in "pauses"—and descriptions that happen outside of story time, in the discourse only. The former should be called descriptive; the latter should be called commentative because they convey the narrator's commentary. Thus, in my view, the shots of the very opening of *Adieu Philippine* are erroneously labeled "bracket" (p. 150). Though it is true that they "are merely chosen as representative of a certain reality: work in a television studio," this is not a studio out in the real world but precisely the fictional studio in which the protagonist works and which becomes the setting for the first part of the film.

17. Charles Dickens, *Great Expectations* (1861), ed. Angus Calder (Harmondsworth: Penguin Books, 1965), chap. 1.

18. *All About Eve* (Twentieth Century–Fox, 1950) is available on Magnetic Video.

19. *The Oxford Companion to Film*, ed. Liz-Anne Bawden (New York: Oxford University Press, 1970), p. 614.

20. For an excellent account of the operant conventions of the classic Hollywood narrative film, see David Bordwell, *Narration in the Fiction Film* (Madison: University of Wisconsin Press, 1985), a book that I discuss in detail in Chapter 8.

21. Gérard Genette, *Narrative Discourse*, trans. Jane Lewin (Ithaca: Cornell University Press, 1980), pp. 109–12.

22. See Chatman, *Story and Discourse*, pp. 63–65.

23. Malcolm Lowry, *Under the Volcano* (1947; New York: Signet Books, 1965), p. 29.
24. *The Passenger* (1975) is available on MGM videocassette.
25. Noël Burch, *Theory of Film Practice*, trans. Helen R. Lane (New York: Praeger, 1973), p. 28. This effect is well known in perceptual psychology: it is difficult to tell whether an object seen through a peephole is large and distant or near and small. Since context has been eliminated, we have no way of knowing. See Bordwell, *Narration in the Fiction Film*, pp. 100–104, for a good discussion of the relevant literature on perception.
26. See Michelangelo Antonioni, *Il deserto rosso* (Bologna: Capelli, 1964).
27. The frame is reproduced in black and white in Seymour Chatman, *Antonioni; or, The Surface of the World* (Berkeley: University of California Press, 1985), p. 127.
28. E. M. Forster, *Aspects of the Novel* (Harmondsworth: Penguin Books, 1962), p. 34.

Notes to Chapter 4

1. David Bordwell, *Narration in the Fiction Film* (Madison: University of Wisconsin Press, 1985), p. 235; David Bordwell and Kristen Thompson, *Film Art: An Introduction*, 2d ed. (New York: Knopf, 1986), chap. 3.
2. Christian Metz, *Film Language: A Semiotics of the Cinema*, trans. Michael Taylor (New York: Oxford University Press, 1974), p. 194: "It is not because the cinema is language that it can tell such fine stories, but rather it has become language because it has told such fine stories."
3. John Fell, *Film and the Narrative Tradition* (Berkeley: University of California Press, 1986), documents the rise of the cinema out of nineteenth-century narrative genres—the novel, stage play, and the like.
4. This is not true of television, which, from its very beginnings, has been a multitextual medium. Many commercials and some documentaries have explicitly argumentative structures. Even so, non-narrative programs have always had to struggle for prime time, and several cable channels show nothing but movies.
5. An exception is the final title in some films, such as *A Cry in the Dark*, which cites postdiegetic facts bearing on the film's moral issue.
6. The film is available for 16mm rental and on videotape (Embassy 4065); the scenario—more precisely, the cutting continuity or *découpage*—appears in Alain Resnais, *Mon oncle d'Amérique, L'Avant Scène du Cinéma*, no. 263 (March 1981), 30, 47–72.
7. For what it's worth, here is what Jean Gruault said in an interview

about his and Resnais's intentions: "This may sound pretentious, but we *used* Laborit, although not to make a didactic film. It's like Proust using the notes of his father—who was a doctor—to create his characters, especially their medical histories. Laborit for me is a bit like Marx was for Brecht: an illumination for telling a story" (Annette Insdorf, "French Uncles," *Film Comment* 16 [September–October 1980], 23). It would be interesting to know whether Laborit felt that *he* had "used" Gruault and Resnais as a way of communicating his theory to a mass audience.

8. *Le Monde*, September 13, 1980, as quoted in *L'Avant Scène du Cinéma*, no. 263 (March 1981), 72.

9. That Laborit is self-consciously *in* the discourse is amusingly emphasized by the fact that he, unlike the fictional characters, can hear what the *speakerine* says about him. He playfully amplifies her commentary by mentioning his Vendéese origin.

10. This view is articulated by, e.g., Metz in *Film Language*, pp. 67, 116.

11. The overtness of the struggle between René and Veestrate is a function of their petit-bourgeois class (also signaled by their beefiness and unstylish suits). Struggle for dominion at the upper bourgeois level is less physical: the battle between Jean and Michel is discreet and repressed. But Laborit is not interested in class; he wishes only to show that ostensibly different behaviors manifest the same biological imperatives.

12. Reviewing the film in "French Uncles," *American Film* 16 (September–October, 1980), 22, Jan Dawson wrote: "The fragmentary narrative technique itself—in leaving us constantly wanting to see more, and in making us constantly aware that we are permitted to view only moments selected to illustrate a theory . . . serves to put a question mark at the end of Laborit's matter-of-fact pronouncements." But the knife cuts both ways: Laborit's discourse similarly puts the fiction into question. And both are put into question by the final sequence: a traveling shot through an American slum.

13. Ibid.: the film endows nature with "an aching beauty that cannot be explained away—not even by the fact that its powers of adaptation and survival are manifestly so much stronger than those of the humans attempting to find their niche within it."

14. The effect is further complicated by the fact that as she pretends to storm out, Jean won't let her leave. But then she is genuinely frustrated— she weeps the frustrated tears of her childhood as she sits in her own bedroom, held captive for the wrong reasons, prevented from doing the noble thing. When she breaks one of her own vases, she is both *acting* angry and *feeling* angry.

15. In an interview published with the screenplay, Resnais acknowledged the resemblance to *Blow-Up* and also to certain paintings of Paul Signac.

Notes to Chapter 5

1. See Wayne Booth, *The Rhetoric of Fiction*, 2d ed. (Chicago: University of Chicago Press, 1983); Shlomith Rimmon, "A Comprehensive Theory of Narrative: Genette's *Figures III*," *PTL* 1 (1976), 58 (a critique of Genette's omission of the implied author from his narrative system); Shlomith Rimmon-Kenan, *Narrative Fiction: Contemporary Poetics* (London: Methuen, 1983), pp. 86–89, 101–4; Gérard Genette, who seems to accept a de-anthropomophized implied author in *Narrative Discourse Revisited*, trans. Jane Lewin (Ithaca: Cornell University Press, 1988), chap. 19; W. J. M. Bronzwaer, "Implied Author, Extradiegetic Narrator, and Public Reader: Gérard Genette's Narratological Model and the Reading Version of *Great Expectations*," *Neophilologus* 62 (1978), 1–17; and W. J. M. Bronzwaer, "Mieke Bal's Concept of Focalization: A Critical Note," *Poetics Today* 2 (1981), 193–201, a critique of Bal's attempt to replace the pair "implied author–narrator" by the pair "narrator-focalizer"; Mieke Bal, who defends her position in "The Laughing Mice, or On Focalization," *Poetics Today* 2 (1981), 202–10; and Gerald Prince, *Dictionary of Narratology* (Lincoln: University of Nebraska Press, 1987), pp. 42–43.

2. Susan Sniader Lanser, *The Narrative Act* (Princeton: Princeton University Press, 1981), argues that the narrator is close "to the author's own enterprise and can provide important indices of the author's relationship to the literary act" (p. 141), and that the narrator is the "textually encoded, historically authoritative voice kin to but not identical with the biographical person who wrote the text" (p. 152). In analyzing a story by Kate Chopin, she finds it relevant to discuss facts about the real author; e.g., she claims to know that the covert narrator is female "by virtue of the conventions linking the author's social identity with that of the heterodiegetic narrative voice," and that "by the conventions of authorial equivalence this narrator may also be assumed to share the personality and values—the imaginative and ideological consciousness of the authorial voice" (p. 250).

3. See W. K. Wimsatt, Jr., and Monroe Beardsley, "Intention," in *Dictionary of World Literature*, ed. Joseph T. Shipley (Paterson, N.J.: Littlefield, Adams, 1960).

4. Our understanding of the reader's response has been expanded considerably in recent years. See Umberto Eco, *The Role of the Reader: Explorations in the Semiotics of Texts* (Bloomington: Indiana University Press, 1979); Stanley Fish, *Is There a Text in This Class? The Authority of Interpretive Communities* (Cambridge: Harvard University Press, 1978); Wolfgang Iser, *The Act of Reading: A Theory of Aesthetic Response* (Baltimore: Johns Hopkins University Press, 1978); Wolfgang Iser, *The Implied Reader: Patterns of Communication in Prose Fiction from Bunyan to Beckett* (Baltimore: Johns Hopkins

University Press, 1974); Hans Robert Jauss, *Toward an Aesthetic of Reception*, trans. Timothy Bahti (Minneapolis: University of Minnesota Press, 1982); Stephen Mailloux, *Interpretive Conventions: The Reader in the Study of American Fiction* (Ithaca: Cornell University Press, 1982); Walter J. Ong, "The Writer's Audience Is Always a Fiction," *PMLA* 90 (1975), 9–21; Gerald Prince, *Narratology: The Form and Functioning of Narrative* (Berlin: Mouton, 1982), Peter Rabinowitz, *Before Reading: Narrative Conventions and the Politics of Interpretation* (Ithaca: Cornell University Press, 1988); Susan Suleiman and Inge Crosman, ed., *The Reader in the Text*: Essays on Audience and Interpretation (Princeton: Princeton University Press, 1980), Jane Tompkins, ed., *Reader-Response Criticism: From Formalism to Post-Structuralism* (Baltimore: Johns Hopkins University Press, 1980); and *Critical Inquiry* 9 (1982), a special issue devoted to the "Politics of Interpretation."

5. Recent work in "possible-world" philosophy finds a theoretical corroboration of the implied author in the very nature of fictional discourse. According to possible-world philosophers, an implied or "reader's author" must be postulated to permit the reader to attribute to the fiction beliefs that may or may not be those of the real author. The implied or reader's author is "different from the real author in that all his beliefs are inferred from the fiction and are all consonant with it" (Koenraad Kuiper and Vernon Small, "Constraints on Fictions: With an Analysis of M. K. Joseph's *A Soldier's Tale*," *Poetics Today* 7 [1986], 495–526; quotation p. 498).

6. See *Le Degré zéro de l'écriture*, as quoted by Jonathan Culler, *Structuralist Poetics* (Ithaca: Cornell University Press, 1975), p. 133; Lanser, *Narrative Act*, p. 115; and Paul Ricoeur, "The Model of the Text: Meaningful Action Considered as a Text," *New Literary History* 5 (1973), 91–117.

7. As Kuiper and Small suggest: "We believe that the [implied] author is inferred from the text by the reader (and can therefore be inferred differently by different readers)" ("Constraints on Fictions," p. 498).

8. E. D. Hirsch, Jr., *Validity in Interpretation* (New Haven: Yale University Press, 1967), p. 211.

9. P.D. Juhl, *Interpretation: An Essay in the Philosophy of Literary Criticism* (Princeton: Princeton University Press, 1981), p. 13.

10. Perhaps even more important than Wimsatt and Beardsley's original article, "Intention," are Beardsley's subsequent remarks in *Aesthetics*, 2d ed. (Indianapolis, Ind.: Hackett, 1981), and in "Intentions and Interpretations: A Fallacy Revived," in *The Aesthetic Point of View*, ed. Michael Wreen and Donald Callen (Ithaca: Cornell University Press, 1982), pp. 188–207.

11. Beardsley, *Aesthetics*, pp. 17, 20, 26.

12. Saul Bellow, quoted by Christopher Lehmann-Haupt in a review of Bellow's *More Die of Heartbreak*, *New York Times*, May 21, 1987, p. C 29.

13. Beardsley, *Aesthetics*, p. 26. A reader-response critic, of course, would

change "the evidence of the poem itself" to "the opinions of all other interpretive communities." But the point remains no less valid: a poet cannot *enforce* an idiosyncratic interpretation (unless he changes the text itself by appending his interpretation to it).

14. Ibid. The term "design" is used in a similar sense in Roger Fowler, *Linguistics in the Novel* (London: Methuen, 1977), p. 80.

15. I take the terms from the lucid article by William Tolhurst, "On What a Text Is and How It Means," *British Journal of Aesthetics* 19 (1979), 3–14. Another useful anti-intentionalist statement is Jack Meiland, "Interpretation as a Cognitive Discipline," *Philosophy and Literature* 2 (1978), 23–45. Meiland uses Hirsch's terms—"validity," "cognition," "objectivity"—to argue quite a different conclusion: namely, that "a work can have several different interpretations, all of which may be equally valid" (p. 30).

16. Tolhurst, "On What a Text Is," p. 5. "Utterance meaning is best understood as the intention which a member of the intended audience [or 'implied reader'] would be most justified in attributing to the author based on the knowledge and attitudes which he possesses in virtue of being a member of the intended audience. Thus utterance meaning is to be construed as that hypothesis of utterer's meaning which is most justified on the basis of those beliefs and attitudes which one possesses qua intended hearer or intended reader" (p. 11).

17. Booth, *Rhetoric of Fiction*, pp. 70–74.

18. Italo Calvino expressed a similar view: "The author is an author insofar as he enters into a role the way an actor does and identifies himself with that projection of himself at the moment of writing" (quoted in Christopher Lehmann-Haupt's review of Calvino's *Uses of Literature: Essays* [New York: Wolff/Harcourt Brace Jovanovich, 1986], *New York Times*, October 27, 1986, p. 17).

19. E.g., P. D. Juhl (*Interpretation*, pp. 13–15) excludes from "intention" (a) what the author planned to write or convey, (b) his "motive" in writing (to gain wealth, recognition, or the like), and (c) the "sustained focal effect or textual coherence of the work." He limits intention to "writing a certain sequence of words—in the sense, that is, of what [the author] meant by the words he used." Wallace Martin reminds me (in a letter) that "intentionality" in the latter sense is well established in philosophy, particularly in Edmund Husserl: e.g., in a phrase such as "objective intentionality"; see "Intentionality," in *Dictionary of Philosophy*, ed. Dagobert Runes (Totowa, N.J.: Littlefield, Adams, 1975), p. 148.

20. But see the discussion of the "career-author," below, for a way to account for information deriving from other "authorial" choices in the other works of a given author.

21. Fowler, *Linguistics*, pp. 79–80. Wayne Booth, in *The Company We*

Notes

Keep: An Ethics of Fiction (Berkeley: University of California Press, 1988), p. 91, continues to equate text and implied author: "What is never obvious is any precise line dividing the questions that a given fiction—which is to say, a given implied author—invites, or will tolerate, or will want to reject."

22. Some theorists believe that only human beings can "intend." Why that should be so has never been clear to me. A text is the repository of intentions—or, better, achieved intentions—so why bridle at saying that it *has* intentions? Surely the statement "The Constitution intends to protect freedom of the press" is no less meaningful than "The signers of the Constitution intended to protect freedom of the press." As Booth puts it: "If works of art, like other seemingly inert objects in the world, do have natures in the sense of presenting horizons of potentiality, then they can be said to take attitudes toward our questions" (*The Company We Keep*, p. 91).

23. R. W. Stallman, "Intentions," in *Princeton Encyclopedia of Poetry and Poetics*, ed. Alex Preminger, enl. ed. (Princeton: Princeton University Press, 1974), p. 398.

24. W. K. Wimsatt, "Genesis: A Fallacy Revisited," in *Day of the Leopards: Essays in Defense of Poems* (New Haven: Yale University Press, 1976), pp. 221–22.

25. As Genette writes (*Narrative Discourse Revisited*, p. 148): "If one means by it that beyond the narrator (even an extradiegetic one), and by various pinpointed or global signs, the narrative text (like any other text) produces a certain *idea* (taking everything into account, this term is preferable to 'image,' and it is high time to substitute it for image) *of the author*, one means something obvious, which I can only acknowledge and even insist on, and *in this sense* I willingly approve of Bronzwaer's formula: 'The scope of narrative theory [I would say, more carefully, of poetics] excludes the writer but includes the implied author.'"

26. Wallace Martin (letter to the author).

27. Booth, *Rhetoric of Fiction*, p. 72.

28. Henry Fielding, *The History of the Adventures of Joseph Andrews & His Friend Mr. Abraham Adams* (1742; Harmondsworth: Penguin Books, 1954), pp. 29–30.

29. This represents a change in the position I took in Seymour Chatman, *Story and Discourse: Narrative Structure in Fiction and Film* (Ithaca: Cornell University Press, 1978), pp. 148–51. I no longer believe that narrators and narratees are "optional" and that where the narrator is "absent," the implied author may address the reader directly. That is irreconcilable with the notion of the implied author as silent source, as the perpetually reanimatable inventor of the whole. I am indebted to the discussion of this point by Shlomith Rimmon-Kenan, *Narrative Fiction*, pp. 88–89 (though unlike her, I continue to believe in the utility of a six-part communication model of narrative that includes implied author and implied reader).

218

30. But Susan Lanser argues that "titles, prefaces, epigraphs, dedications, and so on" provide information about the real author's views in "an open forum" with the real reader (see *Narrative Act*, p. 125). And it is true that for some fictions, titles must be attributed to the implied authors, since their narrators could not (out of ignorance or whatever) articulate them (*The Sound and the Fury, One Flew over the Cuckoo's Nest*). But in other cases, titles may be simply one more message from the narrator to the narratee: *A la recherche du temps perdu, Pride and Prejudice, Great Expectations* are quite within the conceptual powers and larger intentions of their respective narrators. It seems excessive to categorize *all* titles as "extrafictional."

31. E.g., Balzac's "republicanism," some claim, emerges only in his fiction. See Genette, *Narrative Discourse Revisited*, pp. 142–43.

32. Wayne Booth, *Critical Understanding: The Powers and Limits of Pluralism* (Chicago: University of Chicago Press, 1979), p. 270.

Notes to Chapter 6

1. Wayne Booth, *The Rhetoric of Fiction*, 2d ed. (Chicago: University of Chicago Press, 1983), pp. 422–34.

2. I take the example of Anne Frank from an unpublished manuscript by Jeffrey Staley, " 'Like Trees, Walking': Reading the Gospels with Open Eyes."

3. W. K. Wimsatt, Jr., "Genesis: A Fallacy Revisited," in *Day of the Leopards: Essays in Defense of Poems* (New Haven: Yale University Press, 1976), p. 206.

4. E. A. Speiser, introduction to *The Anchor Bible: Genesis* (Garden City, N.Y.: Doubleday, 1964), pp. xx–xxi, xxvi. The "Yahwist" referred to God by the personal name *Yahweh* (Jehovah); the "Elohist" used *Elohim*, "the generic Hebrew word for divine being." I am grateful to Robert Alter for the citation.

5. Producer Arthur Freed, quoted by Lillian Ross in *Picture* (New York: Rinehart, 1952), p. 194.

6. *Auteurisme*—the idea that single individuals, typically directors, are the true sources of films of quality—was imported from France by Andrew Sarris (see *The American Cinema: Directors and Directions: 1929–1968* [New York: Dutton, 1968]). The *auteurs*—such directors as Orson Welles, John Ford, Alfred Hitchcock, Howard Hawks—were supposed somehow to have overcome the overriding influence of the studios to achieve largely personal visions.

7. These reviews are all quoted in Ross, *Picture*, pp. 229–31. *The Red Badge of Courage* (1951) is available on MGM videocassette.

8. Bronislau Kaper, quoted in Ross, *Picture*, p. 144.

9. Conversation quoted in ibid., p. 59. Huston was probably right. As a film critic for the *New York Tribune* remarked, "A redundant narration . . . clutters up the sound track from time to time explaining facts already clear in the images" (p. 229). Rheinhardt defended his decision in a wonderfully titled article, "Soundtrack Narration: Its Use Is Not Always a Resort of the Lazy or the Incompetent," *Films in Review* 4 (1953), 459–60.

10. Review quoted in Ross, *Picture*, pp. 229–30.

11. Dorrit Cohn, *Transparent Minds* (Princeton: Princeton University Press, 1978), p. 14.

12. Stephen Crane, *The Red Badge of Courage* (1895; New York: Bantam Books, 1983), p. 64.

13. Adam Garbicz and Jacek Klinowski, *Cinema, the Magic Vehicle: A Guide to Its Achievement*, vol. 1 (New York: Schocken Books, 1983), p. 73.

14. Ross, *Picture*, pp. 215–16.

15. Wimsatt, "Genesis," p. 214. See also David Magarshack, *Chekhov the Dramatist* (New York: Hill & Wang, 1960), pp. 188–89.

16. Rosalyn Krauss, review of Arthur Danto, *The Transfiguration of the Commonplace* (Cambridge, Mass.: Harvard University Press, 1981), *New Republic*, May 25, 1987, pp. 29–30.

17. Marianna Torgovnick, *Closure in the Novel* (Princeton: Princeton University Press, 1981), p. 16.

18. Albert J. Guerard, *The Triumph of the Novel* (Chicago: University of Chicago Press, 1982), p. 294.

19. Irving Howe, *Politics and the Novel* (Greenwich, Conn.: Fawcett, 1967), pp. 73–75.

20. Fyodor Dostoevsky, *The Notebooks for "The Possessed,"* ed. Edward Wasiolek, trans. Victor Terras (Chicago: University of Chicago Press, 1968), p. 12.

21. Ibid., pp. 12–13.

22. Vladimir A. Tunimanov, "The Narrator in *The Devils*," trans. Susanne Fusso, in *Dostoevsky: New Perspectives*, ed. Robert Louis Jackson (Englewood Cliffs, N.J.: Prentice-Hall, 1984), pp. 154–55. Tunimanov goes on: "It is impossible to place [a character] in some sort of category that exhausts his essence. He fits into many categories, and one can expand the number of them almost to infinity. This does not at all contradict the presence of a multitude of facts and 'factlets,' everyday details that create an impression of 'redundancy' and 'needlessness.' On the contrary, the petty details are good in that by their insignificance they countervail the power of categories and make that power illusory."

23. *Newsweek*, May 2, 1988, p. 51.

24. Hence, perhaps, the tiny cigarette, as emblem of the pre-tumescent cherub.

25. Fredric Jameson, "Class and Allegory in Contemporary Mass Culture: *Dog Day Afternoon* as a Political Film," in *Movies and Methods*, vol. 2, ed. Bill Nichols (Berkeley: University of California Press, 1985), pp. 715–33 (originally published in *College English* 38 [1977]).

26. Ibid., p. 719–20.

27. Indeed, the *corporate* interest in public turmoil is probably at the opposite pole, as Jameson points out (ibid., pp. 720–21): the media's "repeated stereotypical use of otherwise disturbing and alien phenomena in our present social conjuncture—political militancy, student revolt, resistance to and hatred of authority—has an effect of containment for the system as a whole. To name something is to domesticate it, to refer to it repeatedly is to persuade a fearful and beleaguered middle-class public that all of that is part of a known and catalogued world and thus somehow in order."

28. Ibid., p. 723.

29. Ibid., p. 728.

30. Ibid., p. 730.

Notes to Chapter 7

1. Gérard Genette, *Narrative Discourse*, trans. Jane Lewin (Ithaca: Cornell University Press, 1980), p. 162 and n2. Genette prefers the translation "pure narrative" (rather than "simple narrative") for *haplē diēgēsis*, arguing that it is so called because it is not "mixed," that is, does not contain direct quotation of dialogue.

2. *Aristole's Poetics: A Translation and Commentary for Students of Literature*, trans. Leon Golden (Englewood Cliffs, N.J.: Prentice-Hall, 1968), 5.1449b (p. 10).

3. Genette, *Narrative Discourse*, p. 163. Why, too, the quotation marks? If a short story contained nothing but the quoted speeches of the characters, wouldn't it be genuinely mimetic in the same sense as a published playscript?

4. Gérard Genette, *Narrative Discourse Revisited*, trans. Jane Lewin (Ithaca: Cornell University Press, 1988), p. 41.

5. Aristotle, *Poetics*, 24.1459b (p. 43).

6. "The very idea of *showing*, like that of imitation or narrative representation (and even more so, because of its naively visual character), is completely illusory: in contrast to dramatic representation, no narrative can 'show' or 'imitate' the story it tells. All it can do is tell it in a manner which is detailed, precise, 'alive' and in that way give more or less the *illusion of mimesis*—which is the only narrative mimesis, for this single and sufficient reason: that narration, oral or written, is a fact of language, and language signifies without imitating. Unless, of course, the object signified (narrated)

Notes

be itself language" (Genette, *Narrative Discourse*, pp. 163–64). And, again, "I believe there is no imitation in narrative because narrative, like everything (or almost everything) in literature, is an act of language. And, therefore, there can be no more imitation in narrative in particular than there is in language in general. Like every verbal act, a narrative can only *inform*—that is, transmit meanings" (Genette, *Narrative Discourse Revisited*, pp. 42–43).

7. In *Narrative Discourse Revisited*, p. 43, Genette does not even acknowledge that the dialogue is "imitated": it is, he says, simply "reproduced" or "transcribed." "Narrative does not 'represent' a (real or fictive) story, it *recounts* it—that is, it signifies it by means of language—except for the *already verbal* elements of the story (dialogues, monologues). And these, too, it does not imitate—not, certainly, because it cannot, but simply because it need not, since it can directly reproduce them, or more precisely, transcribe them."

8. Umberto Eco demonstrates the conventionality of iconic signs in *The Open Work*, trans. Anna Concogni (Cambridge: Harvard University Press, 1988). He makes two points of relevance to this discussion. First, iconicity is always a question of degree: e.g., a Renaissance sculpture is more iconic with respect to dimension, proportion, and contour than to color; a film is more iconic with respect to movement than a photograph. Second, the process of recognizing iconic signs is itself coded, not "natural." Schematic drawings are, in some sense, iconic, but one must understand the nature of the signifieds to grasp that iconicity. Grossly simplified drawings such as comic strips are more easily readable by adults than by children; hence, it is clear that time and energy have been required to learn their codes of representation. In short, "analogous" should not be understood in too simple a sense; an iconic sign is better defined as one that constructs a "model of relations" which is "homologous" to the model of perceptual relations we construct in recognizing the signified itself.

9. In Seymour Chatman, *Story and Discourse: Narrative Structure in Fiction and Film* (Ithaca: Cornell University Press, 1978), pp. 166–69, I tried to mitigate the assertion by offering readers the "option" of treating purely mimetic narratives as "minimally narrated" instead of "non-narrated." But that tactic clearly evaded the issue.

10. I treat the terms "presenting" and "transmitting" as synonymous. See Seymour Chatman, "The Structure of Narrative Transmission," in *Style and Structure in Literature: Essays in the New Stylistics*, ed. Roger Fowler (Ithaca: Cornell University Press, 1975), pp. 213–57.

11. Chatman, *Story and Discourse*, p. 146. I would also now reserve the concept of "mediate" for the action of filter characters (see Chapter 9).

12. Roger Fowler, *Linguistics and the Novel* (London: Methuen, 1977), p. 74. I apologize for once again subjecting this fatigued story to narratological analysis, but apparently we still have something to learn from it.

13. Nor is it clear to whom he is "invisible." To other characters in the story? To us? To "himself"? And is he invisible in the same way as H. G. Wells' character is? Or is there a special kind of narratorial invisibility?

14. Susan Sniader Lanser, *The Narrative Act* (Princeton: Princeton University Press, 1981), p. 266.

15. Lanser, *Narrative Act*, pp. 266–67.

16. Jonathan Culler, "Problems in the Theory of Fiction," *Diacritics* 14 (Spring 1984), 5, writes wisely about this matter: "The argument [of those who insist on assigning gender to narrators] would be . . . that since every person has a sex, and narrators are people, every narrator must have a sex, and to omit discussion of the sex of narrators is to miss important aspects of novels. This argument is plausible only, it seems to me, because we have come to take for granted that we explain textual details by adducing narrators and explain narrators by adducing qualities of real people. . . . The theory of fiction needs to be alert to the inadequacies of this orientation, which strives to convert everything in language to a mark of human personalities."

17. Lanser, *Narrative Act*, p. 268.

Notes to Chapter 8

1. E.g., Jean-Pierre Oudart, "Cinema and Suture," *Screen* 18 (1977–78), 35–47; and Daniel Dayan, "The Tutor-Code of Classical Cinema," in *Movies and Methods*, vol. 1, ed. Bill Nichols (Berkeley: University of California Press, 1976), pp. 438–50—effectively answered by William Rothman, "Against the System of the Suture," in Nichols, *Movies and Methods*, vol. 1, pp. 451–59.

2. David Bordwell, *Narration in the Fiction Film* (Madison: University of Wisconsin Press, 1985), chap. 2. For another good critique, see Noël Carroll, *Mystifying Movies* (New York: Columbia University Press, 1988).

3. See Christian Metz, "Story/Discourse (A Note on Two Kinds of Voyeurism)," in *The Imaginary Signifier*, trans. Celia Britton (Bloomington: Indiana University Press, 1981). Benveniste's views appear in *Problèmes de linguistique générale*, 2 vols. (Paris: Gallimard, 1966, 1974); the first volume has been published as *Problems in General Linguistics*, trans. Mary Elizabeth Meek (Coral Gables, Fla.: University of Miami Press, 1971). For Benveniste, *discours* refers to enunciations that contain references to the speaker and/or listener: thus to sentences with personal pronouns, imperatives, "deictic" adverbs, etc. *Histoire*, on the other hand, comprises enunciations that do not contain such marks, thus giving the impression of a totally impersonal account. This sense is especially strong for French speakers, because French has a tense form, the *passé simple* or aorist, which is used

Notes

solely for literary narrative. For a full discussion of the implications of this distinction, see the work of Ann Banfield, esp. *Unspeakable Sentences: Narration and Representation in the Language of Fiction* (London: Routledge & Kegan Paul, 1982). My own use of "story" and "discourse" is unrelated to Benveniste's.

4. Bordwell goes into detail to show the difficulties of applying enunciation theory to film studies (*Narration in the Fiction Film*, pp. 21–25). E.g., Mark Nash, "*Vampyr* and the Fantastic," *Screen* 17, no. 3 (1976), 29–67, "must reject nearly all of Benveniste's 'means of enunciation' (e.g. verb tense, signs of time) as inapplicable," and the only one left, "person," is given a questionable filmic equivalent ("What would a second-person *image* look like?" asks Bordwell). He finds similar problems in the work of François Jost, Nick Browne, Alain Bergala, Marie Ropars-Wuilleaumier, Raymond Bellour, and Stephen Heath.

5. Bordwell, *Narration in the Fiction Film*, p. 49. As I argued in *Story and Discourse: Narrative Structure in Fiction and Film* (Ithaca: Cornell University Press, 1978), pp. 45–48, causality is not the only logical principle (additional to temporal sequentiality) that connects story events. I proposed the term "contingency" to explain those cases not explained by strict causality. Bordwell (p. 51) seems to be referring to these other possibilities when he speaks of "parallelism." E.g., in *Rear Window*, the courtyard vignettes illustrating a variety of amatory relationships do not, strictly speaking, fit into the causal pattern of either the Thorwald murder plot or the Jeff-Lisa love plot, but they do form a kind of parallel to the latter.

6. What I called *mythos*, after Aristotle, in Chatman, *Story and Discourse*, pp. 19, 43.

7. Bordwell, *Narration in the Fiction Film*, p. 51.

8. Ibid., p. 50.

9. Ibid., pp. 49, 53. Other film theorists who argue against the cinematic narrator are Edward Branigan, *Point of View in the Cinema: A Theory of Narration and Subjectivity in Classical Film* (Berlin: Mouton, 1984); and Brian Henderson, "Tense, Mood, and Voice in Film (Notes after Genette)," *Film Quarterly* 36, no. 4 (1983), 4–17.

10. Bordwell, *Narration in the Fiction Film*, pp. 61–62.

11. Nick Browne, *The Rhetoric of Filmic Narration* (Ann Arbor, Mich.: UMI Research Press, 1982), p. 1.

12. Bordwell's theory puts an odd cast on other terms as well: e.g., "representation." He writes: "The spectator possesses stylistic schemata as well as others, and these invariably affect the overall process of narrative representation" (*Narration in the Fiction Film*, p. 53). But surely the viewer does not "represent"—or even re-present—the film in any usual sense of the word.

13. Ibid., pp. 57–58. For the useful concepts of "aesthetic objects" and

"aesthetic qualities," see Monroe Beardsley, *Aesthetics*, 2d ed. (Indianapolis, Ind.: Hackett, 1981), esp. pp. 38, 63–65. Beardsley reaffirmed his position in 1981 in the postscript to the second edition; see esp. pp. xxviii–xxxi.

14. Bordwell, *Narration in the Fiction Film*, p. 78.

15. Ibid., pp. 57–61.

16. Ibid., p. 62.

17. The concept has suggested many synonyms, as pointed out by Linda Hutcheon, *Narcissistic Narrative: The Metafictional Paradox* (Waterloo, Ont.: Wilfrid Laurier University Press, 1980), p. 1: "self-conscious," "self-reflective," "self-informing," "self-reflexive," "auto-referential," "auto-representational," and her own term "narcissistic." See also Robert Alter, *Partial Magic: The Novel as a Self-Conscious Genre* (Berkeley: University of California Press, 1976).

18. Bordwell, *Narration in the Fiction Film*, p. 58.

19. Ibid., p. 59.

20. See Kristin Thompson, "The Duplicitous Text: An Analysis of *Stage Fright*," *Film Reader* 2 (1977), 52–64.

21. We must be precise in our use of the term "unreliable narration." It is a meaningful concept only when it refers to the actual and overt misrepresentation or distortion of story "facts," by a narrator's guile, naiveté, or whatever. It must refer, I believe, to a narrator's acts of commission, not of omission. The omission of crucial data in the unraveling of a story is not a matter of unreliability but of that special form of analepsis which, as Gérard Genette puts it, "sidesteps" an event and which he dubs "paralipsis." Paralipsis omits "one of the constituent elements of a situation in a period that the narrative does generally cover." For example, in *A la recherche du temps perdu*, Proust recounts "his childhood while systematically concealing the existence of one of the members of his family" (*Narrative Discourse*, trans. Jane Lewin [Ithaca: Cornell University Press, 1980], p. 52). This seems to be the case of Bordwell's example (*Narration in Fiction Film*, p. 84), the film *Secret beyond the Door* (I say "seems" since I have not seen the film but go only by his description). Unlike the unreliable narrator, the paraliptic narrator *ultimately* fills in the gap. But the unreliable narrator sticks to his guns, and it is only the context or the intervention of a later, reliable narrator (as in *Stage Fright*) that sets things straight.

Another film theorist who uses "unreliable narration" in an odd way is George Wilson, *Narration in Light* (Baltimore: Johns Hopkins University Press, 1986), chaps. 2–3. Wilson equates unreliability with "openness" (lack of narrative closure), but that too seems to confuse it with paralipsis.

22. Bordwell, *Narration in Fiction Film*, p. 61, cites Branigan, *Point of View in the Cinema*, pp. 40–49, as his authority for this view.

23. Sarah Kozloff, *Invisible Storytellers: Voice-Over in American Fiction Film*

(Berkeley: University of California Press, 1988), p. 115, has problems with ascertaining the source of the lying flashback by speaking not of the implied author but of Hitchcock, (not "Hitchcock"). In general, Kozloff's position, though enlightened, fails to recognize the more general principle that controls all narrative transmission by whatever means. Thus, she distinguishes between the "silent image-maker" and the "narrator" (voice-over or -on), but she does not fully explain how the two are controlled by a more general agency that instructs them—the implied author.

24. An interesting proposal to account for narrative agency in the cinema has been made by Robert Burgoyne in an unpublished paper, "The Cinematic Narrator: The Logic and Pragmatics of Impersonal Narration." Following Marie-Laure Ryan, "The Pragmatics of Personal and Impersonal Narration," *Poetics* 10 (1981), 517–39, Burgoyne proposes two basic kinds of narrator—personal and impersonal. Unlike the personal narrator, who "simply reports on the world," the impersonal narrator also creates that world "while at the same time referring to it as if it had an autonomous existence, as if it preexisted the illocutionary act" (in what some film theorists call the "profilmic" state). "The impersonal narrator's lack of human personality allows the viewer to imagine that [the viewer] is confronting the fictional universe directly, putting aside any reflection on the form of the narrative discourse." The personal narrator may lie or distort the story, yet the true facts will remain; the impersonal narrator, who has created the story world, cannot present anything *but* the facts.

In arguing that the impersonal narrator creates as well as reports the diegetic world, Burgoyne and Ryan are attributing to it powers that I reserve for the implied author. If a narrator can create the diegetic world, there is nothing left for the implied author to do; indeed, Burgoyne concludes that "impersonal narration thus eliminates the need for the category of the implied author." There are various possible responses to the Burgoyne-Ryan theory: the one that immediately strikes me is that it does not account for the so-called "authorial narrator": that is, a narrator who is heterodiegetic and exists in the discourse only but, unlike the impersonal narrator, may well have a "personal" identity. Further, as I tried to show in Chapter 6, there are other reasons than reliability for recognizing the existence of the implied author.

25. Bordwell, *Narration in the Fiction Film*, p. 49.

26. Kozloff, *Invisible Storytellers*, p. 44.

27. Kozloff (ibid.) describes the problems posed by various alternative names for the overall presenter of a film: "voice" is bad for reasons argued above; "camera" is misleading because it neglects other presentational devices such as "lighting, graphics, processing, staging, sound track," and so on; "implied author" confuses levels; "implied director" makes auteurist assumptions; "implied narrator" risks confusion with voice-over narrators

(as well as with "implied author"); "master of ceremonies" is "sexist and circusy"; and Metz's "grand image-maker" "slights the sound track." But Kozloff herself goes along with Metz and calls this agency the "image-maker."

28. "Voice-over is just one of many elements, including musical scoring, sound effects, editing, lighting, and so on, through which the cinematic text is narrated" (ibid., pp. 43–44). By one estimate (in an unpublished manuscript by Avrom Fleishmann) about 15 percent of all films include narrators who speak or write parts of the narrative.

29. It would, of course, be possible to create a text that shows only black on the screen and communicates its story solely on the sound track. But it is questionable whether such a text should be called a "film," since exactly the same effect could be created by broadcasting an audio recording to an audience assembled in the dark.

30. Kozloff, *Invisible Storytellers*, p. 45: "In many cases the voice-over narrator is so inscribed in the film as to seem as if he or she has generated not only what he is saying but also what we are seeing. In other words, films often create the sense of character-narration so strongly that one accepts the voice-over narrator as if he or she were the mouthpiece of the image-maker either for the whole film or for the duration of his or her embedded story. We put our faith in the voice not as created but as creator."

31. Ibid., p. 12.

32. Kozloff (ibid., pp. 112–15) cites a number of other Hollywood films in which this happens: *Taxi Driver, Gilda, Cat Ballou, Evil under the Sun, Days of Heaven.*

33. Ibid., p. 115. I remember as a child in the 1930s seeing comic short subjects, addenda to the newsreels, in which the camera could act zany and be corrected by the voice-over narrator.

34. Kozloff (ibid., 117–26) discusses at length the question of reliability in *Barry Lyndon.*

35. Ann Banfield, "Describing the Unobserved: Events Grouped around an Empty Centre," in *The Linguistics of Writing*, ed. Nigel Fabb, Derek Attridge, Alan Durant, and Colin MacCabe (Manchester: Manchester University Press, 1987), p. 265.

36. Banfield, "Describing the Unobserved," pp. 266–67.

37. Gilles Deleuze, *Cinéma I: L'image mouvement* (Paris: Minuit, 1983), p. 117.

Notes to Chapter 9

1. Charles Dickens, *Dealings with the Firm of Dombey & Son Wholesale, Retail & for Exportation* (1848; London: Chapman & Hall, 1907), p. 1.

2. Ibid., pp. 2–3.

3. Gérard Genette, *Narrative Discourse*, trans. Jane Lewin (Ithaca: Cornell University Press, 1980), p. 205.

4. I discuss additional problems with the term "focalization" in Seymour Chatman, "What Can We Learn from Contextualist Narratology?" forthcoming in *Poetics Today*.

5. Virginia Woolf, *Jacob's Room* (1922; New York: Harvest Books, 1978), p. 7.

6. Charles Dickens, *Oliver Twist* (New York: Oxford University Press, 1949), p. 1.

7. See the section "Ironic Reading as Knowledge," in Wayne Booth, *A Rhetoric of Irony* (Chicago: University of Chicago Press, 1974), pp. 14–19.

8. The terms, of course, are not self-explanatory in the case of naive narrators or characters who lie in dialogue, but this terminology seems better than, say, "fallible narrator" and "unreliable filter."

9. Wayne Booth, *The Rhetoric of Fiction*, 2d ed. (Chicago: University of Chicago Press, 1983), pp. 347–53.

10. A good selection of articles on the subject appears in *Movies and Methods*, 2 vols., ed. Bill Nichols (Berkeley: University of California Press, 1976, 1985).

11. See Jean-Pierre Oudart, "Cinema and Suture," *Screen* 18 (1977–78), 35–47, and Daniel Dayan, "The Tutor-Code of Classical Cinema," in Nichols, *Movies and Methods*, vol. 1, pp. 438–50, for discussions of the ideological implications of classical Hollywood "suturing." Brian Henderson considers the ideological implications of another kind of film style in "Toward a Non-Bourgeois Camera Style (Part-Whole Relations in Godard's Late Films)," in *A Critique of Film Theory* (New York: Dutton, 1980), pp. 62–81.

12. The Tintoretto painting is in the Samuel H. Kress Collection of the National Gallery in Washington, D.C.

13. Nick Browne, *The Rhetoric of Film Narration* (Ann Arbor, Mich.: UMI Research Press, 1982), p. 3.

14. Ibid., p. 4.

15. Ibid., pp. 6, 8.

16. George Bluestone, *Novels into Film* (Berkeley: University of California Press, 1957), pp. 47–48.

17. The phrase was used by Antonioni in many interviews. For a more extended discussion of how this theme relates to existential anxiety, see Seymour Chatman, *Antonioni; or, The Surface of the World* (Berkeley: University of California Press, 1985), pp. 55–66. See also the article by psychoanalyst Simon Lesser, "*L'Avventura*: A Closer Look," *Yale Review* 54 (1964), 41–50.

Notes to Chapter 10

1. Wolfgang Iser, "The Reading Process: A Phenomenological Approach," in *The Implied Reader: Patterns of Communication in Prose Fiction from Bunyan to Beckett* (Baltimore: John Hopkins University Press, 1974), p. 283.

2. *The Third Man* is a classic case of a film that makes significant narrative improvements on the original text. See Seymour Chatman, "Who Is the Best Narrator? The Case of *The Third Man*," *Style* 23 (1989), 183–96.

3. These difficulties have been recognized for many years: see George Bluestone, *Novels into Film* (Berkeley: University of California Press, 1957).

4. The subject has become a genuine industry. Harris Ross, *Film as Literature, Literature as Film: An Introduction to and Bibliography of Film's Relationship to Literature* (Westport, Conn.: Greenwood Press, 1987), lists some 2,500 items; in English, there are 104 "general studies and anthologies" about adaptation alone.

5. See Martin Battestin, "Osborne's *Tom Jones*: Adapting a Classic," in *Man and the Movies*, ed. W. R. Robinson (Baltimore: Penguin Books, 1969), pp. 31–45. Battestin demonstrates other analogies such as the "dated acting styles" intended to suggest the "Hogarthian" characterization in the novel. He writes: "Just as Fielding indulges in amplifications, ironies, similes, mock-heroics, parodies, etc., so the film exploits for comic effect a circusful of wipes, freezes, flips, speed-ups, narrowed focuses—in short the entire battery of camera tricks" (p. 40).

6. Sarah Kozloff, *Invisible Storytellers: Voice-Over Narration in American Fiction Film* (Berkeley and Los Angeles: University of California Press, 1989).

7. See Bruce Kawin, *Mindscreen: Bergman, Godard, and First-Person Film* (Princeton: Princeton University Press, 1978).

8. *The French Lieutenant's Woman* (1981) is available on videocassette, Fox F4586.

9. Linda Hutcheon gives a good account of the special "self-consciousness" of the novel in a chapter titled "Freedom through Artifice: *The French Lieutenant's Woman*," in *Narcissistic Narrative: The Metaphysical Paradox* (Waterloo, Ont.: Wilfred Laurier University Press, 1980), pp. 57–70.

10. Peter Conradi interestingly argues that the theme of the novel's assault on Victorian mores is carefully matched by its assault on conventional narrative technique: "In *The French Lieutenant's Woman*, itself a species of historical romance, albeit an ornately mannered and self-conscious one, Fowles addresses the problem of repression and liberation as aspects both of the evolution of modern ethics, so that its major characters defy social convention, and also of the emancipation of the poetics of his chosen fictional form, so that the revelation and denunciation of the inauthenticities of his hero are accompanied by the attempt to expose the conventions and

hypocrisies of the form" ("*The French Lieutenant's Woman*: Novel, Screenplay, Film," *Critical Quarterly* 24 [Spring 1982], 42).

11. Joy Gould Boyum, *Double Exposure: Fiction into Film* (New York: Plume, 1985), p. 105. A more accurate characterization of the "transformation from narrator's comment to actor's voice" appears in Guido Almansi and Simon Henderson, *Harold Pinter* (London: Methuen, 1983), p. 96.

12. The exceptions are such *outré* moments as in chap. 61, when the narrator himself time-travels back to participate in the Victorian action.

13. John Fowles, *The French Lieutenant's Woman* (New York: New American Library, 1969), pp. 47, 324.

14. Peter Conradi, *John Fowles* (London: Methuen, 1982), p. 60. Conradi's is the most sophisticated discussion of the novel.

15. Fowles, *French Lieutenant's Woman*, pp. 80–81.

16. Ibid., p. 365.

17. E.g., Sarah's strange drawings, the meeting in the cemetery, the lightning and thunder as she flees to the ruined barn—none of which occur in the novel.

18. Fowles, *French Lieutenant's Woman*, p. 14.

19. Ibid., p. 351. There is evidence in the novel, especially in the way Sarah handles Mrs. Poulteney, that Dr. Grogan's diagnosis of her as a hysteric is not accurate. The mad drawings introduced into the film, contrarily, support his diagnosis.

20. Whatever the reason, the filmmakers did not honor Fowles's injunction to "keep her inexplicable" (quoted in Conradi, "*The French Lieutenant's Woman*," p. 43; Fowles made the remark on *The South Bank Show* on British television).

21. Fowles, *French Lieutenant's Woman*, p. 140.

22. Ibid., p. 138.

23. Ibid.

24. Boyum, e.g., writes: "Charming and clever as Fowles's narrator might be, he interrupts too frequently, often with much coyness. Many readers in fact have complained of his inconsistency, of his 'bad faith,' and that he is little more than a 'boring red herring.' There are times we couldn't care less what this chatty fellow has to tell us about the *nouveau roman*, about truth and reality in fiction—we just want to get on with the story. It's already quite clear that this is all a fantasy and there's no need for him to belabor the point" (*Double Exposure*, p. 107).

25. Fowles, *French Lieutenant's Woman*, pp. 138–43.

26. Ibid., p. 135.

27. John Fowles, introduction to Harold Pinter, *The Screenplay of "The French Lieutenant's Woman"* (London: Cape, 1981), p. xii.

28. Susanna Barber and Richard Messer, "*The French Lieutenant's Woman*

and Individualization," *Literature/Film Quarterly* 12 (1984), 229. As Glenn K. S. Man notes, "There is no particular reason" to make such an inference: see "The Intertextual Discourses of *The French Lieutenant's Woman*," *New Orleans Review* 12 (1988), 54–55.

29. Boyum, *Double Exposure*, pp. 106–8. Man, too, oversimplifies by arguing that "the film's happy resolution to the Victorian love story parallels the book's first ending, while Anna's decision to separate from Mike in the modern story parallels the second ending" ("Intertextual Discourses," p. 59).

30. Fowles, *French Lieutenant's Woman*, p. 354.

31. But their exchange does corroborate, in a "narratorial" way, the scene in the Victorian story which it immediately follows: Anna reads the startling statistics about prostitution just after Sarah has accepted the proposal to work in Mrs. Poulteney's ménage. In that context, even the most wretched job would be better than her fate should she go to London. As she says later to Charles in the cemetery, "If I went to London I know what I should become. I should become what some already call me in Lyme."

32. Christian Metz, *Film Language: A Semiotics of the Cinema*, trans. Michael Taylor (New York: Oxford University Press, 1974), p. 128.

33. As Conradi notes (*"The French Lieutenant's Woman,"* p. 50), the imbrication of the two love stories suggested by the screenplay is "significantly reduced" in the film itself. Virtually half the modern scenes originally proposed by the screenplay do not appear in the film.

34. These shots were doubtless intended to correspond to the novel's explicit description of the Undercliff (chap. 10), especially to evoke its semitropical character.

35. Both Ernestina and Sarah have their own musical themes. Sarah's is heavily Romantic, carried mostly by the deeper strings; Ernestina's is lighter, more English, but subject to a sad, minor variation when the relationship breaks up.

36. In the novel, Charles is much more restrained, using a "quiet voice," showing only "a flash of hurt resentment" (Fowles, *French Lieutenant's Woman*, pp. 350–51).

37. See Metz, "Mirror Construction in Fellini's *8 1/2*," in *Film Language*, pp. 228–34. The term *mise-en-abyme* was used by André Gide to describe novels such as *Paludes* and *Les fauxmonnayeurs*, which contain within themselves a replica of their own stories. Metz's translator proposes the English equivalents "mirror construction" and "inescutcheon construction," since Gide's original term was a metaphor drawn on the presence in heraldic shields of a small shield duplicating the containing shield. For a full discussion of *mise-en-abyme* in literary narrative, see Lucien Dällenbach, *Le récit spéculaire: Essai sur la mise en abyme* (Paris: Seuil, 1977).

Notes

38. In an interview (Harlan Kennedy, "The Czech Director's Woman," *Film Comment* 17 [September–October 1981], 25, 30), Karel Reisz acknowledged this intention: "In the Victorian scenes we very consciously went for an academic kind of lighting, the sort of high definition that you see in Victorian paintings. We used front light and side light—a pre-Impressionist kind of light to paint the object. We had our own shorthand motto for this: 'Constable, not Monet.' "

39. Curiously, Almansi and Henderson take this to be a *fault* in the movie, rather than one of its intentions: "Where the script does not seem to work is in the modern love story . . . Here, inevitably, the melodramatic impetus of the original story, the Victorian love-affair, so forcefully opposed and slow to come to life, is much more fascinating than the modern one, which appears facile and uncommitted. Every time the film moves to the modern love-scenes, the audience hopes that they will soon be over so that they will get back to Charles and Sarah's fate" (*Harold Printer*, p. 97). But that "uncommitted facility" of modern love—what has happened to Eros is one hundred years—is finally what the whole film is about. The audience's discomfort seems precisely what the implied author intends.

40. A good example: to explain Charles's disdain for commerce and his desire to remain a gentleman, the novel's narrator asks the narratee to think of possible modern parallels: "You have just turned down a tempting offer in commercial applied science in order to continue your academic teaching? Your last exhibition did not sell as well as the previous one, but you are determined to keep to your new style? You have just made some decision in which your personal benefit, your chance of possession, has not been allowed to interfere? Then do not dismiss Charles's state of mind" (Fowles, *French Lieutenant's Woman*, p. 234).

41. Again, analogies are drawn too easily by critics: "Like Charles . . . Mike displays a passion that is obsessive; while like Sarah, Anna proves ultimately elusive" (Boyum, *Double Exposure*, p. 106). But the film Sarah is not elusive; her return to Charles for romantic reasons is all too predictable. Interestingly, in the shot in which Charles says goodbye to her in Exeter after they make love, the screenplay gives him the line "I shall come back for you, my sweet . . . mystery." But the last phrase, "my sweet . . . mystery," is not spoken in the film. Nor do I agree that "the film's happy resolution to the Victorian love story parallels the first ending, while Anna's decision to separate from Mike in the modern story parallels the second ending" (Man, "Intertextual Discourses," p. 59). We don't know what Anna "decided"; perhaps she did not decide at all but simply left in ambivalent terror. In the novel, Sarah offers Charles a *kind* of relationship; *he* elects to leave. In the film, Anna just disappears.

42. We do sense, however, that she is a much weaker character than

Sarah. It strikes me as a flawed reading of the film to argue that "the contrast between the wild and needy Sarah and the more controlled and independent Anna carries much of the book's commentary on the Victorian woman, on her evolution into the modern" (Boyum, *Double Exposure*, p. 108). The woman who expresses her envy of Mike's wife's "gardening ability" is hardly "independent," and the woman who drives off without giving her lover a word of explanation is hardly "controlled."

43. Fowles, *French Lieutenant's Woman*, p. 213. The whole of chap. 35 is an expository-argumentative essay on the Victorian male's strangely conflicting attitudes toward women, the narrator discussing the repression of sex in the context of Freud's theory of sublimation.

44. Charles Scruggs, "The Two Endings of *The French Lieutenant's Woman*," *Modern Fiction Studies* 31 (Spring 1985), 95–114.

45. Of course, the film exists in consort with the novel, and many viewers cannot help embroidering the former with their memories of the latter. Boyum (*Double Exposure*, p. 64) and Man ("Intertextual Discourses," p. 55) are right in calling our attention to the "palimpsest" quality of films adapted from novels. The film "is distinct," says Man, "yet it derives its fullest possible meaning from its nature as a transformation of the literary work." It is not only that a picture speaks a thousand words but that even the briefest shot in a film based on a profusely discursive novel echoes some of the novel's commentary and background.

46. Conradi, *John Fowles*, p. 68, quoting from Lorna Sage, "Profile 7: John Fowles," *New Review*, 1974, p. 34.

Notes to Chapter 11

1. Terry Eagleton, *Literary Theory: An Introduction* (Minneapolis: University of Minnesota Press, 1983), pp. 205–7, argues that a revitalized rhetoric should be the alternative to literary theory, which in his view has become a "non-subject."

2. Christine Brooke-Rose, *A Rhetoric of the Unreal: Studies in Narrative and Structure, Especially of the Fantastic* (New York: Cambridge University Press, 1981), p. 12.

3. Paolo Valesio, *Novantiqua: Rhetorics as a Contemporary Theory* (Bloomington: Indiana University Press, 1980).

4. Chaim Perelman, *The New Rhetoric: A Treatise on Argumentation* (Notre Dame, Ind.: Notre Dame University Press, 1969).

5. Wayne Booth, *The Rhetoric of Fiction*, 2d ed. (Chicago: University of Chicago Press, 1983), p. 409.

6. Ibid., p. xiii.

Notes

7. Kenneth Burke, "Lexicon Rhetoricae," in *Counter-statement* (Berkeley: University of California Press, 1968), p. 135.

8. But didactic fictions are studied by Sheldon Sacks, *Fiction and the Shape of Belief: A Study of Henry Fielding, with Glances at Swift, Johnson, and Richardson* (Berkeley: University of California Press, 1964); David Richter, *Fable's End: Completeness and Closure in Rhetorical Fiction* (Chicago: University of Chicago Press, 1974); and Susan Suleiman, *Authoritarian Fictions* (New York: Columbia University Press, 1983).

9. See Ross Chambers, *Story and Situation: Narrative Seduction and the Power of Fiction* (Minneapolis: University of Minnesota Press, 1984). For all its own seductive appeal, however, it remains to be seen, as Porter Abbott points out in his review of Chambers, *Story and Situation* (*Poetics Today* 6 no. 3 [1985], 544), whether "the terminology of love will [in fact] bond to the critical language."

10. The statement, quoted from David Lodge's review of the book in the (British) *Modern Language Review*, appears on the back cover of the paperback version of the first edition of Booth's *Rhetoric of Fiction*.

11. The same problem seems to occur in some of the early stories of Joyce Carol Oates: e.g., "By the North Gate," in the collection *By the North Gate* (New York: Fawcett, 1971), pp. 195–208.

12. Booth, *Rhetoric of Fiction*, p. 415.

13. Glen McClish, "Rhetoric and the Rise of the English Novel" (Ph. D. diss., University of California, Berkeley, 1986).

14. Booth, *Rhetoric of Fiction*, pp. 105, 50.

15. Ibid., p. 69.

16. Ibid., p. 70.

17. See Seymour Chatman, *Story and Discourse: Narrative Structure in Fiction and Film* (Ithaca: Cornell University Press, 1978), pp. 215–19; quotation, p. 216.

18. Virginia Woolf, *Jacob's Room* (1922; New York: Harcourt Brace Jovanovich, 1978), pp. 139–40.

19. David Daiches, *Virginia Woolf* (Norfolk, Conn.: New Directions, 1942), p. 42.

20. Woolf, *Jacob's Room*, p. 44.

21. Ibid., p. 33.

22. *The Passenger* is available on MGM videocassette. For a fuller account of the film, see Seymour Chatman, *Antonioni; or, The Surface of the World* (Berkeley: University of California Press, 1985), pp. 182–202.

23. Otto Rank, *The Double: A Psychoanalytic Study*, trans. Harry Tucker (Chapel Hill: University of North Carolina Press, 1971), p. 6.

24. Alan Watts, *Psychotherapy East and West* (New York: Vintage Books, 1975), p. 114.

Index

Abbott, Porter, 234
Aesop, 11
Allen, Woody: *Annie Hall*, 129, 159, 164; *Manhattan*, 157
Almansi, Guido, 232
Alter, Robert, 225
Anti-intentionalism, 78
Antonioni, Michelangelo, 130, 154, 162, 211, 213; *L'Avventura*, 42, 160; *The Passenger*, 52–53, 200–202, 213, 234; *Red Desert*, 53–55
Arabian Nights, The, 182
Arguer, implied, 76
Argument: in film, 56–73; as text-type, 10
Argument at the service of narrative, 12–15
Aristotle, 109, 111, 185–86, 207, 211, 220
Arnheim, Rudolf, 7, 206
Arnold, Matthew, 167
Asyndetism, 32
Austen, Jane, 88, 167; *Emma*, 78, 149, 151, 152, 194
Auteurisme, 219
Authorial intention, debate over, 77

Babenco, Hector: *The Kiss of the Spider Woman*, 164
Bach, Johann Sebastian, 78
Bakhtin, Mikhail, 118, 184
Bal, Mieke, 208
Balzac, Honoré de, 27, 212; *Père Goriot*, 32, 44

Banfield, Ann, 137–38, 224, 227
Barber, Susanna, 174, 230
Barrymore, John, 112
Barthes, Roland, 25, 76, 206; *S/Z*, 192
Battestin, Martin, 164, 229
Beardsley, Monroe, 74, 78–80, 215, 225
Beaujour, Michel, 9, 206
Bedeutung, 77
Bellour, Raymond, 224
Bellow, Saul, 78, 216; *Herzog*, 78
Benveniste, Emile, 124, 223
Bergala, Alain, 224
Bergman, Ingmar: *Wild Strawberries*, 164
Bergman, Ingrid, 46
Bernhardt, Sarah, 112
Bible, The, 82, 91–92
Blair, Hugh, 23
Blessington, Marguerite, 17–18
Bluestone, George, 159, 228, 229
Boccaccio: *The Decameron*, 194
Boileau, Nicolas, 23
Booth, Margaret, 93, 95
Booth, Wayne, 4, 74, 80–82, 84, 87–89, 97, 118, 149–50, 184, 185–203, 208, 217–18, 219, 228, 233, 234
Bordwell, David, 20, 56–57, 124–30, 132, 134–35, 162, 207, 208, 212, 213, 223, 224, 225, 226
Boyum, Jay Gould, 166, 230, 231, 232, 233
Branigan, Edward, 224
Bresson, Robert: *Diary of a Country Priest*, 134, 136, 164
Broderick, James, 107–8

235

Index

Brontë, Emily: *Wuthering Heights,* 182
Brooke-Rose, Christine, 184, 233
Brooks, Cleanth, 17, 35, 208, 211
Browne, Nick, 157–58, 224, 228
Burch, Noël, 53, 213
Burgess, Anthony: *A Clockwork Orange,* 164
Burgoyne, Robert, 226
Burke, Kenneth, 185–86, 188, 197, 234
Byron, George Gordon, 17–18

Cagney, James, 56
Callenbach, Ernest, 43, 212
Calvino, Italo, 217
Campbell, George, 185
Camus, Albert: *La Chute,* 149
Capra, Frank: *It's a Wonderful Life,* 2, 57; *You Can't Take It with You,* 3
Career author, 87–89
Carlyle, Thomas, 77
Carroll, Lewis, 167
Carroll, Noël, 223
Celine, Lewis-Ferdinand: *Journey to the End of Night,* 190
Chambers, Ross, 206, 234
Character sketch, 17–19
Chatman, Seymour, 2, 4, 116, 198, 205, 211, 212, 218, 222, 224, 228, 229, 234
Chaucer, Geoffrey: *The Canterbury Tales,* 182
Chekhov, Anton, 197; *The Seagull,* 96
Christ at the Sea of Galilee. See Tintoretto
Chrono-logic, 10
Cinema, expression of thought in, 159
Cinematic narrator, 211
Clayton, Jack: *The Great Gatsby,* 163
Clemens, Samuel: *Huckleberry Finn. See* Twain, Mark.
Clough, A. H., 167
Cohn, Dorrit, 94, 220
Conrad, Joseph, 16; *Heart of Darkness,* 123, 144; *The Nigger of the Narcissus,* 86, 87; *Outcast of the Islands,* 112
Conradi, Peter, 229, 231, 233
Coppola, Francis Ford, 163; *Apocalypse Now,* 164
Crane, Stephen: *The Red Badge of Courage,* 92–96, 220
Croce, Benedetto, 77
Cry in the Dark, A, 213
Culler, Jonathan, 216, 223
Curtiz, Michael: *Mildred Pierce,* 56

Daiches, David, 198, 234
Dällenbach, Lucien, 231

Danto, Arthur, 96, 220
Darwin, Charles, 167
Davis, Bette, 48
Dawson, Jan, 69, 214
Dayan, Daniel, 223, 228
Deleuze, Gilles, 138, 227
Dépardieu, Gérard, 59
Description: assertive, 28; of characters, 25–26; "dangers" of, 23–24; definitions of, 9–10, 15–21; and "dynamism," 29; elliptical implication, 28–29; in film, 20, 38–55; "irreducible narrative finality," 21; nonassertive mention, 28; of places, 24–25; "pulverization" or "distribution" of, 16
Dickens, Charles, 141, 227, 228; *Dombey and Sons,* 141–43; *Great Expectations,* 47, 130, 212; *Hard Times,* 75; *Little Dorrit,* 16, 208; *Oliver Twist,* 148
Didacticism and moralism in film, 58
Dietrich, Marlene, 131
Discourse, 9
Dostoevsky, Feodor: *Crime and Punishment,* 16–17, 208; *The Notebooks for "The Possessed,"* 220; *The Possessed (The Devils),* 25, 97–99, 209
Dowden, Edward, 80
Dundrearies, 39
Durning, Charles, 107

Eagleton, Terry, 184, 233
Eco, Umberto, 222; *The Name of the Rose,* 199
Effet de réel, L', 25, 40, 70
Eisenstein, Sergei, 129, 172; project for *Das Kapital,* 58
Elohist, Bible, 92
Encyclopédie méthodique, 23, 45, 209
Evans, Maurice, 112
Exposition as text-type, 6

Fabula, 9
Faulkner, William: *The Sound and the Fury,* 152
Favored view, 156–57
Fell, John, 213
Fellini, Federico, 154; *8½,* 11, 164, 180
Fielding, Henry, 208, 218; *Jonathan Wild,* 13; *Joseph Andrews,* 12–14, 84–85; *Tom Jones,* 84, 152, 161–62
Finney, Albert, 162
Fitzgerald, F. Scott: *The Great Gatsby,* 148
Flaubert, Gustave: *Madame Bovary,* 16, 27, 44–45, 212

Ford, Ford Madox, 16; *The Good Soldier,* 90
Ford, John, 154, 219; *Stagecoach,* 157
Forster, E. M., 54–55, 213
Fowler, Roger, 81, 119, 217, 223
Fowles, John: *The French Lieutenant's Woman,* 4, 146, 161–83, 211, 230, 231, 232, 233
Framing, in painting and cinema, 156
Frank, Anne: *Diary,* 90
Freed, Arthur, 92, 219
Frege, Gottlob, 77
Fusion of description and narrative, 29–30

Gable, Clark, 40
Garbicz, Adam, 95, 220
Garcia, Nicole, 59
Gardner, Martin, 167
Gelley, Alexander, 29, 210
Genette, Gérard, 4, 16, 18, 21, 22, 26, 50, 109–11, 118, 127, 128, 144–45, 206, 208, 209, 211, 212, 218, 219, 221, 225, 228
Genre, 10
Gibbons, Cedric, 95
Gielgud, John, 133
Godard, Jean-Luc, 163
Gorky, Maxim: *Mother,* 190
Grant, Cary, 159
Griffin, Merv, 153
Griffith, David W., 175; *The Birth of a Nation,* 57, 129; *Intolerance,* 57
Grualt, Jean, 59, 213–14
Guerard, Albert, 97, 220
Guide bleu, Le, 19

Hamon, Philippe, 22–24, 209, 210, 211, 212
Hardy, Thomas, 167
Harris, Frank, 78
Hawks, Howard, 154, 219
Heath, Stephen, 224
Hemingway, Ernest, 25, 163, 192; "The Killers," 115, 119
Henderson, Brian, 224, 228
Henderson, Simon, 232
Hepburn, Katherine, 159
Hirsch, E. D., Jr., 77, 216
Histoire, 9
Hitchcock, Alfred, 46, 130, 154, 219, 226; *The Lady Vanishes,* 50–51, 157; *Notorious,* 46; *Psycho,* 50–51; *Rear Window,* 45–46, 47, 79, 129–30, 138; *Sabotage,* 156; *Shadow of a Doubt,* 129; *Stage*

Fright, 131–32, 134; *Strangers on a Train,* 159
Homer: *Iliad,* 32–34, 211
Housman, A. E.: "1887," 78
Howard, Trevor, 112
Howe, Irving, 220
Huston, John, 51, 220; *The Red Badge of Courage,* 92–96
Hutcheon, Linda, 225, 229

Implied author: as "choosing evaluating person," 81; as creator as opposed to creatures, 81; defense of, 74–89; examples of, 90–108; as inventor, not speaker, 87; as neutral person real author wants to be, 80; no "voice," 85; as recorded invention of the text, 82–87
Innes, Michael, 88
Intention, 74
Intentionalism, 77–78
Intent of a work, 74
Irons, Jeremy, 165, 170
Iser, Wolfgang, 161, 229

James, Henry, 1, 4, 87, 88–89, 144, 188, 190, 192, 194–96; *The Ambassadors,* 195; "The Liar," 149–50; *The Portrait of a Lady,* 195; *The Turn of the Screw,* 87, 182; *The Wings of the Dove,* 148
Jameson, Fredric, 105–8, 210, 220
Jost, François, 224
Joyce, James, 195; *Dubliners,* 151–52, 192; *A Portrait of the Artist as a Young Man,* 25, 209; *Ulysses,* 10, 11, 147
Juhl, P. D., 77, 216, 217

Kaper, Bronislav, 92, 95, 219
Kawin, Bruce, 164, 229
Kelly, Gene (with Stanley Donen): *An American in Paris,* 136; *On the Town,* 153; *Singin' in the Rain,* 180
Kelly, Grace, 46
Kennedy, Harlan, 232
Kipling, Rudyard: "The Man Who Would Be King," 44, 212
Kittay, Jeffrey, 31–33, 210
Klinowski, Jacek, 95, 220
Kozloff, Sarah, 133, 136, 164, 225, 226, 227, 229
Krauss, Rosalyn, 96, 220
Kubrick, Stanley: *Barry Lyndon,* 136; *Lolita,* 164; *2001,* 9
Kuiper, Koenraad, 216
Kurosawa, Akira: *Rashomon,* 164

Index

Laborit, Henri, 59–73
La Fontaine, Jean: *Fables*, 207; "Phoebus and Boreas," 11–12
Landis, John: *Trading Places*, 8
Lanser, Susan Sniader, 121, 207, 215, 218, 223
Lardner, Ring, Jr.: "Haircut," 76, 90, 149, 152
Larousse, Pierre, 23
Lawrence, D. H.: "Love among the Haystacks," 191
Lehmann-Haupt, Christopher, 217
Lesser, Simon, 228
Lessing, Gotthold Ephraim, 32, 206, 210
Lewis, Ben, 93, 95
Lincoln, Abraham: "The Gettysburg Address," 10
Logan, Marie Rose, 206
Logic: argumentative, 10; descriptive, 10, 23–26
Lorentz, Pare: *The River*, 10, 57, 207
Lowry, Malcolm: *Under the Volcano*, 51, 213
Lubbock, Percy, 185
Lucas, George, *Star Wars*, 57
Lukács, Georg, 23, 26–27, 209, 210
Lumet, Sidney: *Dog Day Afternoon*, 105–8

McClish, Glen, 208, 234
Makaveyev, Dusan: *Montenegro*, 137
Malick, Terence: *Badlands*, 136
Man, Glenn K. S., 231, 232
Manckiewicz, Joseph: *All About Eve*, 47–49, 134, 212
Mann, Thomas: *The Magic Mountain*, 11
Marmontel, Jean-François, 23, 209
Martin, Wallace, 20, 21, 29, 208, 209, 210, 217, 218
Marvell, Andrew: "To His Coy Mistress," 10
Marx, Karl: *Das Kapital*, 167
Mayer, Louis B., 92
Messer, Richard, 174, 230
Metonymy as descriptive logic, 24
Metz, Christian, 42, 46, 57, 58, 124, 174, 210, 211, 212, 213, 214, 223, 231
Mill, John Stuart, 167
Milton, John, 78
Mitchell, Margaret: *Gone with the Wind*, 40
Morrissette, Bruce, 208, 211
Movement, as a component of description, 31

Mozart, Wolfgang Amadeus: *The Marriage of Figaro*, 8
Murphy, Audie, 94
Music in the movies, 8–9

Narrative: vs. other text-types, 6–21; at service of argument, 12; at service of description, 19–20
Narratology, 1
Nash, Mark, 224
Newman, John Henry, 167
Nichols, Bill, 220, 223, 228
Nicholson, Jack, 200–201

Oates, Joyce Carol, 234
Olbrechts-Tyteca, L., 207, 233
Olivier, Laurence, 112, 114
Ollier, Claude, 38–42, 211
Orwell, George: *Animal Farm*, 56
Oudart, Jean-Pierre, 223, 228
Overbury, Sir Thomas: "A Pedant," 18–19, 208
Oxford Companion to Film, The, 212

Painting as text, 7–8
Pakula, Alan: *Sophie's Choice*, 164
Pearce, Richard: *Country*, 57
Peirce, C. S., 111
Perelman, Chaim, 185, 207, 233
Peters, Hans, 95
Pinter, Harold, 164
Plato: *Republic*, 109
Plutarch, 163
Pre-Raphaelite Brotherhood, 174
Proust, Marcel, 16, 225
Pynchon, Thomas: *The Crying of Lot 49*, 88; *Gravity's Rainbow*, 88; *V*, 88

Quennel, Peter, 17

Ramsel, Robbie, 101–2
Rank, Otto, 200, 234
Reagan, Ronald, 141
Récit, 9
Reed, Carol: *Outcast of the Islands*, 112
Reinhardt, Gottfried, 93, 94, 95, 220
Reisz, Karel: *The French Lieutenant's Woman*, 164, 229, 232
Rembrandt van Rijn, Hermenszoon, 96, 97; *Polish Rider*, 96
Resnais, Alain, 213, 214; *Mon oncle d'Amérique*, 3, 56–73; *Providence*, 132, 134
Rhetoric of fiction, 5, 184–204

238

Richards, I. A., 185
Richardson, Ralph, 112
Richardson, Samuel: *Clarissa*, 193
Richardson, Tony: *Tom Jones*, 57, 164
Richter, David, 234
Ricoeur, Paul, 216
Riefenstahl, Leni, 154; *Olympiad*, 20
Rimmon-Kenan, Shlomith, 218
Robbe-Grillet, Alain, 208, 211; *La jalousie*, 20, 208–9; "The Secret Room," 34–37
Roosevelt, Franklin, 141
Ropars-Wuilleaumier, Marie, 224
Ross, Harris, 229
Ross, Lillian, 93, 95, 219, 220
Rossetti, Dante Gabriel, 167
Rosson, Harold, 95
Rothman, William, 223
Rouen, description of, 19
Rozier, Jacques: *Adieu Philippine*, 46
Russell, Bertrand, 138
Russian Formalists, 125
Ryan, Marie-Laure, 226

Sacks, Sheldon, 234
Sage, Lorna, 233
Sanders, George, 47
Sarris, Andrew, 219
Schary, Dore, 95, 95
Scruggs, Charles, 182, 233
Service, textual, 8, 10–11
Shakespeare, William, 163; *Hamlet*, 110, 111, 114
Shelley, P. B.: "Ozymandias," 10
Sinn, 77
Small, Vernon, 215
Speech-act theory, 76
Speiser, E. A., 92, 219
Spingarn, J. E., 77
Staley, Jeffrey, 219
Stallman, R. W., 82, 218
Stanislavsky, Konstantin, 96
Stanzel, Franz, 118
Star effect, 159
Steele, Charles, 198
Stendhal (Henri Beyle): *The Red and the Black*, 14, 208
Stephens, Leslie, 168
Sternberg, Meir, 24, 127, 206, 209
Sterne, Lawrence, 145; *Tristram Shandy*, 123
Stewart, J. I. M., 88
Stewart, James, 46
Story, 9

Strauss, Johann: "Blue Danube Waltz," 8
Streep, Meryl, 166, 170, 172
Suleiman, Susan, 11, 207, 234
Suture theory, 157
Swift, Jonathan: "A Modest Proposal . . . ," 10, 76
Syuzhet, 9

Tableau, 32–33
Temps mort, 54
Tennyson, Alfred Lord, 167
Text: definition of, 7; design, 86; implication, 86; instance, 86; as self-existing thing, 81
Text-types, 10
Thackeray, William Makepeace: *Vanity Fair*, 24
Theophrastian character, 18–19
Thompson, Kristin, 20, 57, 225
Thurber, James, "Unicorn in the Garden," 56
Tillotson, Kathleen, 80
Tintoretto: *Christ at the Sea of Galilee*, 155, 228
Todd, Richard, 131
Tolhurst, William, 79–80, 217
Tolstoy, Leo: *Anna Karenina*, 14, 26, 208; *War and Peace*, 29, 31
Torgovnick, Marianna, 7, 97, 206, 220
Transmission, narrative, 3
Truffaut, François: *Day for Night*, 180
Turnimanov, Vladimir A., 99, 220
Twain, Mark: *Huckleberry Finn*, 29, 31, 82, 149, 191–92

Utterance meaning, 79
Utterer's meaning, 79

Valéry, Paul, 23, 209
Valesio, Paolo, 185
Value, as opposed to *valeur*, 83
Vertov, Dziga, 138
Voice of narrator, 76
Voice-over narrations, film names, 164

Warren, Robert Penn, 17, 35, 208, 211
Wasiolek, Edward, 97–99
Watts, Alan, 202, 234
Welles, Orson, 219; *Citizen Kane*, 50, 51–52; *Touch of Evil*, 43, 212
Wellman, William: *Public Enemy*, 56, 57
Wells, H. G., 223
West, Jessamyn, 80

Index

Whitmore, James, 94
Wilson, George, 225
Wimsatt, W. K., Jr. 74, 82, 91, 96, 215, 218, 219, 220
Woolf, Virginia: *Jacob's Room,* 146, 198–200, 228, 234; *Mrs. Dalloway,* 198–99; *A Room of One's Own,* 200
Word-sequence meaning, 79

Wyman, Jane, 131

Yahwist, Bible, 92
Young, G. M., 167

Zola, Emile: *Nana,* 26–27
Zweig, Stefan: *Letter from an Unknown Woman,* 165

Library of Congress Cataloging-in-Publication Data

Chatman, Seymour Benjamin, 1928–
    Coming to terms: the rhetoric of narrative in fiction and film / Seymour
Chatman.
        p. cm.
    Includes bibliographical references.
    ISBN 0-8014-2485-2 (alk. paper). — ISBN 0-8014-9736-1 (pbk.: alk. paper)
    1. Narration (Rhetoric) 2. Fiction—History and criticism. 3. Motion picture
plays—History and criticism. 4. Motion pictures and literature. 5. Motion
pictures—Semiotics. I. Title.
PN212.C47 1990
809'.923—dc20   90-55119